The Girl Who Said No:
A Search in Sicily

Travelers' Tales Books

THE GIRL
WHO SAID NO

A Search in Sicily

Natalie Galli

Travelers' Tales,
an imprint of Solas House, Inc.
Palo Alto

Travelers' Tales and Solas House are trademarks of Solas House, Inc.
Palo Alto, California 94306
www.travelerstales.com

Cover Design: Kimberly Nelson
Interior Design and Page Layout: Howie Severson and Walton Mendelson

Portions of this book were previously published in the anthologies
Travelers' Tales Italy: True Stories of Life on the Road (1998), *Italy, A Love Story* (Seal Press) 2005, and *The Best Women's Travel Writing*, 2008, 2009, 2010 (Travelers' Tales), three of which were awarded gold and silver prizes by Bay Area Travel Writers in 2008 and 2010.

Library of Congress Cataloging-in-Publication Data is available upon request.

ISBN 978-1-60952-172-1 (paperback)
ISBN 978-1-60952-173-8 (ebook)
ISBN 978-1-60952-174-5 (hardcover)

First Edition
10 9 8 7 6 5 4 3 2 1
Printed in the United States of America

*For the many other Francas who have
gone by other names in other places at other times.
And for the most patient of midwives:
Claire Fraschina and Stanley Steinberg.*

Table of Contents

We rowed on.
The Rocks were now behind; Kharybdis, too,
and Skylla dropped astern.

    Then we were coasting
the noble island of the god, where grazed
those cattle with wide brows, and bounteous flocks
of Helios, lord of noon, who rides high heaven.
From the black ship, far still at sea, I heard
the lowing of the cattle winding home
and sheep bleating; and heard, too, in my heart
the words of blind Teiresias of Thebes
and Kirke of Aiaia; both forbade me
the Island of the world's delight, the Sun.
So I spoke out in gloom to my companions:
'Shipmates, grieving and weary though you are,
listen: I had forewarning from Teiresias
and Kirke, too; both told me I must shun
this island of the Sun, the world's delight.
Nothing but fatal trouble shall we find here.
Pull away, then, and put the land astern.'

The Odyssey
Homer
Book Twelve, lines 261-279
Robert Fitzgerald translation

I shall re-view Sicilia, for whose sight I have a woman's
longing.

The Winter's Tale
William Shakespeare
Act IV Sc IV, 670-1

I thought the twenty professional Sicilian mourners were a
bit much.

Angels in America
Tony Kushner
Perestroika

Prologue

I could so easily have missed the tiny item in the *San Francisco Chronicle*, but sometime during the spring of 1966, on the hunt for a Current Events article to bring to sixth-period Social Studies, I came upon the three-inch filler:

RAPED SICILIAN GIRL REFUSES TO MARRY
Trapani, Italy

A young woman has shocked her countrymen by refusing to marry a man who raped her. Franca Viola, 18, has defied more than 1000 years of Sicilian tradition by rejecting nuptials with Filippo Melodia, 25, who tried to force her into marriage by the time-honored custom of abduction and rape. Convention dictates that Viola must accept a "reparation marriage" with Melodia to restore her broken honor. The tradition is still part of Italian law, which provides that all charges be dropped when a woman weds the man who has kidnapped and carnally violated her. The girl has publicly avowed that she has no intention of changing her mind, despite the forceful opinions of many of her townspeople. She has not left her family's modest white home for several weeks. They have endured repeated vandalism and threats of violence.

I did not cut it out—we had to bring something front-page to class—but I never forgot the Sicilian woman's story.

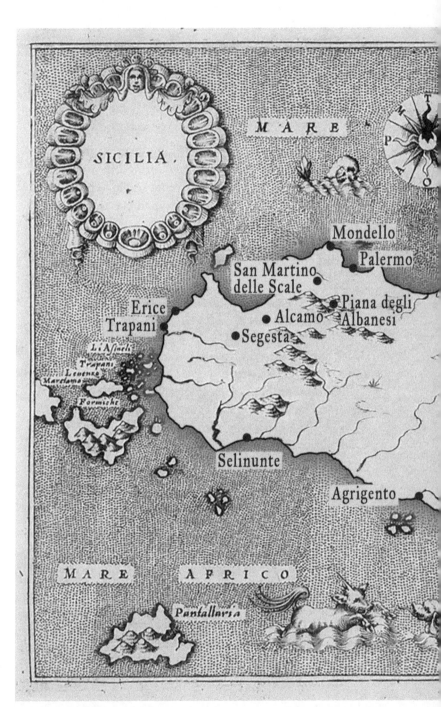

Chapter I

A Hot Pink Hell—1969

When we vaulted the purple-blue Strait of Messina by ferry toward the island of Sicily, home of our southernmost ancestors, and stood on the bright deck in our lightweight American summer clothes that August, the crew surrounded us, curious, chattering, full of questions.

"My parents came from Contessa Entellina on the Greek-Albanian Plain and from Palermo," my mother answered in Sicilian dialect, emotion brimming in her eyes, "and we are returning for the first time."

"Welcome home, *signora*!* Welcome back."

The captain himself came down from the bridge and extended his hand to my father. "Congratulations, my American friend."

"For what?" asked my dad.

"For landing on the moon last month."

"I can't take credit," he laughed, "but thank you."

"To walk on the moon! An achievement we all watched on the television. Sincerely, I salute your great United States. I would like to visit some day. I have cousins in Yonkers."

The adults carried on while we three teen-aged sisters leaned on the railing, dazzled by the almost violet color of the

---

* English translations of Italian words can be found in the Glossary on page 337.

Mediterranean, hoping for dolphins. My younger sister Tina ran ahead to the prow to look for them.

"Hey, Louise," my father called out, "just double-checking that you've got the satchel with the passports, right?" My older sister held it up for him. "And gals, first order of business: acquaint yourselves with where the lifejackets are located. Make sure to tell Tina." He turned back to the Captain.

The grown-ups could concern themselves with travel details and safety. I was still young enough on that crossing not to have some of life's worries. I might not ever experience this newness again, not quite like this, and as we skimmed the sparkling, bouncing sea of unimaginable hue, I revelled in it.

Strolling the deck during that passage, I saw her for the first time—the island flag of the Trinacria—snapping in the wind. She nabbed me with a look. Medusa's half-smile was hard to interpret: encircled by her three running legs, her wings, her serpents, her sheaves of wheat, the face teased and dared. Are you ready? she seemed to ask, scrutinizing me. We were about to set foot on an ancient, magical island, with an ancient woman at the center.

Captain and crew cheered as our rented Fiat was hoisted off the boat by a creaking rope contraption. The car swung out over our heads. When it bump-landed on the pier and the ropes were pulled away, they all waved and called out safe journey.

We headed west into the interior hills, where the twentieth century fell away. Every aged stone village dotting the road or extruding upward from rock outcroppings was shuttered against the blanching late summer light. The sun had long since faded them—centuries ago. Surprised by a Fiat with a northern license plate driving through, *contadini* stopped to tip their caps. Donkeys carried loads bulging out much wider than themselves along the coarse road, their tasseled heads down in the heat. The lulling thump of the tires had us hardly speaking while a remote and rugged landscape revealed itself.

From the car we watched old women balanced on their terra-cotta roofs, crushing and spreading bursting ripe tomatoes across broad pallets to dry in the sun. They used wooden paddles as big as oars to tame and smooth flat the fruit of the land into what would become red paste. Up high, with their feet fixed on the roof tiles, they gave an appearance of slowly rowing through red pools of Sicily's agricultural lifeblood. The toil of these women, in black headscarves, dresses and stockings covering everything but their faces and hands, was hard and long under the seared blue sky.

Below them, we saw teenaged girls seated just outside their front doors. Facing in, hands folded in their laps, heads bowed and hair banished behind modest pastel scarves, they were forbidden to look at anything but the walls. Encircling female relatives made certain they stayed contained. In village after village we saw this stark sight of the elder black silhouettes perched one story above and the fixed virginal presence at road level. These girls were our ages. While we goofed off in the back seat with the windows down, dousing ourselves from glass water bottles to cool off, barely tolerating the weight of sleeveless cotton shifts on our skin—well, that morning Tina had put on a hot-pink sundress, with the vee-front and the scooped back—they were covered up to their throats, down to their wrists and over their knees. Not one turned to watch our lone car go by. They were trained against it.

We entered the city of Agrigento. My father wanted to get a feel for the *centro città* before we visited the famous Valley of the Temples that afternoon, so we parked and wandered into a large piazza. Banks of old men sat fused to metal chairs outside their bar, staring at us. A soft sound like a breeze through dried grass sailed across the square, ssss. It seemed like a tone of nature, maybe a light wind picking up, though the air stayed still. The odd noise grew. Ssssssss. A release of steam somewhere? We kept strolling the grand piazza. It sloped a little.

Suddenly, I saw women in black running toward us from every direction. Some carried brooms. "Sssssssssss," they hissed, and were upon us. The crowd tugged at my fifteen-year-old sister Tina's long dark hair, swatted at her bare arms and hot pink sundress. Then they swallowed her up.

"What the"—my dad yelled—"hey wait a minute!"

"It's the dress!" Louise quickly figured. Our paler-colored shifts spared her and me the direct assault, but the widows spat at our sandals, and tried to sweep all of us out of their piazza with the brooms. Tina pushed through them and grabbed for my father's arm, but the swarm closed in again, and she vanished.

"Let my daughter be," my mother pleaded.

The women ignored her, and the noise in their throats deepened—a communal, low wail. For an instant, we glimpsed hot pink flashing through the swirl of black fabric.

"Tina," I yelled. "Over here!" If we could extract her, we would then face an outer ring of waiting men. We had to get her back to the car. "Tina! Where are you?"

Time limped to a stop when she didn't answer. The women were squeezing in on her in some sort of ritual frenzy when, at once, they broke apart. A tall man in an elegant silk suit and tie had appeared. He held his black-gloved hand up to the mob, which silenced itself and fell away. Salvation: women quickly retreated into their homes and men went back to their caffè seats.

My sister teetered, still on her feet, part of her hem torn down. Her hot-pink plastic headband lay on the paving stones. Louise scooped it up.

"Come with me," he said. Tina was immediately under his protection. He escorted her by the elbow to the door of an establishment and we stumbled along after them. We found ourselves in the dining room of a darkened restaurant. She shivered, her teeth chattering, her recent tan gone pale.

"Sit, *signorina*, please," he pulled out a chair for her.

A waiter jumped up from the table where he was eating lunch with the cooks and dashed over, chewing and swallowing.

"*Prego*, Doctor," he bowed, "how may I assist?"

The man with the glove ordered ice cream for us girls and coffee for my parents.

"*Subito, Dottore*," promised the young man, scurrying towards the bar.

He addressed my father and mother, apology edging his voice: "Your daughter's bright dress they do not accept. Nor do they understand. They do not tolerate bared female skin."

"If we had only known!" my mother answered, fanning herself with her fold-up travel hat to calm down. "We do not mean to offend. We will have to be more respectful and careful from now on."

My dad pulled out a handkerchief to clean his eyeglasses. The barman popped open a bottle of water and pressed it into my sister's hands.

"Where do you come from?" our rescuer inquired. My father told him. "Ahhh, San Francisco, one of the most beautiful cities in the world!"

"Have you visited there?" My mother, still fanning herself, strained to keep up her part of the conversation.

"No, but I have heard," he pinched his fingers together, rotating his wrist in the gesture of appreciation. The glove was gone.

"So sir, you are a doctor?" my father asked.

"Yes. I travel all over Italy for my work."

"What sort of medicine do you practice?"

"I am a doctor of soap."

"Oh," my parents nodded, and earnestly launched into full conversation with him in Italian. We daughters couldn't follow it, being second-generation. Really, we knew so little back then.

"What does he mean doctor of soap?" I whispered to Louise.

"A hygienist, maybe?" she whispered back, "or a chemist who creates new formulas for detergent?"

I glanced at the man who had just saved my sister Tina from a mob. He seemed courtly; my parents appeared engaged, though my Mom kept bringing the demitasse to her lips, hesitating, then setting it back in the saucer. I pulled at my father's sleeve. "What's he saying, Dad?"

He waved his hand under the table. "That he's a merchant, a traveling salesman of sorts."

Tina was fiddling with the slender spoon, pushing the melted pistachio around, making a green pool.

"Why don't you eat it?" Louise prodded her. "To be polite."
She still shook. "Too cold."

Intent on distracting us, the gentleman made sure that we girls were enjoying our *gelati*.

"*Delizioso!*" we answered. "Thank you kindly, *Dottore*."

Louise pulled Tina's dish towards her and started to spoon it up. My younger sister, normally an ice cream fanatic, kept her head bowed and her hands in her lap. I extended my long spoon over to taste the pistachio. Thoughtfully, he had ordered each of us a different flavor. Hazelnut, Lemon.

He finally had us all laughing, nervously, before he paid the bill, bowed, kissed my mother's hand and disappeared.

"*La Mano Nivora*," she murmured, letting out a breath.

"Meaning what, Mom?"

"Shhh, gals," cautioned my father, "not here. We'll tell you kids later."

Through the windows we could see that the piazza had emptied completely. Covered with all four white lace scarves we'd been carrying around to hide our hair and shoulders in churches, the singled-out sister, surrounded by all of us, was rushed back to our car. At the *pensione*, reserved months before, my mother requested an early check-in. We would get ourselves situated before going out to see the Great Temples of Agrigento. We would rest a little bit in the worst of the heat. Louise double-locked our door and closed the green shutters of the stifling room.

I mouthed the letters, "m-a-f-i-a."

"I know how to spell it!" muttered the torn daisy in a low, emptied-out voice.

"He actually wore a black glove," Louise whispered. "The Black Hand."

"He made them go away," Tina said, mostly to herself.

"Well of course, he runs the place." For some reason I wanted to sound like I knew how the Mafia worked.

Tina took off the condemning sundress and put on a slip, a white shift with cap sleeves, and a sweater. She filled the sink and plunged the garment in. The shocking pink fabric darkened in the water, the turquoise dot at the center of each Carnaby Street daisy turned purple.

"Doctor of soap—he launders money, get it?" Louise said.

"Whatever he does, I don't care," I answered. "He could be the soap pope or soap emperor if he wanted. He stopped them."

Louise tiptoed over to the window, opened the shutters and leaned out. Only scarlet geraniums and loud, slow Sicilian bumblebees in the swelter. She unlocked the door and checked the hallway. No one and nothing, except a pair of men's loafers on the marble floor across the hall, waiting to be polished. My parents had been assigned a room down at the other end of the corridor. We all lay out flattened on our beds.

"He was nice. He helped me. What if he hadn't been there?"

"Can you believe that a mafioso would do that? What are we in for on this island?"

"Not just any old mafioso," I asserted with fake authority. "A major Don."

"How do you know that?" Louise shot back. "You don't know that."

"He saved me." Tina squeezed out the water and hung the dress on our nifty travel clothesline, stretched between one of the armoire knobs and a bedpost.

"Oooh, it's dripping on me!" Louise whined.

"Sorry. I'm sorry."

"No, don't move anything. It feels fantastic. This damn heat!"

The drying pink dress, daisy-strewn, hung suspended in the room like a penance.

The wonder of the Greek temples that late afternoon, considered as well-preserved as any to be found in Greece, helped to melt away some of the sting of the incident. But I believe we carried it around like a concealed bruise of shame. We belonged here in the land of our ancestors, didn't we? Yet our foreignness had already caused a ruckus. None of us dared to overstep again. The next morning Tina neatly folded the hot pink dress, placed it flat in the bottom of her suitcase and never wore it again.

In cosmopolitan Palermo, my mother's first cousin Maia welcomed us joyously, with tears and kisses on the right cheek, the left cheek, the right cheek. She ushered us into her elegant living room. We stopped to admire antiquities that she and her late husband had dug up in the Madonie mountains. Small ceramic handheld lamps once filled with olive oil to light, and iridescent glass vials from Roman times.

She urged us to put our feet up on the lounge chairs of her patio while she served *Amarena*, a cool refreshment of mountain cherry juice and mint in bubbly water. We were floating high above most of the city on her modern penthouse terrace, gazing out at the monumental mass of Monte Pellegrino and over the ancient, busy harbor. Even having just arrived, the feel of Palermo's lush, endless history made my hometown, San Francisco, look like a newborn. Maia's world-wise city pulsed from centuries of ripeness and decline, endurance and rebirth. Our California metropolis by the bay suddenly struck me as the western outpost of a very adolescent country. Yes, the cries of gold and silver in the mid eighteen-hundreds turned her quickly international, but nothing like this place.

What did I know at seventeen, anyway? Certainly not enough Italian to ask Maia directly about the girl who said no three years before. To risk suggesting that Sicily was somehow backward would be the worst breach of manners. I could not offend this very generous woman. Nope. We had already taken one cultural misstep.

When Maia made sure we had been revived with refills of *Amarena*, we followed her Fiat for the crazy ride up to the great Norman cathedral at Monreale. Her sons, our cute older boy cousins wearing their dark glasses and their pressed white shirts, tailed us all the way into the hills on a Vespa, then zipped off, waving, while we peeled out of the cars to enter the eleventh-century mosaic wonder. Later that evening they rejoined us for dinner at an outdoor *trattoria* near the Giardino Inglese, filled our glasses with white wine as if that were normal. The first time I had more than a watered-down sip of *vino* happened that balmy night in a piazza strung with lights. Intoxicating. These cousins knew very little English, yet we laughed and mimed our way through the meal, united by our shared badge of youth, while the grown-ups caught up on half a century of family history at the other end of the table. A beautiful night—the fronds of the palm trees catching a breeze we couldn't, a jasmine scent hanging in the air.

Chapter II

Packing

"So you're going to Sicily. If you've gotta minute, give me a ring, awright? Love ya, honey." The voluptuous voice of my mother's old friend Evelyn, kind of like an aunt to me, spilled out of the answering machine.

I shoved aside a pile of travel clothes I'd been building to grab the phone. "Ev?"

"Hey Kid, you're there. I'm so excited for you, honey!" With Evelyn, it took just one syllable of her warm tone to conjure up the complete image: the figure-eight-and-a-half-curves and bouffant caramel hair, the full mouth coated with Coral Joy lipstick, her signature color. "What's the occasion?"

"Well, a bunch of us got laid off last week and—"

"Not from writing your Consumer Alert column, I hope?" she blurted. The urgency, the concern, the worry. So Sicilian, one generation into the diaspora.

"No, I still write the column. I meant the other boring accounts payable one. I'm grabbing the opportunity while I'm free. I've been wanting to go back for a million years. So I thought, what a great chance to see the Easter celebrations and visit my relatives in Palermo again, and also . . . I've got this wild idea to go looking for a woman I read about when I was in junior high."

"What woman?"

With Evelyn, brevity was key. I described what I remembered of the filler.

She drew air in and held it. "Oh my."

"Yeah. I know."

"What year was that?"

"Nineteen sixty-six, I think."

"You can't look her up here?"

"I've tried all the Main Libraries and called the *Chronicle*, but their archive indexes don't go back that far. And they didn't document fillers, anyway, I'm pretty sure. Nothing's been written about her that I can find."

"You know, Kid, I know something about marriage customs too. My mother didn't want to marry my father, but she had to, anyway. Her parents and his parents arranged the wedding and that was that, do you know? She didn't have any say."

"Wow."

"Absolutely. However, as a consequence, that became her ticket out. They took a boat to America when Ma was in her early twenties, and never went back. Things were pretty hopeless there. The poverty for one thing. And for another, she used to tell me how every Saturday someone would be gunned down in the city. What a world, I'm telling you."

"Which city?"

"Agrigento."

"Oh! The Mafia."

She lowered her voice. "Shhh, don't say it out loud. They called them 'retaliation killings'."

"Yeah. Vendettas."

"Don't say it. Deadly. They'd stay inside terrified. I remember her words. She said, 'every weekend our hearts were in our throats.'"

"Whoa."

"So you're doing this on your own? Is that handsome boyfriend of yours going with you?"

"Nah." I hesitated about Boothe. He was as much a reason I was leaving as the Easter processions I intended to see. I so much hoped by traveling to make our relationship paler, and when I told him last week I was flying to Sicily, he—always wanting to keep his options open—offered, "oooh, maybe I can get off work and meet up with you, though I'd really rather go to Northern Italy." Well, then go to Northern Italy, Boothe. Who invited you on my trip to the deep south anyway?

"He's not that handsome anymore, Evelyn," I finally answered, "not with the way he throws it around." Even while he was distracted by the next woman, and the next, Boothe's talent lay in making you the rapt focus of his lens. He was a photographer, after all, enamored of the world's endless visuals. When I figured out that I formed part of a very long chain chain chain of women he turned his high beams onto, I backed away. That's when he reapplied his focus on me, double-strength. Naturally I responded, having been smitten by the guy, but any renewed interest from me was all it took for him to pull away again. He was too scared to stay in one place with anyone. I told him so to his face. He listened and he even agreed, but that didn't change his slipping in and out of involvement.

My weakness for him kept me all caught up in the chronic tug of advance and retreat. Putting a North American continent and an Atlantic Ocean between us seemed like the maneuver that could put an end to this two-way madness. I needed to get far away from him. Then I would quit him. For good.

"I have to admit he's one soxy dreamboat. Even a lady of my advanced age noticed."

Oh Evelyn, I suppressed a laugh. Soxy?

"Let's face it, Kid, aside from being so smart and funny and lively, with that beautiful speaking voice perfect for radio, he's a real good looker."

"Yep, he was looking everywhere, all the time. I've lost interest, Ev. It doesn't matter anymore. Let's change the subject." I could feel myself heating up. "He plays his games and takes deadly chances, you know, with HIV on the loose."

"Of course, Kid, you stay away from him. I'm just sorry to hear it hasn't worked out. I was so hopeful when you found someone you liked after separating from what's-his-name, the doctor."

Oh him. Breaker of the Hippocratic Oath. I really didn't want to talk about that earlier philanderer.

"And then the actor before him, your first real heartbreak, who went and did himself in, poor kid . . ."

OK, that's enough. "I'm going on my own, Ev, and I'm very excited."

"Well, we've gotta keep moving. Anyway, let me get to what I was calling about. I've got a very old cousin there—well, in actual fact we're not directly related, but my cousin Maria is—who I haven't seen in oh, thirty years. And I just wondered if you happen to go to Agrigento whether you could do me an enormous favor and bring something important to her. See, honey, I know it's a lot to ask but I don't trust the Italian mail."

"But Evelyn, I'm staying in Palermo with relatives. I'm not going to Agrigento. Is it a bulky or heavy thing?"

"No," she laughed easily. "Just a packet of letters, a few photos. Personal, sentimental things that belong to her. It won't take up any space in your suitcase. My guess is it weighs six ounces tops."

I stalled. "It's pretty important, huh?" I was already feeling the weight of everything that needed taking care of before Wednesday morning.

"It's one long story. I tell you what—I'll send the package with an addressed envelope to her and I'll write you a little note of explanation."

"They don't still have murders there every weekend, do they?"

Her voice turned quiet. "No."

"You've gotta express mail it to me today, though. I'm leaving in two days."

"Sure, and if you don't travel to Agrigento, well then, go ahead and just mail it from Palermo. You wouldn't mind insuring it, would you? You're such a doll, kid."

"All right. Listen Ev, gotta go!"

"Have a super trip," she trilled, "and don't forget to send a postcard!"

"Of course. Love you, Ev."

My cat sauntered over. "No way am I going anywhere near Agrigento," I told him. He yawned.

Essential travel items still to check off the list: rush passport and wedding ring. In the morning I'd sprinted to Telegraph Avenue, yet with all the jewelry stalls lining the sidewalks, no one had plain gold bands. I told one vendor that I was not getting married but needed it for travel, so it could be cheap and plated and just a couple of bucks.

"Let me guess," she countered. "You're going to Italy, right? Whenever women say they need a ring for a trip, turns out always to be Italy. What's the deal?"

I didn't have time to explain Italian men and anyway, she had nothing for me. I jogged back home and rummaged around in my dresser for a goofy Crackerjack plastic ring that I won at a carnival once. The adjustable bauble looked so phony with its two stand-up rhinestones and gold painted aluminum band, who would I ever fool? I turned it so the "diamonds" aimed into the palm. Only if the lighting were bad and if it were nighttime could the ruse possibly work. "Don't laugh," I told myself, "this trinket could save your life."

So why not bring the other plastic prize in the top drawer too—the mini orange water pistol? Just in case.

"Blend in," I reminded myself, staring at the clothing pile my cat was busy kneading. I wanted to walk down the streets of Palermo and have nothing telltale about me. Ergo, I had to put aside my sloppy, casual California ways and give over to *La Bella Figura*: the longstanding Italian cultural rule that how you dress, and beyond that how you carry yourself in public, is foremost. I squelched a rising memory of the hot pink mistake, straightened my shoulders and lectured my cat, "Comportment, above all." He narrowed his eyes.

I was likely to lose my footing on the built-in tightrope of southern Italian form. I needed to appear somehow fashionable yet modest, *alta moda* yet traditional, respectable yet not dull. A couple of inches at the hem or the neckline—up or down—could peg me right way, and the shoes—well, they were going to be hopeless. And the whole contradiction had to fit into one piece of carry-on luggage.

Getting the style right, since it changed yearly in Italy, was an almost impossible trick. If I absolutely had to, I'd buy the uniform once I got there, but I'd have to like it, and funding was tight.

"Think of widows." I knew how to dress like one, my grandmother's generation having been full of them. Even though they had immigrated to this brighter new world, Nonny and her sisters adhered to the tradition. Once your husband died, no matter your age, you wore the absence of color forever, relegated to and protected by a timeless Mediterranean shadow look. For festive occasions—New Year's, weddings, Christmas—you might don the navy-blue dress with the scattered white dots, or dip into gray, but that was about as daring as it got. I invoked my ancestresses to help me pack the suitcase with black—skirt, pants, long-sleeved shirt, walking shoes, hose, sweater, and hey, black underwear. This would form my baseline wardrobe if I ended up in remote villages on the trail of the girl who said no. Not wanting to offend, alert, or draw attention to myself, black would be my *carte blanche*.

I shoved the entire pile plus my parrot-colored swimsuit into the case and couldn't zip it closed. Shaking it a few times to get any air pockets out made no difference. Neither did sitting on it. The final test would involve walking around the block, wheeling the bulging thing while wearing my all-weather jacket, strapped in with shoulder purse and satchel criss-crossed over my chest. If there was no pain at the end, I could take everything. Otherwise I had to lighten up. This was a test I had not yet passed in all my traveling life.

So of course, in defiance, I remembered the lemon silk blouse that Boothe had bought me last October on the harvest moon evening. He noticed it in the window of a vintage clothing shop just west of College Avenue during one of our multi-mile night walks. They'd lit it from two angles with footlights for extra sheen. The bodice was gusseted in that artful forties way which no one takes the time to do anymore. And it was cut on the bias.

"Wow," he grabbed my hand, "it's the same color as the moon. I bet that'd look great on you. Go in and try it on."

"Who, me?"

It fit perfectly, a subtle concoction with little cork buttons down the front.

"I wanna get it for you. So silky," he murmured, peeling fives and ones out of his wallet. "Don't take it off. Wear it now."

I felt anointed that night. Chosen. He had laid down ready money for what I secretly considered to be a kind of engagement blouse. I went to the closet and slid the lemon silk off its clothes hanger. Two vertical darts had opened up on the delicate material, and the long pleat down the back had begun to pull away. The newly gaping areas showed the original, deeper hue of the fabric. I got out some of Nonny's old silk thread to mend it. Tiny, committed stitches were required.

Tailoring is a triumph of artifice. By means of hiding certain areas, binding them up in darts and tucks, a masterful effect, a finished look, a dazzle, results. Our failed relationship had been similarly fashioned: plied together for a period of time by means of all the hidden intents, hopes, and illusions I had and he might have had, sewn within the limits of seams now loosened, now exposed. One could repair a fragile blouse, or a doomed romance, only up to a point.

Still, I was attached enough to take it with me, full knowing that to wear anything like it in Palermo would mark me as the foreigner I did not want to be. I poured the slippery Boothe blouse into my suitcase and carefully zipped it in, making sure the teeth didn't chew it up.

I pulled out my atlas and flipped the pages open to Sicily. The triangle looked as though it were forever about to be punted by the high-heeled boot of Italy, with the muscle power of an entire continent behind it. My cat leapt onto the three-cornered island, settled down and began cleaning himself. I was going for sure. I could hardly wait.

Chapter III

Approach From The West

Our Pan Am jet soared out of JFK. The sun smeared rust at the western horizon, only nine hours after it had risen in San Francisco. A million Manhattan windows lit up glinting, melted gold, and I felt that yearning I always have about New York—the metropolis I don't know well enough.

A pack of wild high school kids galloped up and down the aisles the minute the seatbelt signs went off, yelling and plopping in each others' laps. Their chaperones plus all available flight attendants couldn't herd them into order and eventually gave up bothering.

Oh well, who cared? Not lucky me. I was headed to *Bella Sicilia*, the volcanic jewel set in the navel of the Mediterranean—Middle Land of the ancient western world, the mystical island, forever tri-pointing towards Athens, Tripoli, and Cordoba. Sicily, the lodestone composed of magma, rock, and earth, a destination with an unwavering allure, a three-sided magnet.

The muffled sounds of heavy petting and other adolescent silliness did not keep me from my reverie. They came to the island from every direction, drawn into her turquoise waters. The bare outline of succession spanning thousands of years went something like this: The indigenous Sicans were overlaid by Sicels, then Elymians, then Phoenicians, Greeks, and Romans. Vandals and Ostrogoths poured in. Arabs created a great cultural flowering of tolerance, enlightenment and philosophy for a brief time. They invented sherbet made from the sugarcane they planted and the ice they carried down from Mount Etna. Normans brought their red hair, French customs and established universities. This nonstop procession of traders, warriors, explorers, artists, colonizers and pirates, soldiers and poets, learned and lowbrow, mathematicians, architects, tilers, musicians, royalty and refugee from every port rimming the sea, steered in with the currents. They came following the antique trade routes and dateless crossroads. It wasn't peaceful in the least. Blood spilled and spilled throughout the centuries, diseases coursed through populations, famines and enslavement recurred. Everyone who landed made Sicily and changed Sicily. And always, throughout, peasants tilled the land, and fishers plied the waters.

The Spanish were mean—they did their best to subjugate and destroy, much like they did in the New World. The Austrian Hapsburgs played some kind of role in the Kingdom of the Two Sicilies, but I didn't even know what the second Sicily was exactly. The British built villas and cultivated Marsala wines with the names of Florio and Ingham Whitaker. Dry and sweet. Interestingly, I read somewhere that Napoleon once tried to conquer the island but didn't pull it off. And I was ignorant of the details, but when Garibaldi and the northerners came down and claimed the island for the newly founded republic of Italy—the unification—it was one more land grab, one more assault. What I did know for sure was that the Nazis had succeeded for thirty-five hellish days, because my grandmother's sister died when they confiscated her insulin at the port of Palermo, insulin that Nonny's brother, grand-uncle Peppino, a pharmacist, had been sending her regularly from San Francisco to keep her alive. It was her daughter, Maia Miracolo Santilli, whose houseguest I would be at the end of this long overnight flight.

A spitball landed on my sleeve. I turned and glowered for a while into the darkened cabin, then opened up the reinforced paper regurgitation bag and maneuvered the wad in without touching it. The engines grew louder, grinding on themselves. I shifted my weight, trying to sleep, but it was only late afternoon California time. The waning moon appeared distorted in the bend of my window, trailing a long silver thread on the skin of the Atlantic. The cabin temperature dipped. I dug in my suitcase for another layer to throw over my shoulders. Evelyn's red white and blue eagle packet snagged on the zipper, prompting me to take it out and unseal it. She had drawn a heart around my name on an inner manila envelope. I pulled out a letter scrawled in her big, exuberant loops.

Mon. aft

Dearest N: And you ARE a complete 100% DEAR to take the time to do this for me. Enclosed you will find a number of photos. Feel free to look at them if you so desire. The reason I'm asking you to bring this package to Sicily is complicated, but I'll try to keep it simple. Must be inside post office door by 5.

Anyway honey here's the deal. Years ago—1956 to be exact—I went to Agrigento to visit my grandmother and cousins. As I just told you on the phone, my mother never went back—she referred to Sicily as quella brutta terra—but I wanted to meet my relatives, so I went to stay with them for a couple of weeks. At that time I had broken off the engagement with Silvio, and I hoped to forget all about him, how was I to know our engagement would last another sixteen years? But that's another story as you well know.

Anyway, my cousins were poor poor farmers and shepherds. They lived in let's put it this way, Very modest stone homes with dirt floors, no electricity or running water. Indoor toilets? Ha. They walked to get their water from the fountain down the street. They had no kitchens. They cooked outside in earthen ovens. They all lived in one neighborhood where they kept an eye on each other (still do) both protective and nosy, do you know? To give you an idea my cousin Maria put me up in her bed and slept on the floor my whole visit. She insisted—it meant that much to her to welcome a cousin from America. And my grandmother who lived directly across the way would bring me an egg in her pocket every day, again in honor of me. Food was NOT abundant—on the contrary, every MORSEL was accounted for. This was ten years after the war mind you, but things had always been tough for my relatives, IE when my mother was young girls weren't allowed to attend school. So she never learned to read and write. Much to her chagrin for the rest of her life.

Another example: One day I told my relatives I wanted to see the Greek temples outside of Agrigento. Mind you, they had not heard of any Greek ruins. The women had never gone out that far away from their houses! So I splurged and rented a big car to take my grandmother, Maria, and as many others as could fit inside. Well, they had never been inside an auto, and they were quite nervous about it, crossing themselves, praying, gripping the handles and so on. My nonna, poor thing, became carsick. We got to the valley of the temples, and they commented on "the big stones" but weren't keen on lingering. They felt nervous being away from home.

Anyway, one day near the end of my stay Maria told me we would pay a visit to her cousin Zi' Arcangela who "lived in a real house." We walked to the center of Agrigento that afternoon, which took us quite a long while. Arcangela lived right on a main piazza in a two-story house with green shutters. Already I could tell she was categorically better off than any other relations I'd met, and believe me I'd met hundreds by that point. We knocked on the door and waited. Finally we heard the lock turn and a petite lady dressed in black from head covering to toe answered.

She was a handsome woman with pale skin like she was never out in the sun, but her eyes I saw right away had a hollow look and when she smiled it faded quick, you know that kind of smile, the kind that's a strain to maintain. (hey I rhymed without trying!) She wore her black and silver hair pulled tightly back. At her feet stood a little whippet or greyhound with golden eyes. Fawn-colored with spots on its chest (literally just like a fawn) and ears pointed straight up. She told me proudly it was a special Sicilian breed called Cirneco dell'Etna. Maria hid behind me when the dog sniffed in our direction as she was not accustomed to animals being inside the home. It was very well behaved, didn't growl or bark at all, very meek, an ideal companion. Nonetheless Maria was edgy in its presence. We followed Arcangela up a white marble staircase—not grand or anything, but marble nonetheless—to her darkened and frankly bleak parlor. The animal sat obediently at her feet always watchful of his mistress, and every once in a while she'd pat him on the head. Who is this cousin I kept asking myself that no one had told me about? I wish I didn't have to give you ALL these details because it's already 3:30 and if I miss the pick-up this whole plan will go poof.

Avanti!!! We had a pleasant enough, formal, I would say somewhat awkward visit. She had prepared a tray with tea which sat on the marble stand next to her chair, and a few biscotti. "You drink tea in America, cousin, isn't that correct? I've heard they drink tea in

America."I could tell she wanted to be hospitable and to show that she had given thought to my tastes. She wanted me to understand she knew something about the outside world. I was very touched by that. I was also about ready to explode from being fed nonstop by my cousins for a week and a half. Even though they had barely enough for themselves, they insisted that I eat and eat. And even though I didn't necessarily want to, I felt obligated to out of respect. You know they'd serve meat when obviously they didn't normally eat it because of the high—for them—price. Believe me when I saw how the meat was cured by hanging it out in the sun where a jillion flies landed on it, I lost my appetite. But they insisted. It was a matter of pride. Crazy huh? Well, when you're in that situation you just have to go along with it, right? Meanwhile, my clothes were getting too tight. So I took uno solo biscotto from Arcangela out of politeness. Watch out for that from your cousins. They're going to try to stuff you alive, mark my words.

Anyway, Zi'Arcangela spoke mostly about her husband, "mio marito" she kept repeating with a far-off expression in her eye, a successful fabric merchant who was older than she by many years and had died twenty plus years prior. She spoke in a hush of the materials that he imported from the Veneto and Piemonte, and from France, India, and the Orient, the silks, and brocades, chiffons and challises, the linens and velvets. You would have thought they had personalities the way she went on.

She made no mention of any children. I remember wondering at the time which cousins would be the recipients of her wealth when the day came that Zi'Arcangela died. Certainly they could all vastly benefit from any financial help. The contrast between her life and theirs was starker than stark. Kid, to give you more of an idea of the poverty we're talking about, one of my cousins lived in a stone hut with dirt floors and one wall that I thought was painted black until I walked up to it close and saw it was covered with flies, not paint. That's why it was such a surprise to be in the house of a well-off relative. I was truly amazed that none of my cousins had spoken of Arcangela to me before that day, and my mother back home certainly hadn't. Arcangela isn't an easy name to forget right?

She asked me about my life, why wasn't I married, I was such a pretty girl she said why wasn't I engaged blahblahblah. Kid, I wasn't about to explain the whole long fiasco with Silvio, so I told her I worked full time as a medical transcriber in a hospital in San Francisco. She said that was all well and good but why didn't I find a husband to do the work in an office so that I could stay home and have children. I simply answered that I was keeping my eyes open, but in America we wait longer to have husbands and children, and that some women never marry. I could tell she was incredulous. Her expression said it all.

Evelyn's little note of explanation! I stretched my neck and gazed up, fixing on the bland woven wallpaper pattern curving towards the luggage bins. The desired effect, the beige coziness of a parlor, didn't fool me, not with the enormity of dark ocean and ethers just the other side of the Plexiglas windows. USE BOTTOM SEAT CUSHION FOR FLOTATION. This practical suggestion brought to mind the final message my mother had left on my machine late last night. She phoned to reassure me—herself actually—that Pan Am had an excellent safety record.

So we said our Auguri and our Arrivederlas, and on the long walk home Maria told me the whole story. Arcangela had had a daughter named Lucia who she razed by herself. Her husband had died when the girl was eight.

"Evelyn," I said aloud, "you're a professional transcriber. You meant 'raised', not 'razed'."

Lucia had all the prospects for a good life because she was devout and educated in the convent. She would make a good match for someone and to that end her mother brought a young eligible man to the house, a son of another merchant family, but Lucia rejected him. She had already fallen in love with a boy in town, a gifted medical student named Roberto. Arcangela reluctantly agreed to their engagement at first because his family wasn't exactly in the correct social stratum, but over time as she got to know him she became moderately pleased about the pairing. However, Maria said she wasn't ever overjoyed about it.

Don't ask me how they found a way to be alone together because I can't even imagine under those circumstances in those times how they managed to even have a private conversation for two seconds. To make a long story short you guessed it, Lucia got pregnant.

I unbuckled my seatbelt and stood up to stretch.

When Arcangela found out, she called off the engagement. She closed Lucia up in that house and when people asked about her, Arcangela told them Lucia had decided to enter a convent in Catania. She lived in an agonizing fear that the townspeople would learn about the pregnancy.

Every time the boy came calling Arcangela would shut the door in his face. The letters he wrote to Lucia were returned unopened. Lucia remained inside her mother's home for the whole nine months. Maria surmised that Arcangela had already made plans to give the baby to a convent, probably in faraway enough Palermo, Catania, or Messina so that word wouldn't leak back to Agrigento.

When the time came for the baby to be born, Arcangela wouldn't let any doctor or midwife attend since of course the baby wasn't supposed to exist, so Lucia was on her own. The thing is she developed complications during the labor, probably a breech birth Maria told me, and she pleaded for help. Now meanwhile her fiancé somehow knew what was going on, and pounded the front door begging Arcangela to let him in so he could help her. He had medical training after all. But Arcangela did not yield—she bolted the door and closed all the windows and shutters, still pretending that there was no pregnancy and that her daughter had left for the convent. The thing is the screaming could be heard in the piazza. She called for Roberto. She begged for mercy. She cried Aiutame. Maria herself heard it. The girl must have lost a great deal of blood. Arcangela later confided to Maria that she put a cloth between her daughter's teeth and told her to bite down on it every time the pain came. Arcangela did not leave the room—she sat clutching Lucia's hand, carefully removed the cloth between her teeth and stroked her daughter's face. Despite her help, Lucia had a whole lot of spasms and then stopped breathing.

The baby and Lucia died while Roberto, in despair, stood downstairs, clinging to the door, begging "Let me in, let me in to save them." No priest gave the last rites. No funeral took place. How could they when

Lucia hadn't 'died'? To this day my cousins still are not certain what became of the bodies, although most likely they were laid to rest in an unmarked grave.

Oh no. My eyes filled. I looked out to see rosy-fingered dawn appearing much too soon over an oceanic layer of flocked clouds. We had to be near Europe by now, possibly Ireland or Normandy? The plane began to rattle from turbulence.

So you see, that horrible hollowed-out look I saw in Zi' Arcangela's eyes was the look of a mother who had inadvertently destroyed four lives—her daughter, her granddaughter, her son-in-law-to-be, and her own—all in the name of preserving honor and appearances. Could she have done differently? Sure, from our perspective we think so, but from hers, probably not. Not in that society at that time. She was completely cornered.

A heat now coursed through me. I opened the air valve fully to cool my forehead. Consciously or not, Evelyn had meant 'razed'. Arcangela, what a soaring name for the sole beleaguered survivor. The fuselage continued to shake. We were never going to make it to Europe. We were about to plunge into the freezing water and that would be that. I was too young to die. A tragic story from the past would be the last thing I read. I would not find out whatever had happened to the girl who said no. Did she survive. What did they do to her. Was she still alive. I wished I hadn't opened the envelope and had been studying the Moors and the Norman Conquest of Sicily instead. I wished I could fall asleep sitting upright.

"Coffee or tea with milk, lemon or non-dairy creamer?" asked a flight attendant.

"Tea," I squeaked, "and milk."

"Sugar or sweetener?"

I cleared my throat. "No, ma'am." I stared at the weak whorls of high altitude steam lifting off the grayish tea. The circular cup indentation in the tray looked like a crater of the moon, and about as far away.

I asked Maria if Arcangela had really truly kept her secret from the townspeople. She said everyone knew because they could HEAR it taking place, but to her face they feigned that they did not. Yet Arcangela stuck to her story that Lucia had become a Carmelite nun in Catania, and therefore could never be seen or spoken to again. As for Roberto, he refused to leave the front door being that he was quite hysterical. Some friends came to help him away. When he was finally able to pull himself together a few months later, he left Agrigento, some thought for Palermo and some said for America, never to return.

Poor Arcangela, on the surface it would be easy to blame her, as my cousins and yes I admit it, I did too, for many years whenever I thought about it. She was the obvious villainess. But that's the easy answer. She only did what she knew she had to do. If she had publicly acknowledged that her daughter had been dishonored, they would ALL have been shunned and humiliated in Agrigento—never mind their wealthy status, and possibly because of it—and the child labeled a bastard. You know what that would have meant—permanent forever HELL. You may ask why she didn't just arrange for the marriage in a hurry? The two loved each other. But I suppose she could not forgive either Roberto for quote ruining unquote her daughter or Lucia for letting him, so she punished them both. Punished them, too, before the Agrigentesi could do it.

Believe it or not, the dear lady's still alive. Do you know she leaves her house as little as possible, a recluse for the last forty years. My cousin said that she wraps herself in her shawl, goes out to church for matins. A girl comes to cook for her. That day we visited her was most unusual, and only happened because I was there from America, and she wished to meet a relative from another country. Otherwise, she has avoided my cousins, and they her. This packet contains photographs of the couple when they were engaged, of Lucia as a young girl, of the family portrait before Arcangela's husband died. Go on look at them. It's sad as Hell.

When I first laid eyes on them I cried buckets, believe me. It just did me in. You must be wondering how I ended up with photos and why I'm entrusting you to bring them back to Sicily. When we returned to Maria's house, she climbed up on a chair and pulled a box off the shelf. Inside were these photos. She said, "Take these, Evelina, take these to remind yourself how lucky you are to live in America. I pray every day for their souls. But I don't want to keep these pictures anymore. It is best you have them." So I did, out of courtesy and respect. I am returning them now because when I phoned Maria last Christmas she said that Arcangela had started asking for the first time for photographs of "mia Lucia." At the time she had apparently destroyed all the reminders, she was so grief-stricken. Maybe she is ready at age 89 to look at them again. Maria claimed that no cousins had kept copies of any photos. Frankly, I find that a little hard to swallow. She says some had thrown them away because they were bad luck, and some couldn't find them after all these years. Maybe they just weren't fessing up to Arcangela. You can imagine how much bad blood there's been between her and the family and it hasn't diminished much over the years. I was the only one who freely admitted to still having copies and so she

asked could I please send them back to Zi'Arcangela.
Naturally, when I heard you were going I put 2 and 2
together, because I was not about to trust them to the
Italian Postal System. Don't worry honey, I've already
had good duplicates of everything made for myself.
I felt I could not refuse her request—an old woman
who has suffered every single day for the last 40 years,
as one of her last wishes in this life. Maybe it will help
ease her guilt-riddled mind.

Oh God - it's 4:50. United States P O here I come.
Thanks, doll.

Your loving friend, Ev

PS A few misspellings no doubt because rushrushrush
no time left to proof it. Big hug and best of luck finding
your woman. E

I opened the manila flap and poured out the photos. Evelyn
had sounded so cheery and casual on the phone. The brownish
pictures which spilled onto my lap sent a shiver skittering across
my skin. Lucia and Roberto, so young and fresh looking, posed
next to a tall palm plant. He stood behind her on her right;
she sat in an ornate chair holding a small bouquet of narcissus.
They smiled uncertainly, the camera registering their fragile
engagement, soon to be dissolved.

An earlier family portrait of Lucia, Arcangela, and the
fabric merchant, taken against a formal painted backdrop of
Mount Etna. Lucia wore a white lace dress, her curls held
down with bows; she clutched a porcelain doll, also dressed in
white. Her parents behind her gazed straight ahead, unsmiling
in the style of the day. Arcangela wore a modest fur collar, the
merchant a tailored suit and patterned sash in place of a belt.
His mustache was twirled at the ends, and a pocket watch
looped down. In another, Lucia, in confirmation dress and

veil, gripped a white rosary. A serious little girl, her arched brows over dark eyes with deep lids looked fated. But maybe I was imagining that fated look since I had just read what happened to her? Or was she truly doomed, being a Sicilian girl of that era, the darker probability. Had she ever had a chance at her own life?

"Refill?" A different attendant leaned over, gripping a pot of tired, simmered water drawn from a municipal tap at JFK in Queens. For something to do, I held out my cup. The tea paled.

"Thanks."

"What interesting old photos," she remarked.

"Aren't they?" I answered quickly to keep my emotions in check. How like Evelyn to drop a bomb in my lap. She could have insured the package and sent it herself, but then the courier wouldn't have been privy to this tale. The memory of the primitive hot pink dress drama in the piazza of Agrigento and the rescue by a Mafia Don crowded in. The same town where this sorry tale took place. I slid all the papers and crisp-from-age pictures back into their envelopes, gripped the armrest and hoisted myself up. No way was I going anywhere near the entire province of Agrigento; I'd mail the package with the highest postage possible from Palermo sometime early next week.

Staggering down the aisle offered a view of open-mouthed sleepers, twitching insomniacs and still-perky teenagers. Everyone looked so vulnerable and rumpled. VACANT said the bathroom door latch, which summed up my state too. All these sleepless hours I could have been brushing up on five thousand years of Sicilian history with my assortment of guidebooks, instead of going into a tailspin reading the letter. Wait a minute—Evelyn *had* written a genuine piece of Sicilian history. Cold water on face, brush through hair, toothpaste on travel toothbrush, more cold water on face. Cruelty-free red lipstick for that adult, put-together look. Hah. I squeezed back into my seat and worked the red white and blue mailer down to the bottom of the suitcase.

A few hours later a flight attendant tapped me awake to buckle up for the descent. Blearily, I gazed down on electrifying blue water, the northern coast of Sicilia slowly rotating into view. Monte Pellegrino, looking like the broad back of a sleeping elephant from up here, lay beached, as always, at one end of the sumptuous, immortal bay. Palermo, the wild, unappreciated queen of the south glistened in an afternoon Mediterranean haze. I'd phoned Nonny at her rest home yesterday to tell her about my visit to her sister's daughters in Palermo. "I'm so happy, *tesoro*. Who's calling, darling?" she'd answered.

We drifted down over the city lazily, closing in on an effortless landing, until the blunt surprise at the last moment when we dove into a narrow valley and the mountains rose up to encompass us, as if a magnet were pulling at the jet. The runway chomped at the tires. The Sicilian tarmac chided, effortless, you think? Easy landing you expect? You must have forgotten who you're dealing with. And what took you so long to come back, anyway? Where have you been, *tesoro*?

Chapter IV

Arrival

Just inside the terminal gate of Punta Raisi Airport, a pair of *carabinieri*—handsome, official, crisp in their navy blue wool uniforms—stood smoking together under a sign *VIETATO FUMARE.* Travelers surged past, clutching Easter breads shaped like doves and bells. They laughed and chatted in their beautiful language. *La Bella Figura* was apparent right away in the styled way they wore their suits, and how they carried themselves. Americans just didn't compare. I lugged my stuff straight to a caffè and set my foot on the rail.

"Sir?"

The white-jacketed, long-aproned bartender was busily buffing his chrome espresso machine with a cloth.

"Excuse me, *signor?*"

"*Prego, signorina.*"

"Do you accept American dollars?"

"We do."

"*Uno cappuccino decaffeinato, per favore.*"

"What?"

"Can you make one without caffeine?"

He stopped polishing to stare, his palms aimed heavenward. "Why would you want to do that? Ruin a perfectly good coffee? You might as well ask for grapes with no seeds or, or wine with no alcohol, or bread with no flour!"

"We have those things in the USA," I admitted. "We Americans think we can improve on nature."

"No! Really? What a disaster."

"You're right. Pardon me. A regular cappuccino, please."

"Immediately."

Two security guards walked a pair of German shepherds who were straining against their heavy black leashes and thick leather chest strappings, their expert noses testing the air.

The bartender set down the foamy cup with a flourish, adding a little stainless steel spoon. "They're looking for bombs, *signorina*. They patrol twenty-four hours a day."

"Right. Of course, right." I took a too-fast gulp, singeing my tongue. "A glass of ice water please, also?"

Through the jet-lag that started to hit, I surveyed the crush of Sicilians. This year's fashion uniform for women and girls was very American golf course country club: a tweedy suit, knee-length with boxy jacket, and cream-colored handkerchief exploding from breast pocket. So much for imagining that I would fit in, but I was a little let down; I had counted on Italy to at least have wised up and deflated the shoulder pad by now. They had reigned far too long, accompanying Ronald Reagan through two terms of office. As the caffeine started to work on the edges of my exhaustion, ridiculous buoyant bulging shoulders were everywhere I looked. Then I recovered just enough presence of mind to tell myself that in the larger, wide world, shoulder pads were of no significance whatsoever.

I sucked an ice chip to numb my burned tongue and tracked a short, intent figure striding into the waiting lounge. She'd be the right age for Maia. She was slightly stooped, sturdy, dressed in a tailored brown winter suit cut not at all like the fashion uniform—and no longer in black. She was searching the faces of the crowd intently.

"Maia?" I called out. "Cousin Maia," I waved.

"Cara Natalie!" she beamed, rushing toward me.

We embraced blood-of-my-blood, then pulled back and studied each other before embracing again. She came up to my forehead. Her once black hair was swept back with a tortoise-shell headband, highlighting the generous, open features I remembered, especially the round, intelligent dark eyes that always seemed to be posing a question or observing her surroundings, and the brown birthmark at her jawline.

"I am so glad you have come to see us!"

"I too am so very glad," I gushed.

She reached into her ear to adjust a hearing aid.

"May I buy you an espresso, Maia?"

"Not for me, but take as long as you need to finish. We have all the time in the world. I am retired, after all."

I bolted down the rest of the scalding coffee and chased it with water. In a smooth gesture Maia picked up the bill, pulled out some hundred lire notes, grabbed hold of my suitcase and began rolling it towards the exit. I left an American dollar under the cup.

We climbed into her two-person Fiat, which had no seat belts, then blasted out of the parking lot, the muffler yammering. Small autos honked and darted around us on the coast road, leaving ghosts of exhaust.

"Do you remember Sicilia? We've changed since you were here. There used to be olive groves and orange trees, meadows, goats all along this coast. *Beh*, the shepherds and the farmers disappeared and the buildings took their place." Yes, right up to the edge of the road in a raw cinderblock mishmash.

Maia pointed to a small island not far offshore. "There's the Isola delle Femmine, built by Saracens in the eleventh century. Tuna fishermen in times past would bring their wives and children there at dawn. Notice its easy slope. They would be left for the whole day and picked up when the fishermen returned home in the evening. This way no other men could get to them. So went the reasoning, at any rate."

The Island of Women was deserted and forlorn with a single rounded tower. "Isn't this the town Joe DiMaggio's family came from?"

"Who, dear?"

A driver plowed diagonally across our path, nearly side-swiping us. I let out a yelp. Maia pressed on the gas pedal. Her speedometer shot up to a hundred and five kilometers. The driver turned his head sideways so that we could clearly see his profile, then gestured a yawn of indifference and slowed in front of us, daring her to rear-end him. This seemed to activate my seventy-two-year-old cousin who buzzed close to his bumper. With a toot-toot of his horn he peeled away, leaving us behind. My cousin shrugged, then let out a chuckle.

I strained to follow her commentary above the noise of Palermo, which we'd entered. It was overspilling with traffic, pedestrians, and crazy, chaotic movement.

"The population has flooded in from the countryside since your visit. Too many *palazzi*, too close together." She shook her head.

"You call these new tall buildings palaces, huh?"

"Palaces. We all live in palaces," she grinned ruefully as the tires bounced against the curb. "You can see the congestion they have caused."

A billboard atop the *palazzo* across the street encouraged all to try *ESERCIZIO AEROBICA!* In her pink and white striped leotard with shoulder pads, gold chains, feathered black hair fluffed up behind a stretch pink headband, the pert, toned model beamed from endorphins. *Endorfini?*

While I pulled myself out of her bumper car after she'd parked, Maia hailed a guy pushing a Motta Gelato cart on the street. "Which do you prefer, Natalie, *pistacchio* or *torrone?*"

"Ummm, oh gee, I can't decide."

"One of each," she told the vendor. She insisted I taste both. "*Buono, no?*"

Maia's building—the narrow, dark wood elevator with its dim bulb, the glossy marble floors of the corridor and her penthouse suite illumined in warm afternoon light, her antiques, and even the smell of furniture wax—had hardly changed since our family visit.

But on the terrace looking out, the view I remembered of Monte Pellegrino, majestic from base to top, was now blocked by the haphazard ten-story *palazzi* in all their weird, post-modern shapes, thrown up in the last decade or so. Now, only the long, flat summit of Pilgrim Mountain hovered above the high-rise rooftops.

The first sighting of Pellegrino from this same spot in '69 had fused in my memory, always evoking a sweeping feeling of optimism whenever I summoned it up. The revelation of arriving in the old country and being treated to the thrill of a wide-open panorama on our ancestors' historic city spreading before us had never left me. Their old world was suddenly a new world. My grandparents would not ever have been able to see all of Palermo from above, as the family did that August afternoon; Maia's building was amongst the first post-war high-rises in town.

The change to her skyline shocked me. Now *her* apartment was towered over by concrete and shadows, and she wouldn't be able to pinpoint, as she had that first day, the location of the grotto where Santa Rosalia, the matron saint of Palermo, had sought shelter to receive her visions, and where prehistoric peoples had drawn pictographs ten thousand or more years ago.

"Would you like to rest a little, Natalie? Bathe?"

"What a good idea." I pulled off my travel jacket. "You're not having a drought here like we are in California?"

"Not especially. Sicily always suffers from too little water. Go ahead," she gestured toward the bathroom, "fill it up." She wanted me to feel at home. We were kin, after all.

I balanced my ice cream cup on the edge of her deep blue tub, turned the handles, reminiscent of musical quarter notes, and lowered myself into the steaming water. The soap, so floral in an old world way, lathered quickly, but the stream from the spigot soon gurgled to a trickle. I fiddled with the formal Italian fixtures and flattened myself into the few wet inches: I had arrived. Arrived on Maundy Thursday, the Thursday of Mysteries, the thirtieth day of the third month on the three-cornered island. I finished off the *torrone gelato*. When my fingertips puckered and the smell of jet fuel was finally washed away, I sloshed around for enough water to rinse out all the shampoo. Nope. I propped my foot on the bidet to dry. Bidets! I had forgotten all about them.

Maia had been waiting in the living room, and gestured that I sit at her round table covered with a pressed white linen cloth. She wheeled in a cart with a tureen of steaming vegetable soup, rolls and bottled water.

"How is my dear Auntie in San Francisco?"

"Nonny's pretty well, considering that she'll be ninety-eight in October and lives in a *casa di riposo*." In Italian, it sounded like a gorgeous dream, a place anyone might want to visit at any time, then once refreshed, move on from. Somehow "house of rest" didn't seem anything like "rest home."

"I relish this news from America. Your grandmother is the last one of my mother's generation."

"And Nonny would be so pleased to know that you and I are together here tonight. She's forgotten many things, but not Palermo."

"The redheads," Maia mused. Her mother, my grandmother and the other auburn-haired sisters. "At the turn of the century they would attend the *passeggiata*—the weekly promenade where girls walked in one direction and boys in the other, round and round, so that they could look at each other—here in town at the Villa Giulia on Sunday afternoons, and heads would turn to admire their brilliant hair. Everyone noticed them. They really stood out. *Ehh, purtroppo,* only in the countryside do you see the *passeggiata* now. Red hair is the sign of Norman blood, by the way. I can see that you've inherited some."

I patted down my damp mop. "Not much. Not like my mom had, and certainly nothing like Nonny. It's getting diluted."

"Tell me about your wonderful mother. I adore her. I always feel so close to her, even though we live far away."

"Yes, she feels the same towards you, Maia. Weren't you both born the same year?"

"That was my sister Sofia, who you'll see tomorrow. I'm a few years younger."

"That's right." I filled her in on my mother and everyone else. Maybe because I hadn't eaten a meal since somewhere over Nova Scotia, and taking a bath had grounded me enough to realize I was famished, the rolls tasted nothing like any rolls anywhere else that I had ever eaten in the whole of my life. They were direct, they were real, they were fresh and unsalted, they were simple, honest and moist. They were baked from grain that hadn't seen the inside of a lab but had descended in a straight, un-hybridized lineage from the sheaves of wheat festooning Medusa's complicated headdress. The soup was good too.

Maia stood to clear the dishes and I jumped up to help. "No, no, you're the guest. Sit. Relax." She returned with a bowl of oranges. We shaved thin pieces off a wedge of pecorino cheese on a platter between us.

"Maia?"

"*Sì, cara?*"

"Do you happen to remember someone by the name of Franca Viola?"

"Franca Viola!" She sat upright, looking straight—piercingly—at me. "Of course I remember her."

"What ever became of her?"

"That I do not know." She put her knife down. "Why do you ask such a thing?"

"I've always been curious about her story. Do you think she's still alive?"

"Oh surely she is still alive. If she were not, we would have heard about it."

"Do you suppose she stayed in Trapani all this time?"

"Trapani? That's not where she lived. That's not where the kidnap occurred. It was in Alcamo. This I remember absolutely."

"Ah . . . and how far to Alcamo from Palermo?"

"Just an hour from here, if that, traveling from the airport in the opposite direction."

"So you think she still lives in Sicily, then?"

My cousin grew wide-eyed. "Probably." The conversation, which had been moving along so well, with me feeling kind of confident in the language, halted.

"We don't talk about these things anymore," she finally added. "It happened a long time ago, and it was very sad and hard on the poor girl. People don't like to bring it up."

"No? I would like to find out where she is."

Maia sat rigid, puzzled. "*Perché?*"

"Because she was so courageous . . . so strong."

"But how? There is no means to find this woman, Natalie!" she said urgently, her neck muscles straining.

"No?" I straightened my spine.

With her fruit knife, Maia took an orange and peeled it, rotating it slowly so the skin fell away in a helix toward her plate. "I don't see how you can do it."

"I was thinking I could go to her town—to Alcamo—and ask around."

"I wouldn't do that if I were you." Her knife was poised suspended in one hand, the peel of the orange boing-boinging from the other. "*Tst*," she clicked her tongue and wagged her finger. "It's not done."

I busied myself trying to make an orange peel helix like hers. Red juice splattered all over the plate.

"It could be dangerous," she continued.

"Even though it happened over twenty-two years ago?" I broke the fruit into segments. A blood orange, it tasted like raspberry perfume.

Maia was shaking her head in thought. "I'll tell you one thing: her story was front-page news for a year. I remember very clearly those daily headlines about Viola, oh yes."

"Were most people on her side?"

"In the north, absolutely. But Sicilians were deeply divided on the subject. Some felt that she was completely out of line. They called her the most terrible names out in the street. Ugly things. *Puttana, Strega, Diavola*. Can you imagine? Though many, many Sicilians did support her."

"Did you?"

She twisted a button on her blouse. "I did, of course."

"How common was the kidnap custom? I mean, did the guy just pick out a woman and drag her off? How did it work exactly?"

"*Beh* . . ." Maia shifted in her chair and put the knife down. "Do you know about the *fuitina*? The little flight," she flapped her fingers like wings, "means elopement. Couples who wanted to marry against their parents' wishes—say they had been formally engaged to others, or they had no money for a wedding, or they had to do so in a hurry, if you understand my meaning—made a *fuitina*. It was a pretend kidnap, a sort of a ritual in which the boy stole the girl and they spent time alone together. Now they were considered as good as married."

"How often did *fuitina* happen?"

"It was common."

"And how often kidnap?"

"Often enough, unfortunately."

"How far back did the kidnap custom go?"

"*Ehhh*," Maia whirled her hand in the air, "centuries, well, millennia. Back to the ancient Greeks. They had a term for it: *Kleptogamos*, literally meaning stolen wedding. We can look to the Romans as well, and certainly the Arabs. *Beh*, what about the Old Testament? You ask a big question with a veiled answer. This is an island, after all, where everything that came here tended to stick."

"Does it still happen, Maia?"

"Oh, no. We're very modern now. Viola changed all that."

"Did she? No kidding! What good news. Was her kidnap supposed to be a *fuitina*?"

"No, no! She did not want that man. I'm merely describing those times. Remember, back then a girl always had chaperones. Her honor was of supreme importance. In those days a boy would visit a girl in her living room. Mother and grandmother and aunt would sit down too. The couple never went out for a sweet together. Never. They would not go to the cinema by themselves. Ever. They might have had, effectively, no chance to talk alone and to get to know each other until after the matrimonial ceremony. The girl would have to let the boy know she liked him with a look or a signal of some sort. Such would become the engagement. Or it was accomplished by the relatives arranging everything and the girl was frequently the last in the family to know. Many girls had no choice. But this was not what happened to *La Viola*."

"What *did* happen to *La Viola*?"

Maia gazed out on the summit of the great mountain. "I'll speak to my son when he returns." She paused and pushed her plate to the side. "They're away for a few days and very excited that you are here. I'll see what he thinks about this."

"Ah."

"He may know someone who would know. I can't promise anything, Natalie, you do understand that?"

"*Capisco.*" I understand.

"And I must tell you that for the next four days, every-thing closes. There's not a person you could call who will be at work until Tuesday. It's Holy Week. We have many Easter celebrations to see in these next several days."

"Yes, how thrilling. I can hardly wait!"

"*Oh-kay,* as you Americans say. We begin tomorrow morning." She set the plates on the cart. A zing of excitement rushed through me. I began to clear the table. She wouldn't let me into the kitchen to wash dishes. "Rest," she urged.

I did. I lay down with all my clothes on and woke up around two or three or four, blinking into the Mediterranean night. If I had conducted my life the old Sicilian way, glances and signals, I would have been engaged to countless guys. How absurd. I'd never actually been engaged. Not with the doctor by choice, not with Boothe not by choice. Who knew the best way for people to find each other, to commit to each other? I unlaced my shoes, put on the black nightgown and drifted off.

Waking with a jolt, I remembered where I was and switched on the light to check the time: 6 a.m. Friday in marvelous Palermo, 9 p.m. Thursday in Boothe-infused Berkeley. The apartment was silent, no sound of Maia stirring yet. I rolled onto my side. I'd dreamed something long and elaborate, though the only fragment dragged back from sleep was of Maia driving me in from the airport with a tiny wig on top of her head, like the scrolled ones English barristers wear, only red. Even through a time-zone fog, interpreting that dream was pretty easy: I feared Maia sat in judgment of my curiosity. I did have to calm down about the Franca story and not be so pushy while my whole Sicilian sojourn was just starting to unfurl.

The thing was, I couldn't fall back to sleep again even though it would now be bedtime in California, because Nonny's reaction when I'd first spotted the article was coming back to me. Lying here, the scene re-inflated, the three-inch filler in the *Chronicle* jumping out of its column at my thirteen-year-old self. Marry the rapist? Were they crazy? At least the girl knew what to do, even if her society didn't. As soon as my grandmother jingled her keys inside the front door, I ran downstairs with the newspaper to get her opinion. Every day around three-thirty she let herself in after walking over from her apartment near Van Ness Avenue to save the fifteen-cent bus fare. She'd become a widow before my mother married; you could say she practically lived with us—every afternoon—until she took herself home in the evening.

"Hi Nonny." We kissed each cheek. I held her worsted coat by the collar as she pulled her arms from the sleeves.

"Hel-lo, *tesoro*. But you look so pale today. What has happened to your lips?"

"Nothing."

"*Mi fai vedere.*" Let me see.

"Nonny!" Frosted Lip Slicker by Yardley of London.

"What?" She made a face and felt for the folded handkerchief she kept up her sleeve. "Where do you find such a thing?"

"Woolworth's." Forty-three cents, babysitting money. Nearly two hours of labor for one tube of marvy English glamor.

"This is free country, but in my opinion, it makes you look like a young phantom. It does not become your natural, fresh, youthful complexion."

"That's groovy." I knew she had to restrain herself from wiping off the Yardley. "You're entitled to your opinion." I thrust the front-page section of the newspaper at her. "I found an article about Sicily."

"Ah, si?" she smiled expectantly. In those days the *Chronicle* filled the gaps in its columns with miniature tales of human woe or whimsy, mostly from overseas, or with funny little tidbits about nature. The only time I could remember Sicilian news—filler or not—was when Mount Etna erupted. I hung the worn woolen coat in the closet on the wooden Nonny hanger, while I carefully watched her mouth form the words silently. My grandmother's face crumpled.

"Why would they do that to girls? It's so unfair," I spouted.

"Ehh, injust it is."

"I need to know: will they kill her?"

"No, no." She went white. *"Bedda Matri."* Beautiful mother. "What a thing this girl has done."

"Will they force her into a cave outside the village?"

"No, no cave."

"Will they make her leave the town?"

"I hope so not."

"What if she's pregnant?"

"Madonna mia." A flush filled her cheeks, like the red solution our science teacher had made us produce in test tubes last week by combining two clear liquids. She cringed into her hands, affording a view of her carefully braided and bobby-pinned rosette of silver hair. "Poor girl," my grandmother shook her bowed head. *"Povera Sicilia."*

"It shouldn't be like that there."

"I agree, *cara.* But what about it can we do at this distance? Let's not dwell on it anymore. Let's talk about my beautiful city Palermo, not the provinces. A pearl of the Mediterranean Sea, surrounded with friendly mountains we call The Golden Shell. It has very, very old university—your grandfather studied medicine there—and not only one, but two opera houses, each more beautiful than the other. One has a crown of bronze horses; the other is second biggest in all of Europa, the Teatro

Massimo. Your ancestor made a bronze lion which guards that front door, so that all the music does not fly out."

"Oh Nonny, please—I'm not a child." Usually I loved hearing her recall the exotic city she left at fourteen, my age in a couple of months, but not today.

"Palermo bay have waters of *acquamarina, verde, azzurro, turchese. Che bedda!* Someone you may go and tip your toe into the sea and float on top from so much salt you don't have to kick, not even once. Did you know we drove to school six days a week in the *carrozza* pulled by our shining black horse? He wore a big green feather on top of his head. He was so lovely. We called him Totò. And we would smell the jasmines and orange blossoms in the airs." I knew the plush scent well, thanks to her. "These lovely joys and more you will find in my city."

She had imparted many stories from the time before the family unexpectedly uprooted and had to cross the Atlantic and, after a couple of years on the East Coast, moved to the West Coast. A bay with fishing boats, citrus in winter, and hills. Faintly like Palermo.

"Take off from the piano the world," she instructed. "I want to show you an interesting something."

I grabbed our Rand-McNally globe to humor her and to keep her talking. She located her triangled island, traced her finger along the Mediterranean through the Strait of Gibraltar and the breadth of the black Atlantic, grazing orange, green and pink united states until halting at San Francisco, California.

"You see? The same latitude identical. Read aloud the number, please. I wish to memorize."

"Thirty something, seven or eight." Idly I glided the sphere back and forth between the sisterly cities.

"Did I ever tell you about the nightingale at my window that I tamed with olives and wild blueberries?"

"Yep."

"And the English Garden next door, full of statues. Did I tell you that my father's cousin, Benedetto Civiletti, sculpted some of them?"

"Uh-huh."

"He was famous."

"I know."

"We used to play in his studio. And I'm sure I told you about the blood oranges."

"Ewww. I will never ever eat anything that has blood in the name."

"You wouldn't say so if you tasted one. They were very prized to us. We called them *moro* or *tarocco*."

"Nonny, what will happen to this girl?"

"I don't know."

"What a weirdo tradition! It's so twisted!"

"*Ehh.*"

"At least one person knew right from wrong."

"Let's hope so well for her, *tesoro*. My mother was supposed to marry someone also."

"Your mother was kidnapped too?!"

"No, not kidnapped." A silence followed. "She had to reject someone, though."

"Yeah? Are you going to tell me?"

Nonny fidgeted. I waited for the story. I had to reject someone from school last month who was bugging me, whose attention I did not want. I didn't feel flattered and I didn't want to attract that boy. Yuck. If only the whole thing hadn't happened. The Beatles were my guys. Ringo in particular, though I loved all four with a devotion that time could never tarnish. This boy was in one or two of my classes, but I'd never spoken to him. While I was boarding the bus one day after school he ran to catch up with me and got on too. There were no empty seats. I held on to the bar. He put his hand next to mine on the metal pole and confessed to having a crush on me. I stared at him blankly; I didn't know what to say to someone I'd barely noticed. He angrily told me I was playing hard to get. I didn't know what that meant, but I decided to get off at the next stop.

"Where are you going? You don't live near here," he yelled after me.

I didn't answer but turned my back and walked the rest of the way home. I immediately called Audrey to see if she knew what playing hard to get meant. She didn't know either but would ask her older brother and call me back.

"It probably means . . . I don't know what it means, but I'd rather play 'A Hard Day's Night' than play Hard to Get!"

We guffawed over that one, agreed that he was a drip and a creep. I should tell him I'm not playing anything, she advised. She would shove him away if he approached me again if I gave her the signal. I wondered if this was anything like what my grandmother meant about her mother. Probably not. Probably nothing like it.

"Instead," Nonny resumed, "my mother married the boy she flirted with in church. They looked at each other across the aisle, many glances back and forth."

"You mean your father?"

"Yes, my father, of course. Your great-grandfather, Vincenzo. It all worked out in the end. Someday I will tell you more."

"Why someday? Tell me now."

"Your great-grandmother's story is complicated. Another time. But don't be upset about this dear Franca anymore now. *Basta.*" She folded the paper. The subject was closed.

"Okay, never mind."

"I make you for lunch tomorrow a *carciofi frittata* sandwich. For your friend too?"

"Sure, Audrey thinks artichoke sandwiches are totally fab."

"Ask your friend what she thinks about lips so pale."

Currently, Audrey's lips were paler than mine. She had applied a triple coat of Yardley outside Woolworth's on Chestnut after school. Intention was everything. Audrey was so with it, probably because she had actually been born in London.

My adorable Nonny, so hopelessly old-fashioned, so out of touch with the swinging sixties, couldn't possibly get it. It wasn't her fault she was born in another century. She would never understand what Lennon and McCartney were writing about, or what kind of deep thoughts George was thinking under his bangs. She would never understand about Mods and Rockers. She could not fathom that Audrey and I had bought tickets priced at $8.25 each in January for the concert August 27th at Candlestick Park, where girls would be screaming non-stop, though she did help me lay out the Butterick pattern on top of the pale apricot cotton poplin I had selected for the dress I would sew and wear to the show. She was already worried about who would drive us there and who would pick us up. It would be late, it would be dark, it was on the other end of San Francisco. One couldn't start fretting too soon.

After Nonny left for home, I opened the paper to the filler about the Sicilian girl with the pretty name, so musical sounding, but I didn't cut it out. And here I am resting on a bed in Palermo, Nonny's beautiful home town, with her niece Maia hosting me. What a trip! I dozed off.

Chapter V

Venerdi Santo

Friday, Good. Eleven a.m. I peeked out my door. Under gray skies, the mountain summit caught timid blotches of sunlight. Maia stood on her terrace watering vines of red nasturtium, and tweeting to a canary that hopped around in its cage.

"*Filumenu miu. Carinu. Beddu. Giallu.*" My *Filumenu*, dear yellow beauty.

Then she caught sight of me and strode inside. "Good morning *cara*. I hope you slept well? Have some breakfast."

Fresh rolls, ruby-colored jam and a teapot waited on the white tablecloth in the dining room. She had brewed the tea with citron, making it lemony to the tenth power. I spooned some of the jam onto a pillow of airy, sweet bread. She had canned the jam last summer from black cherries she'd picked in the Madonie Mountains—*amarena* she called it. I added a dab of unsalted butter, not the yellower color of home—it was light, still cool from the refrigerator—which on the tongue tasted so local that the cows it came from might be grazing on one of the hills of the Golden Shell outside. Up here on the seventh floor of a high-rise in this ancient city, the simple pastured essence of *burro* from the province of Palermo probably hadn't changed since my grandmother tasted it as a young girl, which she might have done on special occasions.

"Whenever you're ready," Maia said, nodding towards the front door.

Within minutes she had us speeding through a park.

"La Favorita we call it, the one-time playground of Bourbon kings—Spanish, French and Neapolitan—who ruled The Kingdom of the Two Sicilies from 1734 to 1816. As you can see, they reserved the best for themselves, as royals always do."

The park hugged the base of Pellegrino and soon we were in the depths of its woods. We came to a red light. There was no traffic at all. Dark smoke smelling of creosote pulsed from metal cans spaced along the roadside. I pointed at them.

"They're part of the landscape. They always go, day and night, to light the way to the prostitutes," Maia explained matter-of-factly. A few feet from the roadway, a bevy of middle-aged women in dingy slips lounged on old armchairs with the stuffing falling out. Every one of them had bleached blond hair and cigarettes hanging from their mouths. They turned to look at our car—the only one—saw we weren't customers and looked away. "Poor things," Maia clucked her tongue, "out here shivering in their underwear in this miserable weather."

We glided into Mondello beside the sea, the creamy white paint of its bungalows brightly reflecting the overcast light. Cousin Sofia lived two blocks from luscious golden sand and azure water, perfect for wading way out and floating forever on the turquoise swells. Already I could taste the salty brilliance.

Maia sighed. "You will judge for yourself how my older sister is when we arrive. She wears black-and-white now, which she's been allowing herself lately, though technically she's still in mourning, seven years being the customary length of time for widows in the cities. We do not wear black permanently, as do women of the country. But clothing is not the question, really." She sighed again. "What upsets me is she rarely leaves her house, claiming she can't walk anymore, that she's too weak. Six years now she has convinced herself of *invalidismo*. I call it terminal widowhood. She's only seventy-five, after all."

Maia rang the bell, then let us in with a key. We climbed the steps to Sofia's flat. She sat like a white-haired doll in front of the large oil landscapes and seascapes her husband had painted, clapping her hand over her mouth in disbelief and pleasure that I'd flown all the way from California to see them.

"Come sit next to me, my love, my dear," she caressed my cheek. "Have an almond cookie and an *orgeata* I've poured especially for you. I want you to try a typical Sicilian beverage. Now tell me everything about our family in San Francisco. Everything!"

Dressed in smart black and white checks, she stayed poised on the edge of the sofa, attentive, blinking her alert dark eyes. She was more diminutive than Maia, a little frail. I started with Nonny, most aged matriarch who no longer remembered that she was, and worked up the family tree into the branches. Maia nodded with approval and pressed cookies on me in case I felt faint from exertion.

"We're elated that you've come to see us. We're honored. We're enchanted. And everyone will want to see you. We'll have many happy get-togethers."

Maia said something in dialect. Sofia's smile dropped.

"But why?" she asked her sister.

Maia gestured at me. Sofia stared at my forehead, her mouth frozen in a lower-case o, her sable eyes blinking. She turned to her sister. "We don't have any news, do we, about Franca Viola?" They shook their heads in slow motion.

"I want to learn the full story, which is unknown in my country," I said, sipping the cloudy liquid as sweet as the glucose tolerance test, with just an afterthought of almond. For politeness' sake I worked on downing the entire glass.

"*Beh*," Sofia uttered, "*La Viola* was a genuine figure in our modern history, granted." Like Maia, she had taught high school. "So much changed from that point on. But in a certain sense, one could argue that too much emphasis was placed on her case. If Franca Viola hadn't done it, some other girl would have sooner or later. We were heading in that direction. We were catching up with the times."

"Someone will know where she is, no?" I watched Sofia carefully.

She turned to Maia. "Things must be very different in America."

Maia blinked. Sofia blinked, then said, "But, dear little cousin, here we don't talk. Frankly, you should not go looking for her."

I decided to blink in solidarity. Sofia reached behind the sofa and pulled out a box of Baci chocolates. She broke the seal and displayed the foiled baubles in front of my nose. Candy as interrogative diversion.

"Mmmm, Baci!" I lit up for the women's benefit. "But I'm not sure I understand why."

"We are Sicilians, you see, and Sicilians respect silence, because we must."

"Do you mean people won't talk to me because I'm a foreigner?"

Maia corrected my word choice, *straniera*, with the more commonly used *forestiere*.

Sofia pivoted on the sofa and took my hand. "Our lives depend on silence. Nobody will want to stir up the past, do you see." This was not a question.

"No?" I nibbled the edge of the hazelnut delicacy. The sisterly glances lingered. I couldn't interpret them. "After so long, why does it matter?" I asked.

"So long you say? In America you're on to the next thing," Sofia snap-snapped her fingers, "always new new new. Here twenty years is nothing."

They lapsed into warp-speed Italian. Maia had obviously been using a remedial tempo with me ever since the airport. I'd been making gaffe after gaffe, unable to remember tense and agreement and, most elemental of all: what was masculine and what feminine. *Il dramma, la mano!* It was exhausting. I busied myself with leaning back into the cushions, polishing off The Kiss and on my knee smoothing out the translucent fortune paper clinging inside its foil wrapper:

> By all means marry: If you get a good wife you will become happy, and if you get a bad one you will become a philosopher.

"*Scusa*, little cousin, we don't want trouble for you." Sofia took hold of my other hand with both of hers. Though small, they gripped fiercely. "We want you to be safe here. We would worry so for you."

"No need to worry. I'll use my good judgment."

"I advise you to be very cautious when you ask after her." Maia nodded. "That's precisely what I told her last night."

"I promise."

Maia and Sofia both fidgeted. I was pushing them.

"Is that silence you speak of what you call *Omertà*?"

"*Omertà* is a kind of silence that has to do with not snitching to the authorities. It's the code of honor," Sofia said, "but this topic you bring up pains us."

"I did not realize that. I'm sorry. I don't want to cause pain. Well, how about a quick walk to the beach?" And a break from old lady worry (evidently a family trait spanning two hemispheres), a breath of sea air, and a chance to dispel this sugar. I wanted lapping seashore, a flash of *acquamarina*, a Mediterranean toe dunking. I felt suffocated sitting in this closed-up parlor.

"Oh, no," Sofia frowned. "Even if I had the strength to walk there, I wouldn't, and you mustn't either. Promise me you won't during your visit. The beach has been closed due to pollution. The authorities have posted signs. We never walk on the sand anymore, because heroin addicts throw down hypodermic needles. I used to teach those kids, now I hear that they are lying around with empty eyes. Their parents are destroyed . . . we have lost so many."

A stifling, gravitational silence settled onto the shuttered room. The green and blue waters her husband had captured in oil paint years ago glowed above her head. I wanted to get out of here—to go walk on the promenade or around the block or something. I wanted to see the real greens and blues. "What can be done?" I finally asked.

"Time passing, and a different society." Sofia paused, deciding whether she wanted to say more. "You see Natalie, some people fought to keep drugs out of Sicily, they were only interested in export, unfortunately to your country. But some were so greedy that they didn't even care about their own people. The two factions went to war." Slowly she exhaled. "There were many, many murders—many families left fatherless—until the latter group I mentioned finally won." Her voice lowered as if we were in danger of being overheard. "The Mafia here is '*una piaga*'."

"A plague? Wait a second . . ." I flipped through my mini-dictionary, three inches by two. "I found it: an open wound."

"A wound that won't heal," Maia clarified.

"Things will never change," muttered Sofia.

"*Pazienza*," Maia counseled her sister. "We must maintain the long view. In the meantime," she rose, jingling her keys, "we do need to get going since we want to see the parade from the start."

"Good, good," Sofia brightened and waved us on our way. "You'll notice, Natalie, that the Madonna will be dressed all in black, only for today."

"Won't you come along, Sofia?"

She pointed to her legs. "Have a wonderful time," she squeezed my hand, "then next visit you can tell me all about it."

"If only my sister would resume living," Maia grumbled, driving defiantly back towards Palermo in her free-form style. "I become very frustrated by this. She used to walk four kilometers every morning with her husband no matter what, along the Lido. But when we stop moving, we lose the facility. We must keep going. Don't you agree? It is imperative! *Avanti!*" Both Maian hands flew off the steering wheel to emphasize this important principle, and stayed off. Using its innate sense of direction, the Fiat steered itself onto a broad boulevard, zipping past a cluster of cinnamon-colored apartment buildings three and four stories high.

"Ooh, Art Nouveau!" I squealed. The stucco work on one of them was so delicate that it looked as though lengths of real fabric had been dipped into russet-colored wash and pressed permanently into the facade, like parted drapery.

"Here, we do not use the French term. Instead we say 'Liberty' style."

"Lee-Bear-Tee," I repeated. "It does look liberated—very free and loose. And so elegant."

Maia then launched into a lesson on Sicilian architecture—"a composite of so many styles found nowhere else in the world"—which she illustrated with ready examples unfolding to our left and our right. I whipped my head from one side to the other to take in Palermo's grandeur. "Here we have the Politeama Garibaldi opera house in the so-called Pompeiian style, with its tiara of bucking bronze horses."

"Stupendous!"

"And you now see the Teatro Massimo which is known for its perfect acoustics, the second largest opera house in all of Europe, though still being restored after many decades and therefore closed at this time. We call the style Corinthian, because of the columns. Notice the lion statue with the lady to the right of the step—do you see? Our ancestor, Benedetto Civiletti sculpted her. She's Tragedy."

Far out! "Nonny loved that statue. She had a black and white photo postcard of it on her table that I looked at every time I visited her apartment." A diaphanously clad dame rode the big cat bareback. She was no delicate damsel either, but muscled like a man. Her hair was pulled up in an intriguing top-knot, she gripped a Greek drama mask to her bosom and was on the verge of sliding off the maned animal's back.

"And the sculpture to the left of the steps is Comedy."

"Civiletti did that one too?"

"Only Tragedy."

Comedy was comely enough, but a lightweight. Frothy. "I like Tragedy more."

"Do you?" Maia chuckled.

"Because she's got more substance. I'm not saying so on account of our blood ties." Top Knot was my kind of girl, that's all. More meat on her bones and a tad intimidating.

The boulevard narrowed, its name changing once or twice, until it reached the heart of the fabulous city where it intersected gloriously with another major thoroughfare, the Corso Vittorio Emanuele.

"We are now at the famed crossroads known as I Quattro Canti." At each of the four corners stood a curving baroque marble facade with a fountain, a female figure personifying a season above that, then a king, then a saint on top. Four directions. Four water sources. Autumn, Winter, Summer, Spring. Four royal highnesses. Maia rattled off the four matron saints of Palermo, "Cristina, Ninfa, Oliva and Agata." A crowd surged below these antiquities, jostling for places to squeeze in along the parade route. My cousin accelerated through the intersection to find parking. The rain started to come down, hard. She decided to wedge the car where it really couldn't fit, and she had to climb out my side with me helping to pull her.

"We have arrived just in time, fortunately." Maia was staking out a minimal space for us on the jammed curb at the corner of Spring. The carved marble extravaganza of I Quattro Canti hovered over us. A king looked down. The season gave us a nod. Then we heard drums, and horns blaring a dirge. Maia spied the march moving slowly up the Corso and angled me by the shoulders to glimpse it through the crush.

First, a lone man dressed in a black cape trimmed with white lace strode along the middle of the street, asking bystanders for donations to his organization, the *Società Maria Santissima Addolorata d'Invalidi e Mutilati di Guerra*. The Most Holy Grieving Mother's Society of Invalids and War Wounded. He handed us a small illustrated prayer card of the Blessed Mother and of her pallid Son. Maia gave him some coins for which he bowed low. I did my best to silently translate the prayer: Most Pitiful Virgin, Most Desolate Lady, we condole with You as You watch Your only Son's thousands of spasms and torments unto death upon the Cross.

Two drummers appeared, beating their black instruments. Behind them paced an executioner in a pointed black mask with holes cut out for eyes. He carried a coiled whip. Another man followed, striking two short black sticks together. On his heels came a teenager carrying a black cross with a white silk banner marked INRI draped around it. The crucifix was very black, his lace smock very white.

"Whoa. So serious. In the states we don't have Easter processions led by death figures."

"No?"

"Someone dresses up in a . . ." I didn't know the Italian for fuzzy, so I showed her the inside lining of my travel jacket, "rabbit costume made of pastel pink polyester and carries a carrot and a basket."

"I see."

Little girls in white capes and white berets now marched up, their white waterproof boots scuffing the street.

"The angels!" Maia beamed, clapping her hands together. "How adorable."

Mothers dressed in jeans chaperoned them, carrying purses and plastic shopping bags, balancing umbrellas like colored auras over their heads. IO ♥ I PUFFI was printed all over a blue Smurf umbrella. The drenched angels huddled together at the red light without making a peep.

A brass band marched through, playing off pitch in a minor key. The focus of the procession slowly swayed into view. Three dozen men, paired off face-to-face and embracing each other tightly around the waist, shouldered an enormous bier. Chanting together, they bore the glassed-in coffin, bedecked with red carnations and crimson gladioli. Inside lay Jesus. We could personally examine the full length of his vulnerable, waxy-pale body, knees bent, one hand on his abdomen, his head resting on twin white satin pillows. Four knights in copper-colored armor, face-plates clamped shut, guarded him with spears and shields.

"Christ in a casket?" I whispered. "That's completely new to me."

"The Normans introduced this concept in the medieval era," Maia whispered back.

A voice cried out. The men supporting the massive weight together lowered it off their shoulders onto the boulevard. They uncoupled, took sips from bottles, mopped their brows, massaged their necks, rubbed each other's backs. Another cry went up. Resuming their intimate positions, they hoisted up the load again, advanced maybe twenty-five feet before bringing it down to rest once more. They were really struggling, as if life wasn't hard enough for these middle-aged guys.

"For them, Christ died today, not two thousand years ago. By carrying Him, they become one with Him, do you see? They share His burden."

"Yes. Ouch."

The crowd leaned with them as they turned and disappeared down the Via Maqueda past Autumn's corner. Hundreds of tearful processions had passed under the Season before. Unperturbed, she held a basket of fruit, her head swathed in grapes. I looked at the faces of the crowd. For all I knew one of them could have been Franca's.

La Madonna followed, dressed in black as Sofia had promised. She too was carried aloft by exhausted men, clinched together chest to chest. Encircled by four-foot pure white lighted candles tied with tiny prim white ribbons, all surrounded by masses of long stemmed bobbing pink roses, *Maria Santissima Addolorata* stood tall, column-like, clasping her hands, eyes down, trailing her son, wobbling. Women in black accompanied her, slowly weaving along below her, holding umbrellas, though they could do nothing to keep her dry. She towered above them.

"See how She knows our human sorrows," Maia murmured. "See how the crowds of women adore Her? Today even the sky cries."

Candle flames expired, snuffed out by the wind and the rain. The silvery metal halo radiating from the back of The Grieving Virgin's head vibrated and rattled loudly as she turned the corner.

"That's it. *Basta*. No more. The parade has ended." Maia pulled me by the arm through the throng. "You must be starving. Let's grab a snack from the vendor over here. I want you to try a typical Palermo street food. Two *panelli*, please."

"*Certo.*" The *panelletoio* flipped the handle on his bottled gas and the griddle started spitting hot olive oil. He pressed two golden squares into the middle. I pulled some dollar bills out of my purse. Maia pushed my money away. "No."

"Yes! Maybe he'd like American money."

"Natalie, please."

"Squeeze of lemon?" the vendor asked.

"Absolutely."

The street chef grabbed two round rolls, split them open, and stuffed the *ceci* bean patties inside.

"Excellent," I cooed between bites, "mmm, light."

"*Buono, no?* These got us through the war. Sometimes we had only one thin *panello* each day. We counted ourselves lucky—between bombings." She pointed to the sky.

"Oh," I swallowed. What they must have gone through.

"Let's keep walking, if you don't mind."

Palm trees swayed and swooshed as she led me into the courtyard of La Capella di San Cataldo, with its three cute red domes like pomegranates.

"It has stood since the eleventh century," Maia burst with civic pride. "Notice the caper-vines growing up the wall."

"So that's where they come from. I love capers. Nonny used to make *piccata* with them on very special occasions."

"Did she?" Maia smiled. "So did *my* mother."

Inside, long-bearded priests conducted a solemn service in Greek, the pious murmuring their responses. We observed from the back. The walls and low ceilings shimmered with mosaics of wild animals and palms, goldly reflecting hundreds of candles. An accumulated devotion of nine hundred years hung in the air. I wouldn't have minded lingering, soaking up the peace of the place, but Maia tapped my arm, drawing me out and across the street to a side entrance of the next church, Santa Caterina. We climbed marble stairs.

"Wait a minute," I looked around. "You brought us to this entry-room before! The place where the nuns make the fancy pastries, right? And sell them to the public from behind the window, in silence?"

"Good memory."

"I never forget a pastry that I didn't have. Do we knock? Not that I could eat any more sweets."

"Go ahead, try. They keep very particular hours. It's a matter of luck more than anything."

No one answered the door, locked tight this penitent Good Friday afternoon.

"We must come back sometime, though. These nuns really have a way with almond paste, which they have perfected over the centuries. Next, we'll look at some of the statues that Civiletti sculpted in the eighteen-hundreds." Maia's heels clicked efficiently down the smoothed stairs. "They're all over Palermo, but we can start with a few at San Domenico."

Our raincoats blowing open, Maia advanced us through the piazza still festooned with shriveled palm fronds from last Sunday. We entered the massive doors. Men paced at the back of the cathedral and a soprano warbled Ave Maria.

"*Ah*," Maia said, "*matrimonio*."

The bride and groom knelt on a skim-milk-white satin cushion at the altar. Children fidgeted in their seats while women cried deeply into handkerchiefs, though not the ones in the breast pockets of their Country Club suits.

"The ceremony could last another hour at least. Follow me."

In a side aisle, I snapped a photo of a bust of Civiletti by Civiletti, my whirring camera echoing up and down the walls. "Whoops, sorry about the noise."

"Didn't hear a thing. There's another one this way. Come." Maia marched in front of the altar, where the bride and groom continued to kneel and the priest recited. I scooted out of their way.

She halted in front of a marble figure. "Here it is. *Charity*."

"Muscular," I murmured, taking another picture. "Heroic."

"Our ancestor certainly knew his anatomy." My cousin seemed unaware that her voice caused nearby guests to turn.

The groom pushed the ring onto the bride's finger. More handkerchiefs fluttered like a flock of doves suddenly roused into flight. Maia leaned against a pew, watching the bridal veil being lifted. We studied the kiss.

"How sweet. You know, this is the island where a revolution started when a French soldier insulted a bride as she walked up the church steps. The Sicilian Vespers in 1282," she continued at lecture volume, "at this very time of year—at Easter."

"How did he insult her?" I whispered.

She turned up her hearing aid. "What, dear?"

I tried for medium *sotto voce*. "What did he do to her?" We had the attention of the wedding celebrants. An audience wanted to know her version of the oft-told offense.

"He made the fatal error of searching her for concealed weapons. No Sicilian would tolerate such an affront. They immediately massacred every last Frenchman on the island. That's another little piece of history for you. I must take you to that church outside of town another day. Don't let me forget, *va bene?*"

She linked her arm through mine and nudged me through a side door into the damp afternoon. A woman of middle age was placing a small aluminum plate on a ledge of the church wall. She genuflected and walked away. Maia pointed to other small pans. I went up on my toes to peer inside: albino-colored sprouts huddled together in black earth, naked and embryonic-looking.

"Lentils," she explained, "offerings to the Madonna and to springtime." Inside the churches: grand ceremony. Outside: little dishes balanced on narrow sills, humble legume gifts barely noticeable, a minuscule germinating detail in the hectic and shrill downtown. While car horns syncopated through the air, another woman neared with a bowl, set it down, made the sign of the cross and departed. Never mind she wore a thick sweater jacket, brown wool skirt and nylon stockings—she was like a high-priestess of Ceres performing a devotional. For thousands of years women had been leaving donations like these every spring.

Maia's church-hopping pace didn't slow for the rest of the afternoon. Arabo-Norman, Catalan-Gothic, Sicilian-Baroque were some of the unique architectural gems we stepped in and out of. My cousin was one powerhouse guide, committed to laying down the outline for me, providing a historic rundown of the landmarks she knew so well and took such pride in, so when I returned to each of these places at my leisure, she assured me, I would know something. In every one we visited, the faithful prayed at the fourteen stations of the cross, fingering their rosaries. I was getting tired—my lids fell down three times. It had to have been around eight a.m. Pacific Time.

We finished up at City Hall to see Civiletti's statue of Dante, but the guard wouldn't let us into the building.

"You don't understand. This young woman has come all the way from America to see the artwork of her ancestor. All we want to do is climb the one flight, quickly take a photo and come right back down."

"*No, signora*," said the seated Immaculate Uniform, hands in prayer position, eyebrows flexed sympathetically. "*Impossibile*."

"I'm older than you, young man," Maia bristled. "I remember when this building used to be open to the citizens it is meant to serve. Let us in for one minute, if you please."

"Truly I am sorry, but we've had bomb threats. *Non è possibile*."

"Do we look as though we are carrying bombs?" she asked indignantly, opening up her purse for him. She didn't seem fazed at all by the heightened alert.

Personally, if a clock tied to a fuse was ticking nearby, I

didn't need to risk life and limb to see our ancestor's interpretation of the great poet, as much as I admired Dante. I edged towards the entry, but Maia wasn't budging.

"*Signora*, the discussion is over. By the way, *signorina, scusa*, but is your necklace gold? If it is valuable to you, better not display it or someone might drive by on a *moto* and yank it off your neck." Maia nodded agreement.

"Oh!" My hand shot up to grasp my good luck medallion, a gold Trinacria that once belonged to Auntie Paolina, another of the redheads, that I wore always. I rotated the chain around so that the medal hung down my back, and buttoned the black blouse all the way up to my throat.

Maia finally gave up and we returned to I Quattro Canti through a long and narrow street market, the Vucciria, named for voices, which we were hearing choruses of: "Urchins, clams, tuna! Fresh! Still moving!" The living and the recently living from salty waters for sale. We admired all the Friday fish displayed on beds of shaved ice and kelp. Coral, black, and white, their tails curled up and eyes wide, the schools pointed back to the Gulf where they'd been swimming this morning. Crabs clicked against each other in buckets, squids wriggled in shallow water, oysters glowered from plastic pans. A swordfish, pulled aloft by fishing line in reenactment of the moment the graceful creature had jumped out of the sea, arced over our heads. An orange octopus in an iron bathtub was flicking three of its tentacles around the rim. So beautiful. I reached for its suckers, but Maia pulled my coat sleeve, worrying that I might get squirted with ink.

I stepped back and thought how neat it would be to write a postcard to my ex-boyfriend Boothe with ink from an octopus, and how much he'd appreciate that, then realized I was nearly in a dream state from jet lag, and that writing to him would only get me into trouble. We were done, weren't we? I was done with him, wasn't I?

I snapped awake, we sampled some salted capers, and strolled back to the Corso. On the sidewalk someone had sketched a life-size chalk saint framed in a puffy cloud. Its salmon-colored robes had subtle folds; the eyes glistened with real glitter.

"Italy bursts with so much art that people even decorate the street, knowing rain and shoes will erase it. What dedication!" I raved while we stepped around the drawing.

"*Eh*, someone probably made a few thousand lire doing this," Maia countered, unlocking the car door on my side and climbing through.

"What a great city you have," I enthused, squeezing in. Once she backed out into the traffic without looking, sleepiness overwhelmed me—I could not stay awake. What we'd seen today blended into one big divine thing with a shimmering halo. Maybe Franca Viola visited church today. Maybe she even sat at the wedding in San Domenico. She could have walked right past us, carrying lentils to balance on the edge of the wall. What would she look like? She had to be forty or so by now, but I'd never seen a photo of her to begin with, so how could I possibly ever recognize her?

The elevator was slow to come at the apartment building. When the door at last opened, a tall man glided out balancing a covered plate on the fingertips of his right hand. What a tragic, beautiful face. What Mondello green eyes.

"Good evening, *Professore*."

"Good evening, *Signora* Santilli," he bowed gravely. He wore a teal blue winter sweater, hand-knitted.

"Was that an offering to Demeter too?" I asked when the lobby door shut behind him.

"*Beh*, he feeds some stray cats in the empty lot next door."

As soon as we entered her apartment, I grabbed the metropolitan phonebook from the hallway phone stand. Dozens of Violas were listed, many with initial F, but no Franca.

I threw open my terrace door. Warm gusts thrummed the stems of the geraniums. The great mountain with its paleolithic secrets was going purple in the twilight, and the barely waned moon rested on it, like a bright, glowing egg. I leaned on the terrace railing, breathing in the deep possibility, the Palermotaneity of it all. I caught the city's scent: peppery flowers suspended in marine air tainted with diesel. I was in love with this place again, just like last time.

Undoing the clasp of my necklace, I studied the Trinacria medallion, which struck me as an ancient sort of compass or treasure hunt map. This talented dame could sprint, fly or slither, and somehow, mysteriously, she was going to direct me in my search.

Faint meows drifted up from the lot below. I remembered it last time as a tended orange grove; now rebar and cinderblock were stacked against the old tree stumps. A figure approached a swarm of skinny cats. They surrounded the sweatered professor. The moon had loosened itself from Pellegrino's crest and was floating towards the swirling, dissolving, softening storm clouds over the harbor. As Fridays went, this one was more than good.

Chapter VI

Sabato Santo

Holy Saturday dawned clear and fresh. Tea, *marmellata* and rolls waited on the table again.

"I don't want to rush you, *cara*, but we'd better leave as soon as possible for Partanna."

"Before we go, I'd like to call Information in Alcamo, just to satisfy my curiosity?"

"Go right ahead, but I very much doubt she will be listed." Maia stood close to the chair while I dialed.

A moment later, "Ah, and nothing under the initial 'F' either? Thank you for checking, sir."

"I'm telling you, she will not be easy to find," my cousin repeated.

"Mm-hmm. I see what you mean."

Back in the States on the day before Easter people were soaking eggs in pastel pink, yellow, green and blue baths, while we were rolling into a neighborhood of Mondello to see the Crucifixion up close. We parked on a street with the enticing name Via Circeo—that powerful witch—and walked the curving roadway past a bakery, a tobacconist, a grocer. Drifting through the green plastic strips shielding a doorway floated the distinct presence of cheese—maybe *bel paese* or *taleggio*—pungent, clean and salty.

"I love this. At home, everything comes sealed in plastic." Here foods were properly worshipped, displayed on marble stands, their holy essences sifting through the air. Here the cheese stands alone.

A sign read Macelleria—butcher store. We were eyeball to glazed eyeball, face to muzzle with twelve furry baby goats, killed and hung in a row along the outside wall, their abdomens split open, intestines stolen away.

"*I capretti*," Maia informed me. "Eaten at Easter time."

"We don't see this at home," I stammered. They were hanging by their necks, for Christ's sake. Their delicate hoofs dangled, purplish-gray, little feet of Pan. And their heads, with tiny budding horns, tilting to the side.

"It makes the meat more tender. We eat them only once a year." My cousin kept up her steady clip along the street. "*Ehh, cara mia*, one way or another, animals are killed so that we can eat. It's just that way."

"I know, but . . ."

We turned into a piazza where an outdoor stage had been constructed. Loudspeakers blasted a warped recording of a Handel oratorio to get the crowd in the right melodramatic mood. Two palm fronds like green parentheses framed the Doric columns at stage rear. Whitewashed walls reflected brilliant morning light. The sound grew more and more distorted each time the piece played, three, four, five times on a loop. Everyone milled around and chatted using hand gestures. I breathed in the language of *Italiano*—consonant linked to vowel linked to consonant linked to vowel like twinkling lights suspended across a carnival.

"The play we will see derives from secular theater originally performed in the street: the annunciation, the birth of Gesù, or in this case, the tribunal," explained Maia.

"Mm-hmm. I'm grateful that you are such a historian."

"Historian, *boh*. I have lived my whole life here, naturally I take an interest in the past."

I looked around. The past was evident, still, in every Sicilian face in the crowd: burnished, tawny, pale, olive, sunburned skin; coppery, black, blond, brunette, white, curly, kinky, wavy, straight hair; Coptic, sloe, blue, green, gold, brown eyes; features that came from everywhere.

"*Pinzimonio di carciofo! Ammoghiù. Freschissimo!*"

"What is that guy with the cart selling?"

"Ah, this you'll enjoy. A treat. A true Sicilian street food." Maia hailed the vendor with one hand while pushing my wallet back into my purse with the other. We were given squares of wax paper holding slivers of raw artichoke hearts drizzled with olive oil, salt and lemon, a small basil leaf adorning each one. I couldn't believe it. In all my early *carciofo* training I'd never been exposed to this tender delicacy. West Coast, get with it.

Eventually *Il Spettacolo* began. The cast of dozens, young men, mimed the action while a booming, disembodied voice narrated. Jeering Hebrews in floor-length woven robes, head-dresses and sandals; scowling Roman guards wearing painted metal breastplates and helmets; the Jerusalemites straining to listen, brows wrinkled, then righteously protesting; the Apostles huddling to one side. Pontius Pilate delivered his speech, stabbing the stage with his spear, gold robes glistening in the sun. Carl Orff's "Carmina Burana" pounded from the speakers.

Jesus appeared, manacled, dressed in a white robe, long blond hair, head lowered. They condemned him. The stage crowd showed no mercy, shrieking, hurling rocks which bounced off him—painted chunks of styrofoam. Some spectators cried out, "Traitors, traitors!" Kids ran around playing tag. The guards stripped off Christ's robe to reveal him pasty and naked except for a demure white loincloth. They tied his wrists to a wall, and two henchmen came forward to whip him. His body snapped with each lash. During one spasm the blond wig flew off, exposing the actor's close-cropped black hair. Oh

Christ. The audience guffawed. Maia shot me a bemused look. Jesus continued to recoil with each blow, enduring this new humiliation. An extra in a red costume climbed down off the stage, retrieved the wig from outstretched hands and rushed over to fit it back on him. A pre-recorded rooster crowed three times. Boothe would have loved this.

They pushed the Crown of Thorns onto his head, which began dripping stage blood. *Ecce Homo.* He groaned, heaved the full weight of the cross on his shoulder and began to drag it, haltingly, out of the square. Mary Magdalene followed close behind, nearly horizontal with grief. The stage crowd formed a line after him. Electronic cymbals crashed.

"He carries the Cross and Life. He carries the Cross and Suffering. He carries the Cross and Humanity," the tremulous narrator intoned.

We all filed after the procession out of the piazza and down a long path, which truly seemed dispirited, the powdery earth having no color to it. We ended up on a broad field, littered everywhere with trash. At a distance we could see the action continuing on a hillside. Halfway up the slope two crosses had already been erected, two figures pre-crucified—not statues, but men—and between them, blond Jesus was being nailed to the cross. The hammering went on and on.

"They're not using real spikes, are they?"

"No. We would never crucify anyone. What a notion!" Maia gaped at me.

"They do in the Philippines," I countered, "I read it some-where once."

"Well, maybe there, but here, it is an honor to share in the pain, to relive the agony of the Savior," she whispered, "in a metaphorical sense."

For long, excruciating minutes Gesu Cristo leaned at forty-five degrees while his tormentors struggled to keep the cross from crashing down. Next to me a mother unwrapped a prosciutto sandwich and handed it to her child. He grabbed it and, never taking his eyes off the Passion, sank his teeth in. They finally hoisted the crucifix vertically. The crowd murmured and the music swelled. Maia motioned to another part of the hill where Judas hung by his neck from a tree. Shrubs hid his feet and I could only hope he stood on a stepladder or something. The loudspeaker droned on. Picnics were produced all around, salami sliced with pocketknives, olives chewed and pits spit out, the lazy hiss of Arancina bottletops being unstoppered.

Maia shifted from one foot to the other. "Would you like to stay a little longer?" She shielded her eyes from the sun.

"What happens next?"

"He doesn't die till three. They will remain crucified on the hillside all afternoon, until a certain time tonight when the body will be taken down, and placed in a secret cave in the mountain."

"Let's go then, shall we?"

"*Oh-kay.*" She enjoyed using the American expression.

As we returned to the square, two actors in Hebrew costumes passed us, nonchalantly carrying a huge cross back to the stage. To props? Between the two of them, they didn't struggle at all with its weight. They passed so close that it snagged a wool thread in Maia's jacket and she carefully unhooked herself while the young men held still, apologizing to the *signora*, chatting in Sicilian. A Roman guard on a motorcycle buzzed by with his skirts flapping, spraying us with dust from the road. We returned down Circe's street of the goats. I kept my eyes fixed on the sidewalk when we passed the butcher's.

"Maia?" I wanted to sound as though the idea had just occurred to me. "Are we by chance anywhere in the vicinity of Alcamo?"

"Not really," she answered levelly, "it's a good forty kilometers from here."

"This is a lot to ask, I know, but would it be possible to maybe take a ride out there?"

"No, I am sorry, not today. The cook will have lunch on the stove," her voice constricted, "so we should be getting home."

What cook? Then I remembered that nothing interrupts lunch here, not anything, and how pushy of me to put her on the spot, anyway.

"You see, I do not drive the distances I used to, but possibly next week we can go through there. Or maybe my son can take you one day. Patience, Natalie," she said evenly.

A slim, middle-aged man with freckles named Primo answered her door.

He had been waiting for us, and quickly changed out of his striped, dark blue work coat into a spotless white jacket to serve the meal. He carried out a steaming platter.

"*Pasta con capperi e pomodoro, Signora* Maia." He poured me a glass of white wine—"Corvo Duca di Salaparuta, made near Trapani, *signorina*"—and one for his employer.

"*Splendido,*" I raised my glass to thank them both. It didn't take long to wash down the entire delicious mound of pasta with it. "*Ottimo.*" He rushed to refill my plate and glass. "Please, only a drop more. It's strong, this wine."

"*Eh si.* In Sicily our grapes grow very sweet, because of our volcanic soil. Seventeen percent alcohol by volume."

"Phew, I really feel the volcano."

"The second course will help with that." He cleared our plates.

"There's more?"

"Naturally!" he and Maia answered together, staring at me.

Primo wheeled in a covered dish. "Chicken cutlets with *broccoletti*," he announced. "You are still overwhelmed by the wine, yes? I shall prepare you a coffee, then."

"No thanks, Primo, I'll just lie down for a bit after." To digest a half-kilo of pasta and a quarter liter of magma. "What a wonderful meal. I'm not used to sitting at a luxurious table like this in the middle of the day. Very civilized."

"What does she mean?" he asked my cousin. "They don't eat lunch in America?"

"Well, they do, but usually standing up."

When we finished, Maia retreated to her room, and I dizzily did the same. Leaden, drifting off in the afternoon heat, I dreamed that a kid goat had escaped from its pen and was tapping at my wooden door with its hoofs, bleating. My eyes shot open. Through the slats of the shutters, I could see Primo beating a rug out on the terrace. I couldn't get used to this siesta idea, just lying here, while the sun rode high in the sky. I grabbed my jacket and made for the front door.

The grand proportion of Maia's street thrilled me: big enough to connect from here to anywhere, via any Sicilian road, and therefore to Franca, if only I knew which direction to aim. By pure fortune I wandered into the zone of the graceful Liberty buildings. Decorative stucco tendrils twined and wound around balconies from which lush lavender wisteria dripped, strewing its scent. What kind of lucky people lived in such splendor?

Directionless, happy, pulled along by a faint magnet, I covered a lot of ground. The small streets I was passing through were named for authors and philosophers who Maia would probably be able to quote. I started pronouncing them out loud: the rhapsody of Via Mario Rapisardi, the melody of Via Ludovigo Ariosto, the tongue-tickling Via Torquato Tasso. Who wouldn't fall in love with these names? At the intersection of Via Francesco Petrarca and the Passaggio dei Poeti, I was ready to surrender citizenship. So many writers, so little time. Natalia Galli, most recently of overly-familiar Berkeley in the boring old United States, has euphorically set up shop under a caper vine at Piazza Boccaccio 70. Office hours Tues and Thurs 4 – 6. Otherwise, by *appuntamento*.

I kept on. A trio of old women were climbing the steps of a small church. I followed them in and stood at the back in the shadows while they joined the many black-clad and bowed heads bunched at the front of the chapel. Above the altar a scarlet cloth had been wrapped around the crucifix: Jesus had disappeared under the folds. A lament rose, Latin in words and Moorish in sound. I listened until it began to feel too heavy, too smothering, too suffocating. I needed fresh air, needed to keep moving, so after sidling up to a rack of flickering votives, lighting one candle, dropping two dollar bills into the metal box (I still hadn't exchanged my money at a bank), I prayed for guidance to locate Via Franca Viola, and left.

I grabbed a bus heading downtown. The driver honked and sparred with cars barreling from one side of the boulevard to the other, raucous during the height of the holy afternoon siesta. *Ciao* Tragedy and Comedy girls barely balancing atop your big cats. Hey everyone at the corners of I Quattro Canti.

We had reached the end of the line in front of the central train station. On a whim, I thought I'll just look inside at departure times so that after the holidays I can plan a ride to Alcamo. The schedule read: Acireale-Catania, Agrigento, Alcamo via Trapani. The next train was due to leave in twenty minutes. Oh, what great luck. I'll just go right now.

"One round trip to Alcamo, please."

I found a bench on the platform. Dialect echoed through the station, sounding staccato and spicy, with lots of energy built right into it, especially powered by the "u" that ended so many Sicilian words. Nonny had warned her new world children—my mother and her baby brother Bruno—to never dare slip into it outside the home, or else, the wooden spoon. In public proper Italian first, English would come with school, of course. The shame of being from the south. She had even fetched the spoon to wave around as a warning, though she would never have used it on them. My grandmother was a pacifist. So I knew all of one earthy Sicilian expression that my mom had taught me and hoped that the right occasion to use it would present itself on this trip: *Era beddu, u pitrusinu. Vin'uattu, e ci pisciao.* "The parsley was beautiful until the cat peed on it," I practiced out loud, my eyes closed. "The parsley was beautiful until the cat—"

"—peed on it? What?" The face of a man with a circum-flex-shaped mustache hovered a few inches in front of me. It must have taken a long time for him to clip his mustache so pencil-thin; maybe a barber did it for him. "What are you, English?"

I stood. "American."

"What are you doing here, miss? Where are you going?"

"Alcamo via Trapani."

He struck a match to light a cigarettete. "I ask the question because you look like you're waiting for a train."

"Isn't this the platform for Alcamo?"

"*Eh,*" he gestured with his palms open. "You're on the right platform, but the train will leave you in Trapani and you'll have no way of getting to Alcamo."

"What do you mean?"

"Don't you know there's a strike going on?"

"What?"

"A strike of state bus conductors."

"You're joking."

"*Magari,* I wish. You'll be stranded there in Trapani, there will be no *autobus* to connect you to Alcamo, Miss America."

"How come they sold me a ticket then?"

"*Beh,* they sell tickets whether or not the connecting vehicles run."

"But . . . that's absurd."

"*Ehh,*" he blew all his smoke straight at me.

"How long has the strike been going on?"

"Since last night."

"How long will it last?"

He laughed. "Do you think I am God?"

"No, I don't think you're God." I started back down the platform. "Thank you for letting me know. This trip would have been pointless."

He followed. "I can arrange a ride for you. I have a friend nearby with a car."

"No, no."

"But I can help you out." Smoke plumed all around. "You need to go to Alcamo, *non è vero?*"

"Yes, but not now. Now I need to leave. Goodbye."

He ran in front of me and blocked my way, shaking his head in confusion, his hands spread wide. Being in the company of Maia so far I hadn't bother to put on the plastic wedding ring, but I felt for it in my purse as I clomped along the track. That ticket seller was going to hear it from me, only when I got there he had vanished, leaving a cigarette burning in an ashtray.

"Hello," I called out, "what am I supposed to do with this ticket? Hello?" Strikes sometimes go on for months. Strikes are as common here as unfiltered cigarettes and soccer matches and church bells. "Does it expire today?"

"I can buy it back from you at a discount," Mustache answered. "If you come with me across the street, my friend who's got the car will drive us to Alcamo."

"No." I slipped the ring on.

"But how will you go there?"

"I don't know at the moment."

"I'm trustworthy. You can feel very safe." Now he was blowing smoke rings that were admittedly impressive and carefully timed.

"I cannot accept your offer, sir, excuse me."

"I help foreigners all the time. Every day. I perform a service."

"I'm sure you do."

"C'mon," he pointed across the palm-filled piazza towards a bar. "My friend is right in there."

"No."

"I don't expect money."

"No, thank you."

"Only a donation. Whatever you think it's worth."

"No!"

"But I want to help."

At least the city buses here hadn't gone on strike while I was in the station. I rode back down the wide boulevard and rang Maia's doorbell.

"Natalie, where have you been?" she exploded in relief, her face taut. "I have been so concerned. You didn't tell Primo you were leaving. We worried that you became lost somewhere, or something happened to you. *O Madonna*, please do not ever do this again!"

"I'm so sorry, I didn't mean to worry you, Maia. I just went out wandering and it got late, I guess. I wasn't using my head."

"Ask me to take you next time. I am happy to accompany you wherever you would like. But if you insist on going out by yourself, at least let us know where to and for how long so that we can keep track. Please."

"Yes, of course. Please forgive me." I slunk into my room, feeling like a chastened teenager.

It was dark now. They'd have taken the Lamb of God down from the cross on the hill in Partanna and placed him in the secret cave. Sometime before sunrise someone at the Palermo chapel where I lit the candle would loosen the red shroud and he would be revealed anew. Maybe the bus strike would end in time for all the Holy Day travelers. Maybe we'd all get where we needed to go.

Where might Franca have spent this day? I imagined her having climbed a hill to watch a flock of sheep graze. Or at a train station trying to get somewhere. The mother-of-pearl moon peered over the mountain; maybe she was gazing at it too, right now. I planned to rise before dawn tomorrow morning and watch the same spot, east, where the sun made its return, even more easterly than that, into the heart, the soul of the cardinal point. Easter. With my mind's eye I imagined east-est—the most east—a source of an ethereal, superlative light.

Chapter VII

Pasqua

Easter dawned gray and blustery. To counter it, I put on the pastel yellow Boothe blouse. The Fiat 500 climbed steadily out of Palermo and up through the dry limestone hills known as the *Conca d'Oro*, the Golden Shell, more like tarnished silver than gold this dark morning. Then we were darting across a sweeping high plateau. Gusts batted the car sideways. Cold sneaked through the windows' rubber margins. We zoomed past a road sign: **Hora e Arbëreshëvet.**

"Meaning Plain of the Albanians, in Albanian," Maia noted.

She revealed only that we had a special invitation here in Piana degli Albanesi to watch someone be dressed in a traditional costume. "You'll see, and so shall I for the first time, for that matter." She took a slip of paper from her purse and asked directions from a "Traffic Specialist" standing on a small podium in the middle of an intersection. She'd been given the name by an old schoolteacher friend. "We are about to witness an Albanian custom that has gone on here for exactly 500 years this year," Maia beamed, as we parked and pushed through a crowd bundled up in dark winter coats. One more helpful direction from a local and she knocked on a splintery door of a low limestone house. A little boy pulled it open and stared up at us.

"*Permesso, picciriddu*," Maia said. "We're here for the young lady."

The boy ran in. The men of the family, huddled near a stone fireplace, waved us toward a closed door. Maia tapped on it and we heard a muffled *Avanti!* Inside, a teenager stood still within layers of white petticoats. Her mother, pins clamped between her lips, mimed hello and smoothed an area on the bedspread for us to sit. The smell of starch filled the small bedroom.

"Thank you for allowing us to come." Maia sat quickly. I followed.

"Don't mention it," the girl replied. "Welcome. I'm Martina. We want the distraction. All morning we've been in here. Tell me about America, anything. Michael Jackson sings Triller. I adore Michael Jackson. Amuse me, *per favore.*"

Maia motioned to me to stay quiet. The mother rushed to the ironing board, pressed a small starched square of embroidered white cloth, then hurried back to pin it to one of the slips. We watched this painstaking, one-at-a-time accumulation of white on white repeated for about an hour, accented each time by the hiss of the iron being uprighted. Maia kept her monastic silence on the soft mattress. She and I slowly settled into a trough, propping one another up by the shoulders.

"I'm steaming alive, Mamma!" Within the cocoon of slips Martina was definitely turning a brighter and brighter pink. When her mother bent down, the girl rolled her eyes at me.

"How many?" I asked when I couldn't stand the silence anymore.

Martina shook her honey-colored hair and gestured with the fingertips of her right hand pulled together, "Hundreds and hundreds of pieces. Every time."

"Tell our visitors that you wear it on Epiphany too, and when you marry you will wear it to church," the mother said.

"Tell them how auspicious their timing is, coming to Piana this spring, on the five-hundredth anniversary this very year of the Greek Albanians being given sanctuary in Sicily."

"Wow, we are fortunate to be here," I smiled, taking the opportunity to detach from the unit Maia and I had become sitting in the dip of the bed, and to remove my coat. The heat in here.

"I like your old-fashioned looking blouse," the mother noted. "I remember that style from the war years."

"Yes," Maia spoke up after her silence of the last hour, "I do too. A handsome color on you, Natalie, you know?"

"My boyfriend bought it for me," I blurted.

"What boyfriend?" Maia asked hopefully.

"Oh, I should say ex-boyfriend." Boothe had been on my mind every day so far. He would have loved being in a town with Albanian street signs and hearing this truly mysterious-sounding language. I missed him, though I didn't want to.

"*Beh*, fashion differs from tradition, doesn't it, *signora*? You and I have seen many styles come and go over the decades, but your custom of far more than five hundred years remains constant."

I'm so tired of this, the girl mouthed to me, dabbing at her upper lip. I nodded in sympathy, then glanced at my cousin, who sat patiently, respectfully. I just couldn't make out the significance of the white squares, but didn't want to disturb the ritual with any more questions. Maybe they represented each generation that had worn the outfit. Martina stood miserably still while her petticoats were slowly covered with them.

"Now," the mother declared, snapping us out of a trance. The girl raised her arms in Superman flight position. A pressed-to-perfection white blouse was fitted over her head and lowered with breathless caution, the billowy sleeves fluffed into place, the broad lace collar straightened and smoothed.

"Lovely," my cousin whispered.

"But this is nothing. Wait." The mother opened a wooden chest and lifted from it a white linen casing. "This costume," she hugged the bundle, "was worn by me, my mother, her mother and her mother, and so on. When Martina has a daughter, she will dress her. And so on."

An adolescent tongue stuck out while the woman unwrapped the first garment.

"Oooh," we both gasped at the dazzle of golden flowers embroidered all over the red vest, the first piece to emerge.

Martina was laced into it. "Your great-grandmother must have been a shrimp. Every year it shrinks. I can't breathe, really I can't!"

The *signora* wisely didn't respond as she brought forth a gilded green skirt which she helped Martina step into. Anxious fluttering resumed. "Carefully, carefully. Patience. Don't pull on it, I beg you." They inched it up to her waist together and she was buttoned in. The embossed gold stitching poured from the waistband all the way down to the hem.

"Finally!" groaned Martina. A gold and silver filigreed belt of Saint George and the Dragon—the family heirloom—was cinched around her waist.

"There," her mother plumped the skirt. "*Squisito*."

A green headdress shot with dense gold thread was pinned to her locks.

"Done at last! Goodbye, ladies!" The girl threw a gilt blue shawl across her shoulders and bolted for the door.

"Martina wait! I forgot." The mother ran out with a five-sided red bow to attach at the front of the collar. She came back winded but smiling, then urged us not to miss the promenade. Mentioning the name of their mutual friend, Maia thanked her, saying how very grateful we were to have witnessed the dressing of the girl.

When we stepped out the front door, church bells were bursting into sound and the town had switched to color. After their morning confinement, the costumed women were currents of energy, laughing and talking as they flowed in one direction toward the Cathedral. We ran into Martina and her dressed-up friends, each outfit distinct, all beautiful. The teens were smoking and gossiping in Albanian. She threw her head back with laughter, but when she caught sight of us, she tried to hide the cigarette behind her skirt.

"Please don't tell my mother if you see her," she begged me.

"Of course not, I won't mention anything. *Ciao*, Martina." Just don't burn a hole in that heirloom skirt.

We walked on. "What a contrast to the first visit, Maia, when girls in small towns could not stroll unchaperoned. And they had to face the walls."

"Certainly, that was true twenty years ago in provincial parts of the island. But we're in a pocket here. This is intact Albanian culture, do you see? With its own customs, its own celebrations."

She stopped in front of a crowded *pasticceria*. "The sheep are giving birth now so it's time for you to have *cannoli*."

"*Beh*, if I absolutely must!"

We squeezed inside, found a vacancy against the counter and watched the crispy shells being lifted from the bubbling olive oil and filled with just-cooked ricotta and chocolate bits. That's how fresh, delicate and creamy they were, with slender squiggles of candied orange peel balanced at the ends. Half the size of the *cannoli* from North Beach back home, we had to have two each on a plate, still warm and cool.

When we emerged, bleachers set in front of the great church were filling up for the Benediction of the Red Eggs, where all present were to be blessed in seven languages. The long-bearded church fathers emerged from the portals two by two, swinging censers to purify the piazza and carrying the standard of the Eastern Orthodox Cross. Martina's mother found us in the crowd and plied me with dyed red eggs wrapped in a newspaper nest.

"How sweet of you, *signora*, I'll take just one egg as a memento."

"It is our tradition. You must take them all. Take, please take." Eight ended up in my hands, our *mille grazie* to her dismissed with "it was nothing."

Maia apologized that a task she had to take care of in Palermo meant we needed to leave now, which also meant I wouldn't dare ask her again if we could take that little detour west toward Alcamo. When we roared out of town, the women still jammed all the streets.

Maia hung a hairpin curve. I grabbed the dashboard with one hand, gripping the eggs with the other. She watched me when she spoke, not the road. We screeched around another bend. All of Palermo was laid out below. I shut my eyes and tried to think of other things.

Maybe Franca had left the island for good without the news ever made public, had gone to Rome, Milano or Torino, and not necessarily because she'd wanted to. Possibly her life was so endangered that her family had to put her on an express night train with one small suitcase, cheese, bread, some hardboiled eggs wrapped in newspaper. If so, I'd get on a train myself and find her up north. I had a few weeks.

Maia pulled up to an apartment building in the outskirts of the city. Yesterday while I went nowhere at the train station she had cooked a special celebratory dish for the lifelong friend of her late husband. She pulled it out of the trunk and whisked away the towels protecting it. "*Timballo*. Some call it *timpano*, like a drum."

"Yow!"

In a stained glass effect, translucent bits of *salame* and tufts of *prosciutto crudo*, mushrooms and red pimento, slivered baby artichoke hearts like smiles and also like lyres, huge green olives and sliced rounds of hardboiled egg suggesting unblinking eyes were pressed flat against the wall of a glass bowl by a mass of *ziti* pasta in a *besciamella* sauce. Now that she had removed the towels the fragrance of it came at me as if I'd walked into a delicatessen.

"What a masterpiece, Maia!"

"It means so much to him. To be unmolded on a platter inside, which he has already set on the table. He makes it last for a week. *Aspetta*, I forgot the wine." She balanced the beautiful creation on the Fiat roof and leaned in to grab the bottle from the floor of the back seat. Out of nowhere a whiny *motorino* whizzed up to our car. An arm extended and—zip—seized her bowl.

"Hey!" I yelled, "Hey!"

Maia's bowl in his left arm, his right steering the thing, he zigzagged on.

"Robber!" Maia cried out, "Thief! It's for an old, hungry man. Stop! He's on a pension."

The guy was getting away! I impulsively threw one of the red eggs and missed. I threw another and beaned him on the head but that didn't keep him or the *timballo* from speeding on two wheels around the corner.

"But . . ." I sputtered. "But . . ."

"Poor Tancredo," Maia moaned. "Every Easter I promise him this dish. He so looks forward to it. What will I tell him? *Porca miseria*. They take any opportunity in this city. I'll have to send Primo over with something later. *Beh*, I'll just be a few minutes bringing him the wine and the bad news."

"I can't believe it. The nerve! Whoever eats the Timballo better appreciate it."

"Ehhh . . ." she sighed, giving the resignation gesture. "*Povero* Tancredo."

"And on Easter of all days," I commiserated. "What a jerk." And I muttered other things in English, not knowing how to righteously swear in Italian.

Back home, we waited in her lobby for the elevator. The green-eyed man came out carrying a bowl.

"*Buona Pasqua, Professore.*"

"*Buona Pasqua, Signora* Santilli. Please give my regards to the family." He glanced at the newspaper nest of eggs.

"For the cats." I handed it to him. "They look hungry."

"Yes, always. Thank you kindly."

"I've seen them from up above. How many are there?"

"More than twenty? The number keeps changing. It's birthing season."

In the elevator Maia confided, "The poor man lost his wife a year ago. He's been inconsolable since."

"Oh no."

"His wife was also a professor. Lovely woman. Since her death, he wears only the sweaters that she knitted him. He's an esteemed political scientist at the university. I'm sure he will marry again someday."

"Ah."

Chapter VIII

Easter Monday

Pasquetta, Little Easter, dawned delicate pink, dainty as the inside of a seashell that I might not ever have the luxury of stooping to pick up on the sand at Mondello Lido. Our final day of festivities had us heading west for the hills to a monastery, San Martino delle Scale, which lay in the direction of, but not as far as, Franca's town, Maia was quick to inform me. I'd stopped asking after Saturday anyway.

As the outskirts of Palermo fell away, I noticed a zigzag of buildings—chunky new boxes—teetering high up on a rocky summit. When I pointed, puzzled by the bizarre sight way up there, Maia shook her head.

"A government housing development. They haven't completed it and they won't."

"Why would anyone want to live in such a place? So hard to get to."

"No one would."

"But then why build it?"

Maia rubbed her thumb and fingers together. A muscle in her jaw began pulsing. "Mafia."

"Oh."

"You wouldn't know as a tourist." She grew quiet. The twisting road dipped into a pine forest. Wisps of bluish smoke floated through the trees. "Look. Picnickers are stoking fires to roast artichokes, another of our traditions. It takes hours to prepare the coals, to heat them red hot, to let them cool to white before the *carciofi* can be buried in them."

Wow, getting up in the dark to do a choke justice, now that's devotion. "I've tasted them cooked so many different ways, but never from underground."

"Then you shall today."

"Primo dug a pit? Where? Down where the cats live?"

She laughed. "Primo has the day off. We'll be eating out." Maia parked the car next to a cream-colored stone wall that enclosed the monastery. We followed a path alongside it, her walking shoes clacking against the caked earth. A vision of young Franca strolling home along an untraveled dusty road like this came to me. I pictured her in a navy shawl and dress with small white dots, carrying a basket loaded with onions and chicory from the family garden. Breezes rustled the silvery olive leaves and birds trilled. A shadow crossed the path. She froze. The man jumped in her way, grinning, and clamped his hand over her mouth. She tried to bite it. Her basket fell, the onions rolled away like bocce balls and the chicory leaves were ground into the dirt as they struggled. Taller and stronger, he dragged her into his car and tore away. One of her shoes, the strap broken, remained behind. The birds had flown away.

"*Tst*," I clicked my tongue, "it probably wasn't anything like that."

"Natalie?"

"Oh sorry, just thinking out loud."

We rounded a bend and, as if someone had suddenly turned on the volume, came upon a slew of folk dancers, singers and musicians in a clearing. Accordions bellowed, tambourines shimmied, mouth harps twanged. Someone wearing a red sash kept spinning a painted vase high into the air and catching it, again and again.

"What does the vase signify?"

Maia gave it some thought. "*Allegria,*" she smiled. Happiness.

This celebration was a frolic. The resurrection had occurred, the weight lifted, Lent ended, and vases flew. We heard a song about a donkey—*Lu me' sciccareddu*—and each time the singer heehawed the audience went wild. I had a little donkey, very dear, and then they killed him, my poor donkey. What a beautiful voice he had, like a great tenor, donkey of my heart, how can I ever forget you?

The players beckoned the audience to follow them up the road to a piazza where a brass band and bunches of red and yellow balloons bobbed in the breeze. Antique wooden horse carts painted in bright colors—the famous *carretteddu sicilianu* that my grandmother of course had a two-inch version of on her windowsill—stood waiting in a circle. The workhorses, all gussied up in magenta and green plumes, mirrored cloth, tassels and fringes, stamped and shook their heads, ringing little bells, raring to go. We moved in closer but not too close. Scenes of fierce battles and angelic visitations, dragons and steeds, paisleys and dots, and portraits of saints crowded every inch of the wooden carts.

"Look underneath near the wheels, *cara*, at Hades."

I bent down to see the detail up close. Carved devils clung below, monsters with dangling tongues, winged beasts. There was No Vacancy in Hell. Creatures were painted everywhere.

The drivers, wearing black caps and red pompons at their throats, cracked their whips and the large wheels began to creak. Children in day-glo parkas, pinned in next to their grandfathers, peered over the sides. One cart, decorated with wildflowers and shafts of rye, carried a cage of songbirds and a wooden wine cask. A man following behind turned the spigot to release white wine into plastic cups a little bigger than thimbles, which he offered to everyone. "Made at home," he said, smiling. "Good for the stomach. Don't refuse it." We didn't.

"*Buono, no?*" Maia licked her lips.

And powerful as all get out, especially at 11:30 in the morning. The cart circled around again. We each accepted another thimbleful. This one went straight to the brain. All daytime wine drinking had to stop tomorrow, I vowed. The circle being of modest size and the cask being full, we had a few more refills.

A priest wearing black-rimmed glasses clambered onto the cart, blessed the birdcage, reached inside and grabbed a few frantic, petite birds. He threw them up to the sky. They chirped deliriously and fluttered above our heads. He clutched another wriggling handful, and more birds swirled up into the sunshine. The crowd let out a cheer.

"I want to show you the Benedictine Abbey," Maia announced.

"Sure." I followed her lethargically, heated up from five tablespoons of super-concentrated *vino*. Mass had already begun. Maia motioned that we squeeze in along the back wall onto a dark wooden bench. The congregation, mostly women, mumbled in response to the hypnotic Latin. Then a Gregorian chant, which fell and rose like a tide, reverberated from wall to wall.

I sat marinating in the Gregorian scale, trying to decide whether it was more major key with a minor overlay, or minor with major. Or neither. Could there be such a key, not major and not minor? "Only Greg knows for sure," I may have mentioned to the vibrating atmosphere.

Maia nodded along, hands folded, eyes closed, but then suddenly turned to me. "Time to eat."

The smell of something baked had swung out into the piazza like secular incense. Good thing we nabbed the last empty table at the *trattoria*.

"*Cameriere*," Maia raised her hand to a waiter balancing three steaming plates of pasta on each forearm. "A half liter of red wine, please."

"Right away."

"I've already had enough *vino*, Maia. Really, I'm kind of drunkish."

"Don't worry about it. Drink what you wish, if you wish, when you wish."

Pasquetta celebrants and all their relatives jammed three dozen tables which the waiter worked alone. After forty days of Lent, they were starving and clamoring for his attention. Feed us. Feed us now.

Even my stoic cousin sighed relief when the waiter finally showed up with the carafe and wineglass stems laced upside-down between his fingers, and leaned down to be heard over the din. "We offer holiday specialties today. *Capretto. Carciofo. Pasta al Forno San Martino.*"

"Baby goat for each of us, and an artichoke to share?"

I shook my head, trying to prevent the return of the sight in front of the butcher store two days ago.

"It's traditional today," she lobbied. "You'll like it."

No goat. Never goat! "I'm sure it's delicious, but an artichoke is what I'll have. The kind roasted underground, right?"

"Certainly. My brother-in-law and I stayed up last night making the pit. As a matter of fact, he's still out there overseeing the operation. No first plates to begin with for you ladies? No pastas?"

No, but Maia pleaded for some bread before he raced off. We were grateful, desperate really, when he slid a plate of rounded rolls onto the table. My cousin grabbed one and tore it open. The crust cracked defiantly, curls of steam exhaled.

I broke open a roll. Its stretchy dough gave way, smooth and moist, flecked with bran. "*Croccante*," I said. Crunchy.

"Perhaps you didn't know that Sicily played breadbasket to the Roman Empire."

"I did not. That's amazing." Two thousand years later the

basket hadn't emptied. Sicily kept giving. Two thousand years later the bread kept breathing, body and soul.

"Here," Maia urged, "have a little to wet your throat while we wait. *Salute*."

"*Cin-cin*." I took a sip of wine against any judgment, then bit into the crust. Golden durum semolina grown on the broad breast of the island's interior, flung into last summer's air to separate out the chaff, and ground between meter-wide stones; bubbly yeast kept teeming since Roman times; sea salt in sacks hauled by painted carts from the Tyrrhenian shore; water caught in a ceramic jug from the always flowing monastery spring—I tasted these immediate ingredients. How could a dough kneaded from them not effortlessly grow? Punched down—large and little gasps of air imprisoned inside—would it not triple in volume? Beaten down again, yea vanquished, would it not rise a second, a third time? Brushed with oil of olives from sacred groves, would it not meet its mysterious destiny—raw to cooked, matter to spirit—sealed inside the fiery oven, the rock rolled into place? Snatched at the last instant from that infernal heat, would it not be borne triumphant on platters by monks (who had just completed their morning prayers, thus imparting a heightened spiritual zest to the loaves) through gardens respiring with spiky rosemary under the morning sun, and be delivered unto the *trattoria*'s back door wrapped in cloth? And kept warm next to the oven, guarded near Vesta's sacred flame. This much you could—I did—taste in one mouthful. Everything alive. If a bite could bind a person to a place—to ensure becoming a part of it—this one bound me to the island. I was here for the duration. The reverse of Persephone, committed to hell because of the six pomegranate seeds she chewed, we bit into morsels of paradise. Man, Sicilian wine is strong.

"My *carciofo* is probably still in the ground, down the mountain, miles away," I yawned behind my hand.

Maia was lost in studying the noisy room around us, observer, anthropologist, cultural attaché to her own *paesani*. Every table had ordered before we did and seated a full clan. Generations were crammed together, parents force-feeding toddlers, teenagers wolfing down pasta, sleeping babies cradled by grandparents, everyone gabbing, laughing, eating, swallowing. The waiter powered around the room, delivering plates and platters, more bottles of water and wine. More bread and beer, bowls and bills.

So if artichokes took hours to roast, the brother-in-law, equipped with walkie-talkie, was probably just loading the baskets with the last of the blessed thistles onto a *sciccareddu*'s back right now. I relaxed into my chair with more vino. Treat the donkey well, give him a handful of hay and a drink from a trough, sing him the donkey song, and take your time because, man, those tenors were tiny beasts of burden. I could wait—we had Bread and Wine. An excellent sacramental appetizer. An old favorite. A meal really. A religion. I refilled Maia's glass and added a few centimeters to my own, pondering Franca again.

"Did Viola escape from Melodia?"

"*Cara* Natalie, I do not recall the specifics. It's been too long a time."

"What did her parents do?"

"*Beh* . . . they were upset, like any parents would be. I'm surprised at this zeal of yours, dear."

"Me too. Honestly, I can't explain why I'm so interested. I just want to know that she's still alive, really. That she's OK."

The waiter was nowhere in the dining room. I took another roll, broke through the crackly crunchy stratas, pulled at the elastic, steamy dough, probed and pinched the warm mass. There must be a technical name for the meeting of crust and dough, brown and white, a baking term for the realm between exterior and interior . . . the body and spirit . . . the dead and the quick.

"You know, both my sisters have an allergy to wheat. Can you imagine life without bread?" I asked, my mouth full.

"Why? What happens to them?"

"Oh, they get sleepy, lethargic, yawn a lot. I'm so lucky to have escaped it."

"I should say." She drained the carafe.

I kept chewing. "They even get disoriented."

The waiter stood over us with plates, trying to remember who ordered what: sacrificial kid goat that smelled sort of barbecued, and the huge vegetable like a baked green crown. "*Buon appetito*, ladies."

"Do I worship it or eat it?" I joked. I loosened the first outer charred petal off the subterranean globe—rounded like a basilica dome—and nibbled its meatiness, bittersweet and mineral. Though seared in a mini-inferno, it hadn't given up any moist ghost. I plucked my way through, spiraling in, the marinade of lemon and olive oil, mint and crushed garlic yielding up.

"Fabulous! So delicious I can't tell you."

"Would you care to taste the meat?"

"No, no. I've got this."

We savored without conversing, the best way to manage in such a loud room. A person achieves something engaging with an artichoke. Does any other vegetable in the world have a built-in goal? Leaf, leaf, leaf, leaf, leaf, leaf, leaf, thicker to thinner, exterior to interior, then the prize of the tender heart. All those roasting hours made this apotheosis. At the end I was just sated, full of the island's generosity. When the waiter set our bill down I grabbed it, but my cousin fixed me with a no-nonsense look and demanded the slip.

"Maia, you must stop treating me as a guest, or for sure I'll get on your nerves very quickly."

"We have to eat."

"Exactly, and here's my contribution to that effort."

"I don't want to hear another word about it." She stood, brushed the crumbs off her lap and firmly pulled the paper from my fingers. The woman was not to be messed with.

We crossed the empty piazza, strewn with peanut shells, shreds of burst balloons and horse manure, and circled down the cream-colored monastery walls of San Martino delle Scale to her Fiat. She opened her glove compartment and began rummaging.

"*Senti*, I suppose we might try driving to Alcamo from here, if you help me read the map."

"Really, Maia? Oh that's great! You won't mind missing your siesta?" Together we unfolded the Touring Club Italiano and spread it wide across the roof.

"As I mentioned, it's been a very long time since I have driven this way." She put her glasses on and located the speck of San Martino delle Scale. A couple of inches away lay the fingerprint-sized smudge of Alcamo. The route twisted between them like a small intestine before connecting to the straighter portion of highway 186.

"And then from 186 to highway 113."

"Good eyes. *That's* the number I couldn't remember."

Her car climbed through artichoke smoke of layered blue, an atmospheric parfait. Perfect. Maia would know what questions to ask and how to phrase them discreetly without arousing anyone, and maybe, with luck, we might even find Franca's old neighborhood. She was switchbacking like crazy, jerking the steering wheel to and fro.

"*Porca miseria*." Most of the roadway had a rockslide splayed across it. Someone had stuck a red and blue traffic disk into the loose dirt. "We've had heavy rains this winter. *Beh*, let's see if we can pass around it." I got out and tossed a few loose stones off the road to make room. We nosed carefully past, rounded a curve and picked up speed again. Her vivid driving technique resumed, which is how we nearly plowed into a second rockslide.

"Oh no." I got out to check if there was space for the car this time. "There's no way, Maia."

She opened her door and surveyed. "I'm sorry," she sighed. "We tried. Thank you."

We were well on our way down to Palermo, past the Mafia-Nightmare architecture up on the crest, when a herd of goats—leaping and glorious—filled the road. The unruly mass insisted upon right of way. Maia turned off the motor and nodded along to the sound of their bells. She knew the score.

Chapter IX

The Garden

"I've been thinking." Maia stood dusting her bookcase in the hall next to me. She'd overheard me on the phone to the *Giornale di Sicilia*, her daily newspaper, which I'd just been told would not grant public access to any archives. "My son knows someone who works there. I can't promise anything but I'll talk with him. Meanwhile, let's visit the Botanical Garden, shall we?"

"But I'm keeping you from doing other things."

"*Ma che*, other things. I'm retired. What else do I have to do? My days are free. Let's go."

I'd have to sneak away during siesta to the bus station, my next plan of approach to Alcamo, which I was picturing as a little hilltop town with narrow streets.

"Before we leave I have one other phone number to try," I said.

"Who?"

"Well, I brought her book along. She's an American expatriate who lives in the city most of the time, but her husband has a family farm in the countryside near Alcamo, and I actually found her name in the phonebook."

The author answered right away. She was certain that Franca had left for the north long ago, but suggested that I petition the office of the mayor of Alcamo, whose name and number she gave me. His line rang for over a minute. I hung the phone back in its cradle: no secretary, no answering machine, *niente*.

"*Andiamo?*" Ready now?

The Fiat was breezing along the Via Maqueda with all other careening transit when sirens grew loud behind us. A phalanx of dark cars and police motorcycles bore down. Traffic quickly obeyed, pulling to the sides. Maia must have turned her hearing aid off, because she was one of the last to move out of the way. A motorcade tore past, a blur of tinted windows and guards gripping rifles.

"What's going on?"

"That would be a judge or a police chief or the mayor going to work. At any time they risk bombing or assassination. You've been spared because of the Easter holidays, but now you glimpse everyday life here. Mark my words, you will hear sirens again at one when they go home for lunch, at four when they return to work and at eight in the evening."

When the flashing lights receded down the boulevard, cars immediately refilled the vacuum. Maia drove straight into the chaos again without looking and, when we got to our destination, parked by colliding with the curb at a jaunty angle all her own. She was, deep down, a wild thing.

Street noises disappeared the farther we retreated on foot into the lushly overgrown *Orto Botanico*. Thick-stemmed palms made canopies for chattering birds.

"We have a Botanical Garden in Berkeley too. Last year, an Andean century hoya flowered thirty-five years earlier than anyone expected. It had never bloomed before, so excited botanists came from all over the world to see it. I went every day after work. The flowers at the top, oh maybe three meters above the ground, looked like pale green orchids. The bees went crazy over it."

"Where was this plant?" a voice demanded. My cousin and I turned around. We saw no one and looked at each other, our eyes bugging out.

"Up here." A wizened man was balancing on a branch

over our heads. He dropped to the ground next to Maia, and presented her with a magnolia flower bigger than her face. She chuckled and twirled it between her hands. "Come along please, ladies, I shall show you the garden."

We tried to match his pace and keep up with his talk. He burst like a seed pod with vital details. Every plant entranced him: papaya, palm, hoya, agave, plus each subtropical shrub, blade and stalk which he formally introduced in Latin. The botanist was enamored. He described the dainty flavor of *fichi d'india*, worth the pain of donning gloves to cut the prickly pear from the cactus, singeing the thorns over a flame, carefully peeling away the skin, and removing the hundreds of seeds inside by floating the fruit in a bowl of water. What was left, he raved, tasted superb.

He ran to his next act, "the incredible soap tree. Let me demonstrate." He wet his hands in an already filled bucket and lathered the soap tree nut between his palms. He touched the *Mimosa sensitiva*, which recoiled from the heat of fingertips, folding in on itself, and had us touch it too. He gathered a few *cherimoya* seeds for me, "to 'seminate' in the United States of America. It tastes like all the fruits put together." He collected fleecy strands of kapok, also known as vegetable wool, placing it in our palms. Maia petted hers as if it were a small sleeping creature. He dashed over to the banyan tree to show how huge it was, scaled it in no time and hid himself within its multiple trunks. We clapped.

"Bravo," Maia called out. "You're an acrobat too."

At the end of the walk he pulled us under a veil of jasmine. We swooned from the vapors.

"My grandmother used to go on about the air perfumed with jasmine and orange blossoms here," I said.

"Correct. I remember it well. What year did she emigrate?"

Maia and I both answered, "1904."

"That Palermo is largely gone since the war."

Maia opened her purse to give him a tip. "Your knowledge, sir, is admirable. I wish more Palermitani shared it. Thank you kindly."

"No no, *signora*, I cannot accept money. However, I would much appreciate a postcard sent from your Botanical Garden?" He offered me a slip of paper with his name and address.

"*Sì, sì*, with pleasure."

Since we were in the neighborhood, Maia also wanted to acquaint me with the Villa Giulia, which may have been glorious when The Redheads were driven through in the family carriage pulled by the shining horse on Sundays, but was now a neglected jumble of weeds. Grasses crowded the fountains and statues. A machine went off somewhere nearby, a generator or small engine. I jumped. "What was that?"

"What was what?"

Louder the second time, it prickled the hair on my arms. Some kind of big device was being . . . strangled. "That sounded awfully close by, don't you think?" After the earlier talk about bombings, I suddenly wanted out of the deserted park, but my erudite cousin continued unconcerned along the walkway, identifying flowers in Latin, Italian and even English whenever she knew the names.

"Look at the lion."

I searched around for the next stone statue, then figured out she was referring to dandelions—*dente di leone*—and nodded listlessly, pointing to a clump of them. Really, we were getting much too detailed here, cataloguing weeds. I needed to get on a bus to Alcamo this afternoon.

"No Natalie, I mean the *lion*."

Just a few strides away, a box of thick black metal mesh contained a real live big cat who was watching us. He could have passed for an old taxidermy display—mane stiffened like a huge dried sunflower, coat the color of hay with a nap like moth-chewed felt—except for the stare down we were getting from his unblinking, cloudy eyes.

Four paces to the left, pivot, four paces to the right, pivot. His overgrown claws scraped with a hollow scritch scritch, the tail dragging along the concrete slab like a dust broom sweeping every millimeter of the cruel cage. The gaze stayed fixed on us.

"Poor thing!" I looked to Maia to justify this outrage on her city's behalf. She should have some explanation, some piece of history to help make sense of it.

My cousin patted my shoulder. "He's been here for many years. This is all he knows now."

A little boy came running with a stick and began striking the cage. His father caught up, out of breath. "No no no no, Gian-Maria," he pleaded. The lion didn't falter.

"Yes yes yes yes," the kid yelled gleefully, poking the stick through the mesh. "Yes!"

The tail thumped, full of power. The leonine eyes closed halfway. Then the machine sound, straight from the chest and throat of the great conquered beast, blasted the child backward.

"Waaaah!"

"Oh Gian-Maria, what have you done now?"

I turned away. "Isn't it about lunchtime, Maia?"

She nodded. "Two children on an outing. Let's go."

Primo was ready with "*una pasta proprio Palermitana*."

"It smells out of this world."

"A seasonal dish, taking advantage of the fresh ricotta which has just come in, and the new spring peas."

"If you stayed here a year, we would serve you a different pasta each day, never the same one repeated," Maia beamed, as if my remaining in Palermo indefinitely would be fine by her. Primo suggested what pastas he could make for us tomorrow, and Thursday, and Friday.

"Mmm, I love today's pasta, Primo. I loved Saturday's."

"It's nothing, *signorina*," he rushed to refill my plate.

"Please," I spread my hands over it, "only a spoonful more. I was thinking of taking an afternoon walk, and giving you a little time to yourself, Maia."

"There's not much to see in my district. All the shops will be closed."

"Maybe a museum?"

"Which? Most only stay open until one."

"Just to admire the architecture then. I want to explore the Politeama district."

"Be careful for purse snatchers out there, *signorina*," Primo wagged his finger, "and keep your camera hidden."

"You saw what happened to the Timballo on Easter," Maia added. Primo clucked sympathetically.

"Of course, I'll be careful." I demonstrated wrapping the strap of my bag around my torso. "They'd have to take me with it."

"This is not a joke, *signorina*."

"Better if you don't go today. My son is coming back this evening. Tomorrow I can take you myself to look at the architecture."

"Just a little outing. Maybe I'll mail something."

"Well . . . you're an adult. Of course, do as you wish. You have my phone number written down?" She opened her purse and handed me some bus tokens. "Use these *gettoni*."

I brought Evelyn's package in case I passed a post office. I wanted to stop worrying about the responsibility she'd thrust on me. It'd be a relief to get it taken care of.

My guidebook said the intra-island Pullmans or buses stopped on the Via Paolo Balsamo, around the corner from the train station. Dropping a *gettono* in the pay box, I easily arrived there and looked around. I saw one air-conditioned bus full of Germans heading for Catania, and the driver had no idea about the next bus for Alcamo; he only knew his one

Autostrada route which he had been driving six days a week without fail for years. The municipal bus, banged-up and fibrillating, was destined for Bagheria, the opposite direction from mine. Its driver thought a Trapani bus might come through around three-thirty with a connection to Alcamo, but he didn't want to make any promises. May God grant you a pleasant journey wherever life may lead you, he called out, touching his San Cristoforo statue on the dashboard. He tipped his cap and I blew him a kiss. His bus coughed and shuddered off, leaving behind a grimy dark cloud. I flopped onto a seat.

"*Prego, signorina?*"

"A *spremuta di limone*, please, with ice."

"Certainly."

"Will any Alcamo buses stop here?"

"Sure, lots come through all the time. You're in the right place."

"That's a relief. They're not on strike?"

"Not that I've heard."

My guidebook provided no map of my destination but gave vague directions:

> At the complicated intersection outside Partinico the road bears left (look for signpost) and traverses a flat cultivated plain (beware of tractors and animals). Alcamo is approached on a new road which negotiates the low hills by viaduct and tunnel (unlit).

"How do you say, 'I'd like to hire a goatherd guide'?"

"*Prego, signorina?*"

"Nothing, nothing. Talking to myself is all."

My waiter planted a napkin on the table, then a long spoon across it, followed by a saucer with paper doily, and a metal bowl containing five elongated packets of sugar, decorated with color detail of Botticelli's most famous paintings.

From afar Alcamo is just an innocent sprinkling of bleached houses on the flank of Monte Bonifato. Those who know it, however, are aware that in the 1950s and '60s it was the lair of the notorious mafioso Vincenzo Rimi. He was the head of a dynasty linked with the American Cosa Nostra, which commanded an important drug trafficking route from Sicily to America and whose activities were screened by political protection . . . . A thug and a much convicted criminal, [he] established himself and his family's supremacy in Alcamo by sheer violence. Such was his corrupt power that he was able to have men of his clan elected to parliament; his lawyer Giovanni Leone, an important Christian Democrat minister eventually became President of the Italian Republic 1971-8.

The waiter gracefully balanced a tray above his shoulder, positioned the narrow tall glass of squeezed lemon juice in bubbly mineral water on the doily, and set down a small plate holding the bill. "One iced *spremuta*."

"Beautiful, sir." I smiled.

He studied his composition for a moment, reached into it and rotated the bowl so that the Botticellis aimed crosswise, adjusted the spoon half an inch, snapped his towel over his arm and bowed. "*Prego, signorina*."

"*Grazie*." Along with a sip of sour lemonade, I took in the afternoon—the old guys wearing *coppola* caps playing chess inside the Caffè; the two elderly women arm-in-arm peering into the doorway of an ironmonger; five kids in smudged clothes lying on the sidewalk, taking turns throwing pebbles down a drain and giggling at the echo. The weather had turned balmy, the sky a hazy, bright white that occurs near saltwater, suggesting summer and sultry evenings soon. I stirred sugar from *The Birth of Venus* and Zephyrus, a detail from *Primavera*, into the glass, watched it tumble downward. I took a sweet swallow, stretched my legs, leaned back in the metal chair, and drank in the splendid, indolent moment, lazily sucking a chip of ice. The bus comes when it comes, mused I, philosopher.

Rimi recruited couriers from Alcamo and Castellammare to work on the principal drug route from North Africa to America via Sicily. Drugs and other contraband arrived and left the country undetected via the remote coast of nearby San Vito Lo Capo. Some drugs entered the USA secreted into cavities gouged out of slabs of marble quarried from the foot of Alcamo's hill. Of course the quarry also belonged to the Mafia . . .

A bus pulled up.
"Alcamo?" I called out.
"Messina."

Over the years Rimi's activities have become a part of Alcamo's folklore, and wary foreigners skirt the town transfixed by the possibility that they might acquire a new pair of concrete boots and a permanent home under the waves of the Golfo of Castellammare. But Rimi died in 1975—go and examine his absurd marble sepulchre in the town's cemetery (ironically, he was to die peacefully in his bed)—and in any case the Mafia rarely concerns itself with outsiders.

Good to know. Reassuring. Another bus pulled in. "Alcamo?"
"*Tst.*"
I entered the Caffè. There was no schedule printed on any wall, no brochures or flyers to consult. In the telephone booth,

I shuffled through pages looking for Autobus services, Public buses, Pullman, Transit, Trasporto, Express.

The bartender had his back to the counter. He was murmuring into his hands, which held between them a green pear, "Beautiful beautiful winter pear. I want to kiss you. I want to eat you."

I could not bring myself to interrupt this intimacy between a man and his fruit to ask about the bus. It was way too private.

Back to my post in the sunlight where I waited until six. And I thought I could get there just because I wanted to. Home again, jiggety-jig, straight down the great and grand boulevard by fast local bus. I saluted the two bronze lions, so much more revered than the live one in the mesh cage. As I got off the bus down the street from Maia's palazzo, I remembered that I'd forgotten all about mailing Evelyn's manila envelope to Agrigento.

"*Buona sera.*"

"*Sera.*" The Professor stood at the elevator holding an empty plate. "Someone must have left the door open again," he sighed, pressing the button. Today the Nile green sweater he wore brought out the intensity of his eye color. "Most likely the new family on the fifth floor."

"I watched them from the terrace."

"The new family?"

"No *scusa*, the cats."

He smiled bravely. "My wife took pity on them when they were three pathetic little skeletons and now, twenty-one hungry mouths to feed last count. I carry on the tradition in her honor."

"They must look forward to your visits."

"*Beh*, the appetites never stop." He put his ear to the door. "It could just be slow. We'll give it another minute. You are visiting *Signora* Santilli from elsewhere?"

"From California."

"A very long way away. I sensed an accent. What brings you to Palermo?" He looked as though he might cry. He asked as if I'd been exiled to this outpost.

"I love being here. My wish to know more of our family history, and research on Franca Viola, if you know who she is."

"I certainly know who she is."

"But information has been difficult to come by."

"I would imagine so." He rubbed the cleft of his chin with his index finger, making a fine sandpaper sound.

"Do you have any idea what became of her?"

The orbs beamed straight into me. He shook his head slowly. I found myself mirroring him.

"Not at all."

"My relatives seem upset that I'm inquiring."

"I don't understand why. Franca Viola was a, if not the, major significant figure of *femminismo* in this century. She brought Italy into the modern era, I would go so far as to say. She was a heroine, and not only for women. She made us Sicilians proud."

The elevator banged down to lobby level. "After you," he gestured.

"What floor shall I press, Professor?"

"Fourth. You could try to contact her lawyer, whose name began with a C, but you know, at the moment I cannot recall his name."

"Ah?"

"I apologize," he shook his head, "that's all that comes to me for now."

"Professor, if you do remember his name, we're up on the seventh."

"Certainly."

The elevator bumped to a stop.

"My floor. A pleasure, *signora*."

The stupid ring was on! "Oh this is just for protection—I'm not married or anything." I pulled it off my finger and held the fake thing up to show him.

"Good evening, then, *signorina*." A vapor of a smile flitted across his beautiful, sad, resigned face. Our eyes tarried until the door shut. And to think that this was how some engagements used to be made—just by signaling, by a look. For a second I enjoyed a fantasy that I had just become engaged in the old way.

Chapter X

The Vault

Friday afternoon at 3 p.m. on the *punto*, Maia and I shouldered through the bulletproof revolving doors of the *Giornale di Sicilia* downtown on the Via Abramo Lincoln. Her son had contacted his friend here at the paper who had agreed to give us a little of his time. An armed guard checked our names against his clipboard and confiscated my passport and her ID.

A secretary told us, "The Doctor will be delayed a few minutes. Have a seat please, make yourselves comfortable."

My cousin reminded me not to get my hopes up. "There is no means," she had cautioned that first night. I fixated on an ashtray the size of a dinner plate stuffed with pungent debris and rehearsed my two sentences in my head. An hour passed.

"He must've forgotten."

"*Stai calma*, Natalie, *stai tranquilla*," Maia used the placating, palms-down gesture and a soothing inflection, "he'll keep the appointment." She returned to her meditative pose—the one she'd used in the bedroom of the girl being dressed—looking but not staring in front of her. The eternal Sicilian now of the eternal Sicilian wait into which another half hour dissolved.

The door swung open and a plume of smoke entered. In followed an ignited cigarette held in the hand of a superbly dressed man. His jacket hung from his shoulders, kept in place only by the power of elegant posture which Italian men had long perfected. *La Bella Figura.*

"*Ahh, Dottore,*" Maia greeted him warmly.

"Your son and family are all well?"

"*Benissimi.* You are so very kind to agree to meet with us. I know how busy you are. May I introduce my young American cousin, Natalie Galli."

He bowed. "*Signorina*, a pleasure. How may I help you?"

"Sir," I took a breath, "a deep thank you for your time. I ask for your assistance in researching Franca Viola."

"Of course we realize that given the time elapsed you may no longer have a file on her." Apology saturated Maia's tone. "I myself believe that *La Viola* probably still lives here, though I have no evidence to support that."

The Doctor sat down in his swivel chair and leaned back, tapping his fingertips together. "Agreed, *Signora* Santilli. Most likely she never left the area. In my position surely I would have heard if she had." He too seemed surprised that I sought information on an incident so long past, that nobody discussed anymore. He remained mute, swinging left, swinging right, the springs creaking. "Nonetheless," he pressed his palms together, "let us go to the vault and see what we can find."

His cigarette, a beacon, led the way down the corridor to an elevator. Holding the doors open, punching the button, he chatted with my cousin and puffed. We entered an open area where employees turned eagerly to him. With a few words he dispatched three to the task. Two tremendous floor-to-ceiling steel doors cranked open to reveal a multi-storied interior of catwalks and ladders onto which the workers climbed. They scurried along the metal platforms and yanked open file cabinet drawers. One emerged with a folder. Ten of us crowded around. Articles and eight-by-ten photographs, undisturbed for years, rested inside.

"Here, miss. Franca Viola."

"*Che bella*," I gasped. The beautiful young woman in a shawl, her dark hair spilling down, sat at an official's desk. "And so young."

I gingerly flipped through the pictures. Franca embracing an older man wearing a *coppola*. Franca with a little boy. A packed public room with a Christmas tree. Many men and officers standing together. Three authorities seated behind a high desk.

Commentary flew between Maia, the Doctor and the assistants who were probably too young to have remembered the case.

"Go ahead, select a few of these images to photocopy," he urged. "We'll reproduce all the articles here for you right now."

"Which ones will you choose?" Maia put her arm around my shoulder, whispering, "we don't want to take up more of his time."

I selected six and thrust them into an assistant's hands, and then sifted again through the glossies I didn't choose, hoping to imprint them in my memory.

"*Signora* Santilli, if she wishes copies of all the *Giornale* articles covering the trial she will need to find them at the National Library in the microfilm section. For some reason they are not in this file."

"Of course, *Dottore*."

"So, Maia, they put her on trial?"

"No, no, the *rapist* was on trial."

"Oh! You did not mention this."

"Didn't I?"

"You have no idea what this means to me, Doctor," my voice caught in my throat. "I've wondered about this person for twenty-two years." The massive jaws of the vault creaked closed, a benevolent beast. I vigorously shook hands with everyone in the room, while they eyed me curiously. "*Grazie infinite a tutti!*" I gushed.

Inside the elevator, I was so elated it felt as if we were going up instead of coming down. The tiny filler from the *SF Chronicle* was exploding into a saga. I bought two fluorescent orange sodas from a vendor at the *Orto Botanico* across the street. We sat on a bench in full sunlight, drinking down every bee-sweet drop. "What a gorgeous afternoon, everything is sparkling, isn't it?"

"Truthfully, I was not sure that you would get this far, and even if you go no farther you will still have achieved something," Maia's chin hovered near the top of the *Orangina* bottle. She allowed herself a careful smile. "I am pleased."

I studied the first headline and panicked. It was one thing to converse (poorly), but another to read journalistic Italian in shrunken type, with complicated flowery clauses that lasted a full paragraph. A sigh escaped me, which Maia heard.

She made a pistol with her thumb and index. "'They Burst In Shooting To Kidnap A Girl: Eight Determined Criminals Enter a House with Weapons in Hand.'"

"Oh, I had no idea. I pictured him doing it alone."

"It continues—listen carefully—'In the Scuffle the Girl's Brother Held onto Her Dress So They Took Him Too, Escaping by Auto.'"

Sharing the front page with the article were reports of heavy casualties in Vietnam and six hundred and twelve U.S. road fatalities over the 1965 Christmas Holiday weekend.

"Patience. Italian journalists are known to be long-winded." Maia patted my wrist. "If you don't understand something, you just come ask me. I'll explain everything. *Andiamo?*" She had sacrificed her siesta to accompany me.

As soon as we returned to the apartment, Maia excused herself to lie down "*per un'oretta*," and I spread the articles all over the bed. At 5:45 I was kissing the Cassell's dictionary I'd lugged along from home. At 7:00, the print began to waver and merge before my eyes. At 7:15 I borrowed Maia's magnifying glass from the living room and could read again. At 8:00, the sirens went by on the boulevard. I rushed out onto the terrace to watch the contingent whizz past—five cars within a swarm of motorcycles. From up here it looked like a cross on the move. At 8:30, I felt nostalgic for the American news reporters' economy of words. Maia entered with a tray of pecorino cheese, olives she had cured herself last winter, and a glass of seltzer with *amarena* cherry juice that she had also made herself, "for fortification." By 9:30 I had written out pages of grammar questions. She put on her reading glasses and clarified every point on the list.

I looked up at the wooden *armadio* facing my bed—it seemed like a sympathetic sentinel watching over the translation. By boiling away most of the wordy flourishes, I pieced together on paper a narrative of the abduction:

Alcamo, December 26, 1965
When Police Sergeant Brigadier Giuseppe Mineo passed Sant'Agostino's church on the way to his office Sunday morning, Saint Stephen's Day, he came upon a bleeding woman, Vita Serro Viola, whose clothes were torn. He brought her to the Civic Hospital where she was treated for injuries including a cranial contusion, occipital hematoma, lesions on the "front and anterior" neck, as well as contusions and abrasions to the right knee and forearm. She cried as she recounted her ordeal.

She had spent the morning at home with her daughter Franca and her young son Mariano. At 8:30 a.m. a car stopped in front of the house. The engine idled while two young men knocked at the door, asking for her husband. She told them he had gone out and could be found at the Piazza Ciulla. They left. She recognized neither of them but stated she did not feel especially suspicious.

Half an hour later two cars pulled up and eight young men poured out, leaving the motors running. Filippo Melodia, who Vita Serro knew by sight, approached the entrance. She quickly shut and locked the door. One of the men smashed the door-glass and they shoved their way into her house. They fired shots at the ceiling causing plaster to fall. She realized why they had come, and threw herself at the attackers in a desperate attempt to protect her daughter. Some held her back while others seized the girl, Franca, and dragged her out of the house through the shattered entrance.

Eight-year-old Mariano latched onto his sister and did not let go. The men tried to peel his fingers away, but he clung to her dress. Sister and brother were thrown into one of the cars. Vita Serro ran out after them, and grabbed hold of the rear bumper. With volleys of pistol shots ringing out, the vehicles sped down the street, dragging her along until her strength failed and she fell to the ground.

Other accounts came from eyewitnesses who ran out in front of the communal slaughterhouse when they heard cars racing by. They saw a white automobile speeding past with two men trying to push off a little boy who was hanging onto the door handle.

Police immediately launched a search. By nightfall no trace had been found. Late that evening Mariano Viola, who was let go by the kidnappers at the edge of town, made it the rest of the way home on his own.

THREE OF THE EIGHT HOOLIGANS ALREADY ARRESTED
December 27, 1965

One day after the kidnap, Carlo Costantino, Giovanni Daidone and Ignazio Coppola were taken into custody and interrogated by the police. They confessed that following the kidnap the group had reconvened at the farmhouse of the Stellino brothers in the Scampati neighborhood near Alcamo Marina, where Franca Viola and Filippo Melodia were holed up under armed guard. Provisions were brought by one of the gang.

Almost all of the eight kidnappers have already been convicted of other crimes and have served sentences. Amongst the eight still at large, two are considered particularly dangerous: Ignazio Lipari and Filippo Melodia, the latter being the kidnapped girl's "pretendente," [wooer; fiancé]. It has been confirmed, furthermore, that Melodia organized the kidnap. He was rejected repeatedly by Franca Viola, who was at one time engaged to him. However, her father broke it off because of Melodia's known delinquent conduct.

Just the week before, he had been arrested for illegal possession and carrying weapons, as well as repeated driving with a revoked license. Both men, with long criminal records, had been detained by the authorities on the grounds that they were socially dangerous, including to public safety.

December 28th, forty-eight hours after the kidnap, a frenzied police and carabinieri *search with dogs yielded nothing. Primary search areas were expanded to include Alcamo, Castellamare del Golfo, and Balestrate, where it was believed the kidnappers may have sought refuge, taking Viola with them.*

At the Alcamo commissioner's office in the security rooms, the direction officer and the commissioner (with the patience of a Carthusian monk) continue to interrogate Costantino, Daidone and Coppola, but no details have been released. Further investigations have ascertained that the fugitives reunited at the farmhouse situated in the Scampati neighborhood in the vicinity of Alcamo Marina, which was rented by cousins Giuseppe Stellino and Antonio Stellino, 28 and 26 respectively, and both sought by police.

THE KIDNAPPERS' CAR FOUND SPATTERED WITH BLOOD - ARREST WARRANTS ISSUED
December 28, 1965

Meanwhile, the Giulietta car [an Alfa Romeo]*belonging to Melodia and his partners was found abandoned in the Giardinello area of Castellammare. It was spattered with blood, a pistol cartridge was found inside and a raincoat hung on a nearby tree. A stolen red Fiat 600 was found on the slope of Monte Bonifato, miles from the first vehicle.*

Some of the men questioned confessed the facts in minute detail and in sequential chronology. It appears that Vito Varvaro, besides having taken an active part in the kidnap, was used to supply his companions, and to bring Franca's brother, Mariano Viola, back to the outskirts of the city.

Meanwhile, public interest in the facts of the extraordinary incident and the method in which it was undertaken continues to grow. Every motorized means of the police which passes through the center of town is closely watched to see whether some member of the gang has fallen into the net, but none have been observed being driven through town in a police vehicle, and almost everyone knows what these men look like.

Tonight in Alcamo the electricity inexplicably went out for an hour and a half. By the light of motorcars, groups of men on the street could be seen intently discussing the kidnap. An unidentified source even suggested that the electricity was intentionally halted in order to give the police an edge in their search without being seen, particularly at the periphery of the inhabited sections of the city, where the kidnappers might be staked out.

Chief Police Commissioner Doctor Lorenzo Camilleri, who with great self-denial has been in charge of all the search operations, has personally visited almost all the suspected locations, and is optimistic that he will soon be able to arrest the fugitives.

The homes of these individuals are under continuous surveillance. Later tonight another powerful offensive is expected in the hunt for the kidnappers.

ALCAMO: KIDNAPPED GIRL AND KIDNAPPER NOT FOUND

December 29

On the morning of December 29th, Mariano Viola told officers that the kidnappers had forced the Stellino shepherds to provide shelter for the group. He said that his sister whispered to him to tell their father she was at the farmhouse of "a certain Stellino."

TOUGHS STILL HOLD THE KIDNAPPED ALCAMO GIRL PRISONER

December 31

The Viola household continues to endure anguished hours since the kidnap five days ago, knowing that their daughter is in the hands of dangerous criminals. The extreme menace of the kidnappers adds to the increased apprehension of her parents and family. In fact it seems evident that this kidnap does not fall under the category of the classic fuga d'amore *[flight of love] more or less agreed on by the participants, which inevitably forms a prelude to marriage. Here instead is a case of a rejected suitor who planned in minutest detail, and then with cold precision carried out a criminal plot with the complicity of seven contemporaries, all of whom have penal records (which are hardly reassuring).*

By New Year's Eve, no new developments in the case were reported.

THE GIRL OF ALCAMO'S TEN TERRIBLE DAYS

January 3, 1966

The "beautiful Alcamese girl" was returned home after nine days of imprisonment. Melodia was arrested following a chase over the roofs of the house where he had been keeping her. After her return she remained at home without seeing anyone. Her parents do not want her to marry the kidnapper, who took her with force and against her will. This time, consequently, it should not be an "Italian marriage" which usually ends adventures of this sort.

Photos include the girl being interviewed by the police immediately after her recovery, the kidnapper at the Commissioner's office, and the moving reunion of Franca Viola and her parents.

IN CONVERSATION WITH THE GIRL FROM ALCAMO "I WILL NOT MARRY HIM
—I Am Not Yielding To Violence And Prejudices"
Francesca Viola tells us

January 5, 1966

On the Eve of the Epiphany, she gave a brief interview. A photograph showed her standing straight, her hands behind her back. "I prefer to end up in a convent rather than marry a man who forced me to stay a week with him until I was freed by the police." Speaking like this, using (for some parts of our island) a new, almost revolutionary language, is Francesca Viola, the young woman kidnapped from her home on the day of Santo Stefano under very dramatic circumstances.

Since January 2, she has remained at home, upset and overburdened, without seeing anyone. Her parents, breaking an uncivilized tradition, have already decided that she should not have to marry the abductor Melodia. *At first it might have appeared that the girl was having some hesitation about her parents' decision. An understandable one, by the way, given the general attitude that the honor of a girl rests in her chastity, which can only be saved by marrying the man who used violence against her. But if she ever did, Viola no longer has doubts. That's what she told us in a brief interview, choosing civilized, conscious words, full of maturity:*

"*I will not marry Filippo Melodia. I am not willing to bow to prejudices and to violence. I know that it has always happened this way, but why must my life be imposed upon by a barbaric custom? I've said it, I do not intend to submit to certain prejudices and then to be unhappy for my whole life.*"

While Viola speaks she becomes animated, and on her very beautiful face pass flashes of fire. Marriage would be a reward for violence. First she had said no to Filippo Melodia. Now that he has resorted to uncivilized means, helped by seven other young toughs, shot a gun, and then beat up her mother, must she say yes, maybe even begging for him to consent to marriage? Why?

"*But how do you explain*"—*we asked her*—"*your previous engagement with the man who you now reject?*" *The reasons that at first convinced her to say no to the engagement only became stronger with time.*

"*When I knew him, some years ago, he didn't seem violent to me or lacking in scruples, which he is. When he revealed his true nature, then I decided to break the engagement. And I was right to do so. The confirmation has been given by his recent, forceful actions. I have therefore no reason to turn back on my decision. Yes, I know that we have many prejudices, and I know how a woman's honor is considered. But I have nothing to regret in myself. I am not guilty for what happened.*"

She denied that her parents played a part in this decision: "*There was no imposition from them. Even if the choice may seem dramatic, I made it by myself.*"

Wow. I found Maia in her armchair, feet propped up on the ottoman, looking out at Monte Pellegrino, the stars shimmering.

"The story is raw and shocking."

"*Ehhh.*"

"So they were engaged at one time."

"Remember what I told you about engagement? The family opens the door to a boy, they might sit in the parlor together, and the arrangement is sealed. Nothing more substantial than that in some instances. I'm afraid I can't stay awake any longer. I'm going to bed now, *cara*."

"Good night, Maia." We kissed each cheek. "How can I thank you?"

"It's nothing. Don't mention it."

Chapter XI

The Shoes Weekend

Maia finally allowed me to take her to lunch on Saturday. We stood at the counter of the famous Antica Foccacceria San Francesco, transfixed by a tremendous cylinder of meat rotating on an iron spit, licked by primal flames.

"What exactly is turning round there?"

"A spleen."

"Whose?"

"The cow."

"I see."

"Your order?"

"One normal sandwich and one without spleen, please." I handed the cashier a ten thousand lire note.

"Without meat that's no sandwich! People come from all over the island to taste our *pani cu' la meusa.*" She looked distraught, peering over her steamed-up, grease-flecked glasses.

"Cheese only."

"*Beh*, as you wish," she conceded.

In the noisy eatery, Maia attacked her *pani* while I took in the church and piazza of Saint Francis through the plate-glass window. "I love your city. I looked it up in your big dictionary: Palermo, meaning all doors, all ports, all harbors, from the Greek 'Panormus.' I feel like an honorary resident, even though temporary."

"Maybe better temporary than permanent." She seemed a little out of sorts today. I'd kept her up much too late last night with all my questions. "If you moved here it could take ten years to get your telephone hooked up. Eh, *cara mia*, it's just not like the United States. The government and the agencies have their own ways of doing things, and they will not budge. You don't want to hear about our Sicilian dilemma, how little there is to go around in the south, all doors notwithstanding!

"But," she brightened, gesturing towards the square, "this city continues on. Aren't you going to eat, Natalie?"

"Oh yes." Creamy *cacciocavallo* cheese bulged out of my sandwich when I bit into it. "Explain something to me. Why did the story appear the very day Franca was kidnapped? No one knew that she'd refuse marriage until she came home many days later and said so. You've told me how common kidnaps were, so what made this one front page news?"

She looked around the restaurant, then whispered in low alto: "The men who kidnapped her were hated. Everyone knew who they were. Melodia and the rest . . . were mafiosi, do you understand?"

"Oh." I pressed my lips together.

"If the newspapers had come out with it directly, there could have been consequences."

"Like what?"

"Such as bombing the news building, murdering the editor, any manner of attack, *capisci*? Instead, they called them criminals, thugs, ruffians, hooligans—euphemisms like that."

The *pani* was too filling to eat at once. Maia finished hers, but I saved half of mine in my satchel and we left. We circled the lovely square, her arm through mine, our twentieth-century shoes scuffing the pocked stones laid out in grand chevrons a mere five hundred years before. We halted to face the thirteenth-century church, its perfect rose window a medallion of calm and motion, an instrument of thy peace, my peace, everyone's peace.

"Beautiful, no? Now here's another point I neglected to make last night: I want you to understand the mentality of many southerners, southern women in particular, who thought that Viola was weird because she refused to have her wrong righted."

"But that's exactly what she did do, Maia. She righted her wrong."

My cousin clucked her tongue. "I say weird because she didn't accept Melodia's offer to save her. She didn't beg him to marry her after he raped her."

I made a face.

"I know," she made the placating gesture with palms turned at me, patting the air between us, "but that was the thinking at the time. A tradition of at least twenty-five hundred years did not die easily. Because they themselves had suffered from it, because they had themselves been so suppressed for generations, some southern women could not imagine her audacity, and they resented her. They could not believe that a girl would vocally defy the status quo for everyone to hear.

"Another thing. Right away her parents opposed the kidnap publicly. And since an abduction was considered a direct insult to the father, his reaction made the news."

"A direct insult to the father . . ." I repeated. "What about the direct insult to Franca? She was the one who was dragged away. She was the one whose body was violated."

"Certainly. I emphasize the point that everyone took the incident seriously when *he* stood up to them. If he *hadn't*, it would have been a different story for her. It very likely might not have been a story as far as the press was concerned. Then surely her plight would have been even more dire. Not that it was easy for him, either."

"OK, I get it." I think.

Circling the saint's piazza, we stopped in front of the one shop with its rolling metal shutter still up during siesta. A pair of white espadrilles with big turquoise polka dots nestled in the window display among the dishtowels, espresso pots and cakes of laundry soap. Granted, they looked a little clown-like, but they were genuine Italian footwear, perfect for the beach whenever I got there, and only four thousand lire.

"Mind if we go in?"

The door jingled with bells. Behind the cash register a woman wearing a hairnet straightened to attention. "How may I help you?"

"Those shoes in the window—do you have size 39?"

"Certainly, certainly. Go get them," she barked to her young son sitting in the semi-gloom.

The frail boy steadied himself against the chair. "Which?" he asked.

"White canvas with blue dots in 39. Go!"

He hobbled to the rear of the narrow store. The shop seemed stocked with merchandise from years ago. Dust drifted down from the upper cartons when he pulled a lower carton loose. He brought it forward and thrust it at me.

"I'm so sorry," I smiled. "The ones with blue dots please, not solid blue."

"Get the right ones this time," his mother snarled.

"Which?"

"Dots! Dots!"

Her harshness to him shocked me. "*Signora*, it doesn't matter. We don't mind in the least."

"But we have it, we do," she assured us, clenching her teeth. "Get the dots, Ettore!"

"There's no rush." My cousin was attempting to lean casually against the counter, but chewed her lower lip. "We have the afternoon available. I am retired, after all."

The boy shuffled back with four boxes, his eyes on the

floor. I tried on a pair that I swam in, but decided to end the torture going on. "Perfect," I announced. "I'll wear them right now. Come to think of it, I'll take all these pairs. For my sisters and friends who will be so excited to have shoes all the way from beautiful Palermo. And when they hear that the piazza was called San Francesco, which is the city I come from in the USA, they'll be overjoyed. So thank you very much for your help, Ettore." I stuck my hand out.

His mother nudged him, "Go on, shake hands, I say."

I pumped too energetically and he pulled away. When she gave me the change I put it in his palm. He looked frightened and quickly glanced at his mother. She bowed, held the door upon, and the bells tinkled behind us.

"Oh no," I groaned, "I didn't handle that very well. I should have bought a few more, including in my size."

"*Poveraccio*," muttered Maia. "I doubt that poor boy has ever been inside a classroom. Here, let me help carry those."

My fierce consumerism had delayed her siesta, but she insisted on dropping me off at the bus terminal on Via Paolo Balsamo. I sat at the same caffè table outdoors, ordered the same lemon drink from the waiter who repeated the careful ritual of placement—this time the sugars were Caravaggios—and wadded some tissue into the toes of my new Italian footwear. I made the *spremuta* last, melting one chip of ice after another down to nothing on my tongue. I pulled out the sandwich and nibbled at it. I waited again for the bus.

The jerky gait of a man carrying a large paper bag into the Caffè caught my attention. The bartender who had been seduced by the winter pear a few days ago leaned over the counter to shake his hand. The bag placed on the countertop between them elicited excited conversation.

A piece of ice caught in my throat when I spied the mustache guy from the train station scuttling along Via Balsamo in this direction. Oh damn. I fumbled for my sunglasses and positioned my guidebook in front of my face. At least this time I was married, with the ring in place.

"Hello Miss America." He was close enough that I could, if I had wanted to, count each hair of his twitching, narrow mustache. "Still going to Alcamo?"

I held the book up. "Yes, by Pullman."

"It won't come."

"My book says they leave every hour."

"Not on weekends. I told you, my friend with the car will take you."

"Thank you but no, I cannot accept."

"Why not?" he needled.

"I'm getting there on my own."

"Suit yourself, miss, but you're wasting your time. You must not want to go there too badly."

"Of course I do," I answered in English, "but not with you in a million years."

Now he looked bruised. "I do not understand your language. My assistance will not cost you millions. Several thousand at the most. I am only trying to help you."

"No," I ferociously stirred the drink. "Let's just leave it at that." To break his focus, I picked up a sugar packet of Caravaggio's *Gypsy Fortune Teller*, ripped it open and dumped it into the lemonade.

He noted the ring. "When God grants you an opportunity, American Miss or Mrs., whatever you are, you must seize it." He grabbed at the air with both hands.

"So you're a deity?" This in English. "Thank you, mister, but no." I gulped the lemonade and pretended to read, my cheeks turning hot.

The men with the bag inside the bar raised their voices, drawing his attention away, and causing the chess players to look up from their game. My waiter stood nearby drying little espresso cups with a cloth, trying to insert a word. Suddenly everyone in the bar was adding an opinion on the subject, whatever it was, and the two started yelling, gesturing at the paper bag. What could be inside? Certainly not winter pears. Then I overheard the word *pistolotto* and freaked. A gun? My cue to slip away. I groped for coins and shoved the metal seat away from the table, but my purse strap caught around the seat back. One of the espadrilles fell off. I pulled the chair over with a crash and hopped around on my bare foot just as the guy who brought the crumpled bag reached inside and pulled out—a shiny pair of coffee-colored men's leather lace-up shoes. The bartender tapped the heels with his fingernails, then patted the guy on the back, who looked tremendously relieved. All this commotion over shoes?

"*Signorina*, are you planning to take our furniture with you to Alcamo?" the waiter teased as he helped me right the chair.

"Oh no," I laughed self-consciously, climbed back into the espadrille and swigged at my sweating lemonade glass, "just got caught up in the excitement. Keep the change. By the way, what were they arguing about?"

"Oh, some new sewing machine over at his uncle's shoe repair."

"No kidding! What's a '*pistolotto*'?"

"A loudmouth, someone who talks too much."

"Really?"

Mustache was listening. "Hey," he told the assembled shoe-experts, "this American will never get to Alcamo."

His words proved true. No bus showed up all Saturday afternoon, except the one I grabbed back to Maia's. When I entered her lobby, hoping to bump into the green-eyed man, I realized too late that I could have mailed Evelyn's package. I had taken to carrying it every time I went out, but there never seemed to be a post office anywhere, not that I was trying very hard to find one. I was taking a risk. If a thief ripped the satchel off my shoulder, Arcangela's precious keepsakes would be lost forever. I had to unburden myself from transporting the important archive of someone's life soon.

Chapter XII

The National Library

Early Monday morning, when dawn her rosy cheeks pinched, I boarded the number thirty-eight bus to the National Library. I had already phoned the office of the mayor of Alcamo first thing. Again, no answer, not even a recorded announcement. Maybe I'd written down the number wrong.

Traffic clotted every intersection and the horns complained. No one and nothing was moving, until a black creature the size of a golfball flew into the bus. The joint erupted: everyone ducked and weaved, while the winged thing zoomed noisily like a toy plane up and down the aisle. Some people dove out the back door. Me, I pulled my coat over my head and assumed crash pose. "What is that?" I asked from inside. "A bat?"

"*Moscona*, big fly, carrier of disease and *miseria*," moaned the passenger next to me.

With an enraged buzz it landed on the dashboard and began sunning itself. Inches away, the driver's hands remained frozen to the wheel. He announced, "Please remain calm until the crisis has been resolved. Do not startle it."

"At least they don't bite," rationalized another.

"I had no idea flies could get that enormous," I said, peeking out.

"Welcome to the south," he muttered, rolling up his news-paper and handing it forward, like a baton to pass in a relay race. "I'm sending a *Giornale* up."

"Aim true, whoever uses it. *Coraggio!*"

A Nonna-type fingering her rosary beads took an aerosol canister out of her carry-all, marched to the front and gave the *moscona* a steady, matter-of-fact shellacking. It whirled around a few times, then took off loudly out the door. The lady was praised for thinking to use hairspray.

"You have to improvise in these situations," she shrugged as she walked back down the aisle. People rushed back onboard, shutting the windows. For all the delay, traffic in front of us had hardly budged.

Finally arriving, I swung open the wide door of the *Biblioteca Nazionale*. Inside the grand entrance sat the photocopy area, tented by canvas to keep the light out.

"May I help you?" inquired a man's voice.

"Yes," I answered into the darkness, "I need microfilm of the *Giornale di Sicilia* for all of November and December 1966. Please." Last night Maia's younger son had phoned, recalling that he'd been studying for his winter exams at the time.

"*Aspetta.*" The silhouette disappeared into the deeper dark of an inner chamber. How mysterious. In California you needed a visor to shield your eyes from the over-fluorescence. The figure returned with boxes of film rolls, pointed to a chair in front of an Olivetti microfiche machine and threaded November 2 onto the spool.

"Thank you." I started cranking the handle and squinted at the now familiar print size. I scanned for headlines, tiny articles, notices, anything. Nothing the first week. I threaded the next roll in. This went on through November. First roll of December. Still nothing. December Roll Number 2. A shiver rippled all the way up into my scalp. Bingo. On December 8th, the headline read:

"I SCREAMED AT HIM: IF MY FATHER DOES NOT FILE CHARGES AGAINST YOU, I WILL"

"I will marry the man I love," she said one year ago.
"I will marry the man I love," she repeats today.

For ten days the trial filled the front pages with columns of coverage and dramatic photographs. I filled out my request sheet for the librarian whose features I could now plainly see. He read down the page slowly, his brows lowering, then he shook his head.

"*Domani, signorina.*" Tomorrow.

"There's no way I can take them today?"

"No."

"I'll run the machine myself. I'll be happy to make the copies if you show me where to do it."

"*Domani.*"

"When tomorrow? In the morning?"

"Yes."

"Very good, sir."

Honestly! I left, and fell in behind a group of university students wearing their matching denim jackets and jeans. For a moment I thought I was home until they started singing on the street. Shop owners poked their heads out to listen. When the kids stopped at a *semenza* stall for roasted pumpkin seeds, favas, lentils and chickpeas in a paper cone, I did too.

On to I Quattro Canti where I stood at the crossroads, cracking hulls that glinted with coarse salt crystals, stinging my tongue. A pigeon pecked at the sidewalk under Winter's corner and I tossed it a few seeds. Immediately a flock descended from the high King's statue, fanning their wings.

I emptied the cone. "Here, darlings, take them." They bobbed and strutted, iridescent pink and green on the pavement around my feet. Which direction from here, ye saints and royals, goddesses and allegories? I faced east toward the harbor, north toward Maia, west toward the Conca D'Oro, then south toward the train station. I could not make up my mind. A man leaned against the Baroque wall reading a paper. It was not the *Giornale di Sicilia*.

I returned to the National Library.

"Back so soon?" the librarian could see me in the dark. "I told you the photocopies won't be ready until tomorrow."

"I understand that, but now I need to look up the newspaper *L'Ora*, December 1966, please."

He shrugged his shoulders, but complied.

L'Ora featured many more photographs than *Il Giornale*. Melodia posed, smoking a cigar—"mugging in the manner of gangsters of old America in the twenties," according to the caption—and sticking out his tongue at the cameras when led in handcuffed. Franca entered the courtroom with coats held over her so that the cameras could not capture her. Bernardo Viola, her father, wiped his eyes. The twelve *imputati*— defendants— who happened to be handsome as hell, sat smirking in the dock.

"Sir," I pleaded, "would it be possible for you to photocopy just some of the first articles from each newspaper? I need to learn about this trial right away, if you would be so kind."

The librarian's eyes shot heavenward, his hands adopted prayer position. "We simply do not allow a change of rules."

"If you could make the exception just this once. I'm not going to be in Palermo very long."

"I have a stack like this," he spread his arms wide. "I'm here entirely alone today."

"Yes, but could you do it anyway?"

"Why are you here?"

"To research this story."

"Were your ancestors Sicilian?"

"Oh yes. My grandmother grew up here in an apartment next to the Giardino Inglese. The Civiletti family. And my grandfather was born in the Plain of the Greeks. His father was the postmaster of Contessa Entellina . . ."

At the mention of the small hill town, the librarian's face softened. "My wife's cousin lived there."

"How interesting. So we may be distantly related—by marriage, of course."

"*Aspetta*." He disappeared. I heard the machine thwack back and forth. He emerged with a short pile, some *Giornale*, some *L'Ora*.

"You are too kind, sir."

"It is nothing," he said mournfully, the long, dark and tedious afternoon of copying stretching ahead of him. "Come back tomorrow for the rest."

Primo answered the door in his meal-serving jacket. "Ahh, *signorina*, come, come, hurry, sit. We have today another dish that is truly Palermitano."

Maia was already seated at the table. He carefully spooned onto my plate a pasta with thin slices of fried eggplant and ribboned basil, then poured mineral water for us.

"Tell me, what did you find today?" she asked.

"The whole trial. Also in *L'Ora*."

"That's the liberal daily here. It's something of a *giallo*."

"A yellow?"

"Yellow journalism—more sensational. More tabloid. More photographs, less text. It would definitely have shown greater sympathy to Franca."

"And more willing to talk about the Mafia?"

"*Ehh*, no."

We ate in silence. Eventually I broke it to mention that the librarian didn't copy all the articles for me. "I have to wait until tomorrow for the rest," I complained.

"That's no time at all."

"But the days are passing quickly."

"Natalie, he could keep you waiting for weeks."

"Then I'm blessed with fortune."

"I should say!"

Primo glided in with a salad, and bent to whisper something to Maia. She straightened and nodded, "Speak, go ahead."

"*Scusa, signorina,* I happened to overhear and if you don't mind, I would like to suggest something. I too followed this trial. The name Proserpina suddenly comes to me."

"Who?" I asked.

"Persephone," Primo said in English.

"Of course!" I nodded. "Yes, yes."

"Exactly so," Primo continued. "This is her land. Franca Viola's case is her tale all over again. Permit me." He set the small plates of escarole down. "A beautiful young maiden is abducted and dragged off to Hell. Her parents go begging for news of her. No one knows if she will return alive. When she finally does the family rejoices. But she has been violated. She must again return to the underworld, one could say. Which Franca had to do, that is, she was forced to hide herself. Then she had to undergo the ordeal of a trial."

"Yes, yes! Please tell me everything you remember."

"The family was threatened over and over. They didn't feel safe leaving their house. Their crops in the field were trampled and their barn was set on fire. The pressure to make Franca marry him did not stop all year. By the time the trial started, the public had an obsession about the girl who was still in hell. Each day the news reports held us in a grip. *Signora*, you remember?"

"Certainly I remember. Primo, you make an interesting comparison," Maia mused, "though in the myth, Proserpina must go back and forth for eternity."

"But we *don't* know how it all ended," I said, "or *I* don't. Do you, Primo, know where she is now? Is she OK?"

"That I cannot answer, but silence is better than bad news." He tipped his head, then vanished into the kitchen to make espresso for me, which he had taken to doing.

"Viola was her own person, that is certain," Maia stated, rising from the table for siesta.

"By the way, Natalie, the name Proserpina comes from Proserpentina, for the serpent."

"Well, that deepens things." I felt for my Trinacria medallion hanging from the chain. "Medusa has serpent hair."

"Indeed she does. The important point, Natalie, is that originally Proserpina represented an earth mother, whose forces pervade the underworld and our world."

"Right, snakes go in and out of the ground," I said firmly.

"*Ehh*, in Sicilia we wade through ancient symbolism all the time."

I brought my satchel into the bedroom, and by date spread out the two newspapers' accounts side by side. My job was to note the differences, but ultimately, to blend them.

THE KIDNAPPERS OF THE GIRL OF ALCAMO AT THE RAIL TOMORROW

On December 8, 1966—one day after President Lyndon B. Johnson signed a treaty with the Soviet Union to ban nuclear weapons in outer space—the trial was due to get underway before the judges of the Penal Section of the Court of Trapani. Attorneys from the Bars of Palermo, Trapani and Agrigento "sharpened their weapons" in preparation.

Prosecutor Ludovico Corrao conferred with the Viola family at their home where, in the late afternoon, they met Professor Alberto

Dall'Ora, who arrived from the University of Milano. Outspoken in newspapers and magazines on his opinion of the kidnap and the need to reform the Penal Code, he willingly accepted Corrao's invitation to join the prosecution.

On the eve of the trial, the Violas were threatened with death by some of the kidnappers: "If we are convicted"—they warned Bernardo Viola through a message delivered by relatives—"you're going to get it, or your daughter will!"

Primo knocked on the door and brought in a demitasse. "*Decaffeinato*, just as you like it."

"You're spoiling me, Primo."

The *Giornale's* headline of December 7 - 8, 1966 read:

REFUSING TO MARRY, FRANCA VIOLA DEFENDS HER "NO" BEFORE THE JUDGES OF TRAPANI

Eleven Defendants at the Trial which Begins Tomorrow. [L'Ora *reported thirteen defendants*]. *The list, after Filippo Melodia, included: Ignazio Lipari, 23; Giuseppe Ferro, 24; Carlo Costantino di Benedetto, 24; Carlo Costantino di Giuseppe, 25; Vito Varvaro, 23; Ignazio Coppola, 35; Giovanni Daidone, 23; Francesco Costantino, 22; Vincenzo Melodia, 34; Vito Vilardi, 28; Gaspare Bruscia, 39; Antonino Stellino, 25 [who unlike the preceding imprisoned individuals, was free on bail].*

Melodia's gang, heady with power, assumed it could get away with stealing "the most beautiful girl in Alcamo." Many of the men already had criminal records, had been issued warnings, and had been put under special surveillance before they "disturbed the Christmas peace." The fact that they were indicted and put in prison, however, absolutely stunned them. They would have to answer to charges of criminal association, kidnap, sequestration of a person, aggravated violence, aggravated breaking and entering, armed threats, personal injury, detention, carrying weapons of war, exploding firearms in a residential zone, giving special favors, infraction of traffic laws and of the law of special surveillance; in addition, all of those who had been under special surveillance prior to the kidnap would be subject to the provisions of article 7 of the Antimafia law of May 31, 1965, number 575, which provided for the doubling of penalties.

Filippo Melodia was further charged with the aggravation of having organized all the crimes of which his companions were accused, and with carnal violence. Yet every one of these charges for the thirteen men could be dropped if Franca would change her mind, and agree to marry him after all.

Meanwhile in Rome, the Minister of Justice made a motion to abolish article 544, which automatically drops the charge of rape when a reconciliation marriage is the outcome, as well as other "medieval" laws still existing in the Penal Code. These ranged from sending the adulterous woman to the dungeon (article 559), to giving a man license to kill his wife, sister or daughter if he discovered her carrying on an illegitimate carnal relationship (article 587). Not all Italian legislators agreed with the Minister. One of them would have limited himself to saving only immoral sisters from their raging, offended brothers, but would still allow husbands and fathers to kill for honor. "It would be like reforming the death penalty by dismissing the executioner but keeping the firing squad in service," retorted the Minister of Justice.

L'ORA: *THE LAWYERS SHARPEN THEIR WEAPONS BEFORE THE BAR AT TRAPANI*

The trial opened Friday morning, December 9 in the humid hall of the Court of Trapani, about twenty-five miles from

Alcamo. Seventeen lawyers in total—four for Franca, and thirteen for the defendants, who had been imprisoned for nearly a year. Newspaper correspondents from across the European continent descended upon the courtroom. A dense crowd of Alcamesi packed the corridors without managing to find a place inside.

The three judges of the Court, President Albeggiani, Assistant Judge Di Girolamo and Public Prosecutor Coco, first listened to the twelve defendants insist they were extraneous to the event. Some claimed that they had been labeled suspects only because of the hatred that Franca's mother had for Melodia and all his friends. One of them said with an excited voice, "She [Mrs. Vita Serro Viola] was going around saying that she wanted to arrest the whole village. Aren't we enough for her here?"

Throughout the interrogation, the twelve in the "big cage," or retaining area, were smiling and acting cheeky, as if the whole thing were a farce. Several leaned affectionately on their neighbors' shoulders. All claimed different alibis for the day and hour in which Franca was kidnapped, to such a degree that one of the prosecution lawyers burst out: "But now the fact becomes mystical. Franca Viola was kidnapped in Heaven!"

Twenty-one witnesses for the defense took the stand, a long procession of Alcamo farmers, vegetable vendors, and workmen who were so terrorized to find themselves in the Court that they were hardly able to speak, let alone remember dates and times. One forgot his own address. Another remembered seeing a defendant pushing a wheelbarrow full of cement the day of the kidnap, but could not state where he himself had been. A barber testified that on that morning he gave a haircut in his salon to one of the defendants, but was dismissed as a witness when he revealed that he was raised by the defendant's uncle.

Another witness said that he gave one of the defendants a ride toward Alcamo that morning. They stopped at the house of the defendant's fiancée to drop off a ricotta cheese mold. There he heard talk that a kidnap had occurred, and then drove the defendant "as far as his street corner around 8:30 a.m." But it had already been established by numerous depositions that the kidnap took place at 9 am.

A witness who had employed one of the accused, Giuseppe Ferro, as a bricklayer, declared: "I hired the defendant December 2nd and he assured me that the house would be ready by January 31st. It cost me that he worked during the holidays. I saw him the day of the 26th—I don't have a watch—but I saw him at the workplace around 7 to 7:30 when the milkman came. I reject the idea that even for a moment he could have gone away because I was there checking the materials." Six other witnesses confirmed the bricklayer's alibi that he was working at the house the morning of the kidnap, but they tripped up over the President's questions. They remembered having seen him only on the 26th, but not in the preceding days, and they remained stuck to this date.

The bricklayer Ferro refused to eat a meal with the eleven other defendants, accusing them of having caused him to end up in jail. During the entire hearing he appeared worried and extremely nervous, while the other defendants joked. Turning to the Court he exclaimed: "Mr. President, I have three children! Three! This is child's play."

Defense lawyers then called a Brigadier Ricotta to the stand: "When the girl was liberated," the warrant officer testified, "I was on the terrace of the house in Alcamo, while my colleagues entered the door after having forced it. Three women came out on the terrace, and [Filippo] Melodia and Franca Viola. I held my pistol in my hand for precaution, remembering that Melodia was armed. Franca saw that I had a gun in hand and yelled at me: 'Don't shoot, don't shoot! He's already my husband.' Melodia intervened: 'Brigadier, put away your pistol, I am unarmed and there are women here.' Franca Viola, as soon as she heard that I was an officer, detached herself from the others, as if she were awakening, and came toward me."

The Court called on one Anna Oddo Friday evening around nine o'clock to appear the next morning.

I heard Maia walking along the marble hallway. She tapped on the door and asked, "How's it going?"

"It's going. Well, slowly, but it's great. So much material."

DAY TWO OF TRIAL

Saturday morning, Oddo, 26, with reddish hair, wearing a red jacket trimmed in a fur collar, began her testimony. A prostitute by profession, she had been in Alcamo one year at the time of the kidnap. The "woman of easy virtue" had been Filippo Melodia's steady woman, but also knew all the other defendants, with whom she used to drive around Alcamo.

Interrogated by the carabinieri *shortly after the kidnap, Oddo had at the time signed a written statement in front of Brigadier Ricotta that she was with Melodia and others the day before the kidnap. They went to a house in the country, then returned to town to meet one of the defendants, who had gone to speak with Bernardo Viola in an attempt to convince him to make Franca agree to marry. According to Oddo, Melodia knew that Franca was engaged to someone else and was angered. He was convinced that "he would have to take her away." Before saying goodbye, the young men made a date for seven the next morning at the Calipso bar, to "do that thing." When Oddo saw Melodia, she asked him: "For that reason are we going to eat your confetti?" Melodia brusquely interrupted her: "'Don't listen to what those idiots tell you.'" Nonetheless, the escapade was planned, according to her written statement.*

I stepped out of my room to find Maia in her armchair reading the paper.

"I don't understand this thing about confetti?" I asked.

She studied the quote, then pulled off her glasses. "It means to celebrate a wedding. The confetti are sugar-covered almonds given to all guests at the party."

"Oh right, Jordan almonds. Hard enough to break your tooth on."

"We *never* eat them, but save them as mementos of the wedding day."

"Uh-huh, of course, yes. Thanks." I started back to my room.

"Come, let me show you mine."

"No, please, don't bother to get up."

She pulled herself out of the armchair and turned the key in a glass cabinet door. Delicate, gilded porcelain boxes, looking like edible confections themselves and done up in frothy white tulle, gold and pink ribbons, the almonds sleeping within, lined the shelves, rococo with flowers, poufs and sparkles. One was a pale pink swan, one was a heart. She inventoried hers and Sofia's, her nieces', her sons', and all the others. "They're meant to last forever. Like the marriage."

"Right. It looks like they do. *Senti*, in reading about all thirteen defendants, it seems as though some of them may have been coerced by Melodia. I mean, why would so many people want to join in on this crazy plan to kidnap, or was that normal in a quote *fuitina* unquote?"

"*Beh*, thirteen men was not normal. My feeling is that they did it to gain favor with Melodia. He probably leaned on them. And they never imagined they'd be charged with any crimes. They were part of his gang. This is what gangs do."

I returned back to my room to continue translating.

Saturday morning Oddo was visibly scared. Under oath, the woman declared that she did not know the contents of any verbal statements that she had previously signed: "I do not confirm the declarations I already made to the police. I have nothing to do with it. I asked the Brigadier to read it to me, but he insisted on telling me that there was no need and that I had nothing to fear."

President Albeggiani then recalled Brigadier Ricotta to the stand, who stated: "I confirm the statements made by Anna Oddo in my presence. Oddo found them consistent with what she was saying and I co-signed them freely. I deny that we had forced her to sign."

Public Prosecutor Coco: "Mr. President, proceed against Oddo for false testimony."

President: "First we warn her."

Oddo: "I'm telling the truth!"

President: "That's not true."

Oddo: "They can say what they want. I don't know their names and surnames. In Alcamo I know many of them but they don't tell me their names. I said that I know only Melodia by name, the others only by sight. In the police station Ricotta wrote some pages they did not read to me but made me sign . . ."

President: "You risk being incriminated not only for false testimony but also for slander."

Oddo: "The public opinion in Alcamo says that some are in jail because of me. What do I have to do with it? Have I by any chance arrested them?"

Public Prosecutor Coco: "This woman is lying out of fear! The version of facts given by Oddo makes it evident that she is afraid, that she has received threats!"

The President sent her to another room to allow her time to reflect. When she returned, Oddo remained under questioning by the President, the Public Prosecutor and the lawyers of both sides. For nearly five hours she persisted in her silence, despite the threat of ending up in jail. Finally, the dam cracked. She cautiously began admitting certain circumstances, then others, punctuated many times by "I don't remember." Ultimately she confirmed her original verbal statement and the Prosecutor let her go.

"A case of the code of silence being broken down," I said
to myself, microprinting the word *Omertà* in the margin.

*Upon being summoned to the stand in the afternoon session,
Franca's mother, Vita Serro, stated that on New Year's Day the
kidnappers agreed to allow her and her husband to embrace Franca
for a while at the house of Serro's brother. She said that Melodia's
relatives arranged the "paciata," or peace-making reunion, on the
condition that the Violas not ask their daughter to return home.*

*"My husband," she spoke in dialect, and in a jerky manner
often incomprehensible, "accepted the condition. At my brother's
house we saw the brother-in-law of Filippo Melodia [defendant
Vincenzo Melodia], and another person that I do not know. The
three tried to convince us to celebrate the marriage. We responded
that after what happened, if my daughter was happy, we would
say yes. When Franca saw us, she said she wanted to return home
with us. My husband, given the conditions which had taken place,
advised her to go with Filippo. When we were getting ready to
leave, her godfather said, 'All the better. We thought we would
have to have another elopement.' However, my husband made use
of Franca's temporary return to put the* carabinieri *on the tracks
of the kidnappers."*

*A couple of times under her breath she muttered, "botta di
sale"— barrel of salt—at Melodia, who turned to his companions
in the cage and quipped: "Better twenty years in jail than a moth-
er-in-law like this!"*

*Franca's little brother Mariano was questioned behind closed
doors. Nevertheless, the delicate words of President Albeggiani
could be heard in the hall: "Picciriddu bieddu veni cca, assiettati.
Ti ricordi comu fu' fatto . . . ."*

"Maia? Help. *Picciriddu?*" She was glued to a black-and-
white Totò comedy, laughing along with the canned audience.
He was Italy's "I Love Lucy"—televised every single evening.

"In dialect it means, 'Beautiful child come here, and sit down. Do you remember how it happened . . .' But, as you can see, they didn't report the little boy's words. His testimony was taken privately. To protect him."

A Captain Dell'Acqua spoke of the way Melodia's clan tried to derail the search. On New Year's Day the gang made it known to the captain that Melodia and his prisoner could be found in the region of Corleone. All available police rushed to that territory, allowing Melodia freedom of movement in Alcamo, and enabling him to bring Franca to meet with her parents in the house of her uncle.

Then the officer shocked the Court by stating: "A few days ago, the seventh of December at 11:30 a.m. to be exact, Bernardo Viola came to find me and said, 'Captain, I am in your hands. Protect me, because one of the Daidone brothers and Mariano Dara [Melodia's brother-in-law] let me know that if they are convicted, they'll get me or my daughter.' Bernardo Viola expressed fears for the safety of his daughter and his family. A couple of months before the trial, when I had investigated other serious crimes that had been attributed to the defendants, when Viola suffered the cutting of his vines, a fire, and threats with a gun, he did not speak out about it right away, but after I gave him the names of the presumed culprits he confirmed them."

Bernardo Viola, called to the stand, was questioned on this same point: "I cannot make precise accusations against anyone, but I firmly maintain my suspicion of Melodia."

President: "Suspicion or certainty?"

B. Viola: "Suspicion."

Defense lawyer: "Why didn't you immediately disclose your suspicion?"

B. Viola: "I made a verbal accusation to Inspector Marshall Vizzini of Calatafimi, indicating that Melodia was the author of the damages."

> *Public prosecutor Coco: "Why did you file charges against the*
> *name of Melodia, but then not sign the written report?"*
> *B. Viola: "Because I was afraid. I knew who he was, and then,*
> *in fact, I suffered other damages."*
> *Defense lawyer Ragusa: "But the word passed on to the public*
> *prosecutor of Castellammare is against unknown persons!"*
> *Prosecution lawyer Dall'Ora: "Naturally. Have we not*
> *already understood? Do I have to spell it out for you? He*
> *was afraid!"*

Bernardo Viola wanted everyone to know that he had not received threats directly from defendants Giovanni Daidone and Mariano Dara. During the deposition taken December 7th, he was shaken and did not calm himself even when Captain Dell'Acqua clarified the difference between direct and indirect threats; not even when with pen and paper he [Viola] drew a picture for them to illustrate the difference between "directly" and "indirectly."

When Bernardo Viola left the witness stand to take his seat, he confided to a reporter, "Until I make it to the end of the trial, I will stay in Alcamo. Then what will be is in God's hands." He said that, as usual, Franca remained at home. From the first moment, she had refused to let herself be seen in Court, shunning any contact with the press. He claimed that she was near a nervous collapse. "Last night she didn't eat—her health worries me," he said, and then almost to himself added, "She doesn't even have the strength to stand up." His eyes were reddened. "Only I know what I have gone through. When both of my children were taken I thought they would kill them."

Chapter XIII

Ill Wind

Dawn brought a *scirocco*, the sand-charged wind blown north from the Sahara.

"How romantic—Africa has arrived," I beamed. "I love how close it is."

"I'm sorry not to share your enthusiasm. The atmosphere depresses me and I prefer to stay indoors. Positive ions make me unwell. You've read *The Leopard* by Giuseppe di Lampedusa?"

"I've seen the movie with Burt Lancaster and Claudia Cardinale and Alain . . ."

"Delon. An excellent film by Visconti, but not the same thing as reading the book. There's the famous line, 'looking up at the scorched slopes of Monte Pellegrino, scarred like the face of misery by eternal ravines'." She parted the drapes. The mountain brooded under a dark orange sky. "Would you mind helping me bring the birdcage in? Filumenu is under the weather too."

We carried the wrought iron stand to the living room. The canary was silent. Maia drew the curtains quickly closed again.

"I was surprised that the mainland Italian and European presses covered the trial," I said. "The case really touched a nerve up north, didn't it?"

"Indeed. All of Italy was interested and it sounds like, from what you say, all of Europe."

On the street, powdery salmon-colored sand had collected in the stair corners and piled up against the curbs. It
had coated all the parked cars and paled the vegetation. The
number thirty-eight plowed through choked air and blurred
boulevards. No caffè tables were set out. The few pedestrians
held handkerchiefs to their faces.

Last night's dream came back to me: some important piece
of paper, a document similar to the Magna Carta, was floating
around in the air above a church altar, when an overwhelming
power sucked it out through the center of the rose window.

Later, at the National Library, I waved to the shadow in
the photocopy tent, "Hello there. How are you this morning?
I'm here as promised."

"Your name again, miss?" There was even less light than
yesterday; I could not make him out. "I have prepared a portion of your list. Please return tomorrow for the remainder."
He handed me a thin pile, nothing like the stack I'd walked
away with the first time.

"Is that it? May I come back this afternoon for the rest
of them?"

"Tomorrow, *signorina*," he sniffed. "I wasn't counting on
a *scirocco*."

He wouldn't have been able to see me roll my eyes. "I hope
you feel better. Good day."

"*Magari*," he moaned. I wish.

Since I was already downtown, I could go over to the main
post office on the Via Roma. Maia had advised me it would be the
safest place to insure and send Arcangela's photos. "Otherwise,"
she said, "you'll be taking a gamble." With so few people out,
this might be an ideal day to mail it. But when I swung the
huge library door open, I abandoned the plan: desert granules
made the sidewalks gritty, and in some areas, slippery. The city
had shuttered itself against a scouring force from the south.

Every now and then I'd stop to take shelter in a doorway of one of the fancy shoe stores, or elegant leather goods or luxurious fabric establishments to avoid the wind. No buses or anything else were visible down the Via Maqueda, so I ended up trekking the four miles home.

At the door, Maia's eight-year-old granddaughter jumped up and down.

"Are we cousins? You look funny."

I caught a glimpse of orange-beige me in the entry-way mirror. She was right.

Maia still had her dressing gown on. "Sabina's school is closed today. Since it's Primo's day off I've put her to work—"

"Making *arancine*." The red-headed, round-faced kid held up a platter of rice balls deep-fried in olive oil—the size and shape of oranges—and the same hue as the sky. She tugged on my hand, "Eat one!"

"Sabina, give our guest a moment to collect herself. My granddaughter has so much enthusiasm. Help yourself to the food, please. I don't have much of an appetite. There's salad also. And beer."

"Nonna, can I have some?"

"Beer? Absolutely not."

"Just one sip?"

"Sabina! Pour yourself a glass of water. Did you get your papers at the library?"

"Not all of them."

"In any event you show persistence to go out in this weather."

"Hurry up, Natalie, sit down and eat!"

"Sabina, calm yourself."

The kid walked with me into the bathroom and held out the soap. "How much are Timberland shoes in America and how long do you have to wait on a list before you get them?" She couldn't believe I had never heard of the brand. "But they're made in the USA!" She looked at me witheringly and got the towel ready. "Are you going to live here with Nonna?"

"No. Just visiting for a time."

"I wish you would move in with her and walk me to school every day."

"That would be fun."

"I'll show you where it is." She grabbed my hand and dragged me out to the terrace. "See the billboard *Aerobica*?" The *scirocco* was getting denser, but I could make out the leotard stripes and the headband of the perky athlete. "Well, Natalie, if you made a hole in her belly button you could see our school."

"Not too far then," I coughed.

"You could pick me up from there every afternoon. You could take me to Luna Park and buy me *gelato* and let me ride the Panoramic Wheel."

"I could. Let's plan on it at least once. Shall we go back in now?"

We went into the kitchen, where, "*Uno, due, tre!*", between us we put away a dozen riceballs, some filled with molten mozzarella with peas and some with chopped meat in ragù, then devoured—well, I did—the crunchy, deep-green, bitter chicory salad. She wanted to open a beer bottle for me, but I talked her out of it.

"Nonna, can I take Filumenu home with me today?"

"No *cara*, we have to protect him from the elements. He will suffer to be carried anywhere outside. He's very delicate."

"But that would be all right because I know how to give artificial resuscitation. We learned at school."

"For birds?" Maia chuckled. "Sabina, after our cousin has finished lunch, you must let her do her work without interruption. Will you come in and rest with me then? You can bring your Puffi crossword book." She vanished down the hall.

"Yes Nonna. When you go back home will you find out how much Timberland shoes cost, Natalie?"

"It will be one of the first things I do," I promised, opening my door to enter the translation chamber.

A 'NO' WHICH HAS CHANGED
SOMETHING IN SICILY

Dec 9, 1966

Melodia spoke behind closed doors. Through leaks, journalists learned that he stated he had not kidnapped Franca; rather, she had agreed to stage a consensual elopement before her parents and the people of the neighborhood; that he accomplished the kidnap with the aid of only three casual acquaintances from Palermo whose names he no longer remembered. There was no violence, but only brusque movements when her mother opposed him and tried to hold back her daughter, and that he only saw the little brother Mariano at the last moment, when he was already in the car. After the kidnap, they arrived at the farmhouse of the shepherd Stellino; then to cover their tracks, moved to a farmhouse in the San Leonardo area, staying there until the end.

"To better clarify what happened between me and la Viola, and of the consent on her part . . . I clarify that I was already having sexual relations with her before the staged kidnap. My first sexual relation with the girl goes back to July 1963, which was at the time of our engagement. Such relations continued until about six months before my departure for Germany. In this period, I had been in the habit of meeting with her five or six times and in the course of each encounter, the relations were numerous. Our meetings took place in the Viola house, and both of us took advantage of the temporary absence of members of her family . . ."

When he was questioned immediately after his capture, the kidnapper stated that on the evening of New Year's Day, a peace-making reunion occurred at the Viola house. Franca's father, mother, godfather and other relatives were present. He said that the

Violas demonstrated affection towards him, that Bernardo Viola faced him and jokingly said: "You should be ashamed of yourself. Come sit by me. From now on you are my son." He claimed that her parents did not want the two young people to leave. He said that in the end they agreed that on the next morning, Filippo and Franca would spontaneously present themselves at the barracks to inform the authorities not only of their return but also of the reconciliation event. The next morning, however, came Franca's surprise announcement, and Melodia's incarceration: "Inexplicably, I was arrested." He said he was still in love with Franca and ready to marry her at any moment.

Amongst the other crimes with which he was charged, Melodia engaged in "unauthorized pasturage" a month and a half before the kidnap. He brought his herd of sheep to the Viola farm and allowed them to graze through the tomato patch.

Gripping the bar of the defendants' cage, Melodia shouted, "I had only a small part of the tomatoes. Viola and the other farmers had sold them 'a troffe'—the whole vine together with the fruit—to some Palermitani who had already completed the harvest, leaving only the residual. Permission to graze in the area was given to me by one of the men who had rented from Viola. Anyway the Palermitani didn't come anymore, and there weren't any to keep guard."

The flock tranquilly ate the tomatoes for some days without anyone protesting. "Then," claimed Melodia, "Bernardo Viola arrived and who knows what got into him. He yelled at me things I don't even want to repeat . . ."

The prosecution thwarted the defense's attempt to summon two medical professors prepared to comment on the gynecological examination Franca underwent after the rape. They had concluded that the girl was not accustomed to sexual relations, but they also pointed out that it was not possible to establish the time of her first "rapporto completo"—full relations—with a man.

Maia and Sabina were still in her bedroom. I went to the kitchen to get some bubbly water. The sky was completely orange, the story completely gripping.

FRANCA VIOLA: "IT WAS LIKE THIS"

Franca Viola arrived at the Court closely surrounded by her mother and her aunt, her face covered by her father's coat to avoid the flashbulbs of the cameras, which she hated.

She entered the hall at 5 p.m. and left after 6 p.m. She was glimpsed for only a moment, while she timidly crossed the hall to sit near the President's bench. A slim, graceful girl with long hair loose on her shoulders, and with a sweet expression, she passed under the cage of the accused without lifting her gaze towards Filippo Melodia, who finally struck a posture less contemptuous than usual.

Behind closed doors, the President invited her to narrate the scene of the kidnap, beginning on the morning of December 26th:

"I saw Melodia, Ferro and Lipari enter. They broke the glass and pushed the door to the ground. Others entered but in the confusion I could not distinguish them. I heard many, many gunshots but I did not see who fired them. I hid in my mother's arms, but the aggressors pulled me away from her. My brother was dragged into their car. Inside the car Lipari and Filippo Melodia were yelling at him. Lipari was covering my mouth. As they drove out of town Melodia and Lipari tried to make my brother get out of the auto at the location of the slaughterhouse, but they gave up because he resisted and I was screaming.

"Then Carlo Costantino and the dark one who doesn't have the bad eye [unnamed defendant] got out. I didn't see other cars following us. At the Stellino houses I got out. Stellino was not pleased

about our arrival. I screamed: "Why did you do this to me?" and begged Melodia for my father.

"'If your father'—Melodia said to me—'does not go to the authorities, I will take you immediately back home.' However he would not have taken me back even if my father had done that. I said: 'If my father does not file charges against you I will do it myself.' After a little while someone brought food and vials of penicillin. I said to Melodia, 'I will never marry you.' He said to me: 'Tonight I will take you home.' I believed him. That evening my brother was taken away by the same one who brought the food. I told my brother to inform my family that they could find me at the house of a certain Stellino.

"That same evening Melodia told me to follow him, saying that he was taking me back home. However, he made me go to an isolated cottage in another field where we stayed for two days. He told me that it was his house but I don't know if that is true. Afterwards he accompanied me on the country road and took me to another house. I suffered the carnal violence in Melodia's country house. I was weak because I had been fasting since Christmas night. I almost always stayed in bed in a state of semi-consciousness and Melodia succeeded in having relations with me two or three times. I said to him: 'Vastaso, vastaso!'"

The translation in my smaller dictionary: "Rude, rude." In Maia's big one: "Uncouth, ill-mannered, coarse, boorish, poorly educated, raw, vulgar, good-for-nothing."

"The third day I was moved to Alcamo. A woman arrived whose name I do not know. She said to me: 'Have courage. I am letting you enter because of God's mercy.' I stayed there five days. She begged me not to mention her hospitality and said to me: 'If you want to marry him, marry him, if not, nothing,' that if I wanted to leave I could do it. But I heard Melodia's voice outside and I was too afraid to leave.

"During my imprisonment he gave himself two injections *of penicillin. He gave me two versions: that he was injured on one hand. In fact, he said: 'Do you want to have one also, in case I infect you?'*

"I *was abused two other times. New Year's Eve they con-sented to let me see my parents and I was taken to my uncle Saverio Serro's house by two of Melodia's men. They said to me that I would see my parents on the condition that I consented to return with Melodia, and not to ever say that I had seen my parents at my uncle's house. Before going to the New Year's Eve reunion, Melodia said to the two men, 'If you do not return her to me, there will be another elopement.'*

"As soon as I saw my father again I told him I wanted to go back with him and that I did not want to return with Melodia. My father, I don't know why, said, 'For today, go with him.'

"I never wanted him and I don't want him."

I glided across the cool marble floor to the kitchen, grabbed an *arancino* out of the refrigerator, and stepped onto the terrace. The *scirocco* had vanished, leaving behind a navy-blue velvet sky. I leaned on the ledge and felt the starry shawl of night come down and wrap around my shoulders. The "orange" was even better now that the flavors had melded. Surmising that the sweatered professor did not feed them in the dark, I tossed a fragment of meat down to the skinny cats, down to where sweet oranges had once grown.

What's in an Italian name? I visited Maia's grand dictionary in the living room and, using her magnifying glass looked up, well, first of all, Franca.

Franca - frank, sincere, open, frankly, outspoken, candid, above-board, free, immune, exempted, honest.

The name really suited her. Underneath lay all kinds of attendant, significant meanings:

Francamente - Freely, openly, frankly.
Francare - to release.
Franchezza - Frankness, openness, sincerity, freedom.
Francheggiare - To reassure, to give confidence to.
Francheggiarsi - To take courage, to feel reassured.
Franchigia - Exemption, immunity, privilege.
Farla Franca - to escape scot-free.

Since I was at "F" I looked up Filippo. Filippo derived from the Greek, Lover of horses. Then I had to go to V:

Viola - botanically, a violet, viola; musically, a string instrument.
Violabile - violable, infringeable.
Violamento - violating.
Violatore - transgressor, violator.
Violazione - Violation, breach, infringement, transgression, rape.
Violentare - to do violence to, to force; to outrage, to ravish, to rape.
Violare - to violate, to transgress.

What a language.

Chapter XIV

Summit Plea To Aphrodite

"Good morning sir." I was back at microfiche's dark temple. "Feeling better today? I've come on schedule to pick up the rest of my copies."

"Name?"

I knew the routine by now: act like a fellow shade. Though why he insisted on formality I did not know. We had conversed about family in the town of Contessa Entellina. How much more chummy could we get in these dim recesses?

"*Aspetta*." He melted away.

His shadowness reappeared empty-handed.

"Oh *scusa*, sir. I thought you were the librarian."

"He suffers from respiratory insufficiency as a result of the bad air yesterday. Today I substitute for him. You come from America, don't you? From what province?"

"California."

"*Ahhh*. There is plenty of work there, no?"

"It depends on what kind of work."

"*Ahhh*."

"And so my photocopies, please?"

"Not ready."

"But he promised me they would be here this morning! I just took a one-hour bus ride."

"*Signorina*, I was called in at the last minute. Your order is not completed. I am sorry."

"It's so dark you can't see anything in there. You need a flashlight."

He laughed. "If one were provided it would only confirm what I already know. Nothing here. You will have your photocopies tomorrow. That is a personal vow."

"I can do it myself now. I know how to use copy machines. We have many different kinds in my country, each one has its own little tricks. We have photocopy opportunities in the US and I can coach you on the most common names—Canon, Epson, IBM, Xerox and Hewlett-Packard—you could pretty much count on getting a job anywhere with that skill."

"No Olivetti?"

"Not that I've seen."

"*Magari!* In any case, If someone saw me allowing you behind the desk, *I* could be fired."

"How much time shall I give you? I'll come back this afternoon. Does four o'clock work?"

"No."

"Five?"

"No."

"But it's terribly important."

"All photocopy requests are important, *signorina.*"

Maia held her hand over the receiver as I let myself in the door. "You remember Emilia, my sister Sofia's daughter? She has spontaneously invited us on an excursion to Trapani. We should go, because it's a perfect day. This could be your one chance."

"I'm already ready!"

We drove through the park, past the metal cans of flickering creosote and the prostitutes, who had turned redhead en masse. I told Maia about the photocopies not being done and she simply repeated her mantra, "Patience. Patience."

As we slid into Mondello, I wished I had remembered to bring my swimsuit—the turquoise sea was shining. Sofia waved from the second floor window. Emilia, her husband and grown daughter chimed in unison, "She never goes out anymore!" We all squeezed into the car and streaked westward.

"What do you think of our island?" Emilia turned and planted her warm eyes on me, perched over the hump between her daughter Pina and Maia.

What words to use in this company—scrumptious, chaotic, beautiful, elegant, sad, deep, hilarious, elegiac, fun? "I adore it. I'm so happy to be here. I love looking at all the faces, the hair of every shade . . ."

Emilia answered with something that everyone laughed at.

"She said," Pina leaned into my ear, "that at different times in her life, *she* has had hair of every color."

"A true Siciliana, my wife," added her husband, Pietro, behind the wheel.

We were just passing Isola delle Femmine, the little island with the tower, when Emilia complained how narrow—"*stretta stretta*"—life in Sicily was, and how she dreamed of immigrating to Australia, ". . . to make a new beginning. Sicily gives me island fever. There's no future here," she sighed. "And the shameful, disgraceful things that go on. It's better not to talk about it." She turned to look at the scenery. "*Cose brute.*" Ugly things.

Her daughter glanced at me and shrugged. The car turned quiet. We skirted the hills along the Golfo di Castellammare, a perfect crescent shoreline of turquoise water lined in white breakers. The *carabinieri* searched for Franca somewhere right around here, in farmhouses and secluded outposts. I leaned forward to snap a shot of the scene, but Maia's gesturing hand kept entering the frame. She and Emilia were discussing the latest teachers' strike, the reason why Emilia suddenly had the day off.

"Well, we're delighted to be on this unplanned adventure with our visiting California cousin. But listen, Auntie, in principle I don't mind striking. My point is when I get a phone call at 5:30 a.m. that I shouldn't show up to my classroom, I'm put out," she fumed. "I've anticipated work, prepared my lessons, filled the gas tank to drive to a town I've never been to. I count on that salary and I've already done the work. But we never get what we strike for. The low pay you already know about, so I won't even mention it. But I have students sitting on the floor. There is no money for books and desks." Emilia straightened the sleeves of her knit jacket.

"Alcamo," Maia nudged me and pointed up the long gradual slope to a broad city. It hugged the base of the hump-like Monte Bonifato, where the abandoned car had been found.

"So close," I murmured. "Much bigger than I imagined."

"From Al-ka-muk, an Arabic name, referring to a variety of melon the area was known for."

"*Scusa*, auntie, what melons?" Pina leaned across me with pinched fingers extended. "Alkamuk means the Magnificent Fortress."

"Well, both may be correct, etymologically. Natalie, do you understand why I advise you against going unannounced? Where would you begin?"

"It's spread out," I agreed. I would begin at the beginning, of course, in the neighborhood of the Church of Sant'Agostino where the brigadier found Franca's mother bleeding and crying, or the Piazza Ciulla where Franca's father had gone the morning of the abduction. I'd buy stamps from a Tabacchi stand or a shopkeeper and ask a few simple questions. If only we could just detour up there, but Alcamo was already retreating behind us.

Pina turned to me. "How much does an American wedding cost?"

"Hmmm, good question. I have no idea."

"I'm engaged. My fiancé's name is Dario. But we can't afford to get married until we save at least eleven million lire, more like eighteen million."

Her father calculated the amount for me: fifteen to twenty thousand American dollars.

"No," I groaned, "A fortune. I would rather elope, consensually of course." Oops, I shouldn't have joked about something so important to her. Pina continued with the costs of the banquet, floral displays, long candles, gown, tuxedo.

"Why not rent the tuxedo?"

"Rent it?" Pina's eyes widened. "*Come mai?*" How?

"We do in America, we're big on renting out stuff in my country. It's an industry."

"Can you rent a husband?" Emilia quipped.

"Can you rent a wife?" Pietro counter-quipped.

"Who knows how many years it'll take!" Pina lamented, not finding humor in any of this.

"Somehow," Emilia answered, "we'll manage to do it. You came from my body, *gioia mia*."

"Do you know Marsala wine, Natalie?" Pietro asked. "We are surrounded by its world-famous grapevines." Bare vineyards mantled the hills.

"Do I? I adore Marsala." I flashed on Nonny's forty-year-old unopened bottle, wrapped in thin coppery foil, tasseled with red and yellow cord, coated with San Francisco Cow Hollow dust. Anything that she honored she never used. The greatest homage she could pay to something precious was to conserve it on her shelf, along with a few other treasures, like her mother's etched blue glass vase. The joy of the bottle was not in the drinking but in the future anticipation of the drinking. That bottled-up joy remained on the shelf since at least my early childhood until we had to move Nonny out of her apartment and into the *casa di riposo*. I couldn't remember whatever became of it, whether it was ever opened, or whether it had dried up to nothing.

We descended into the broad plain of Trapani. The clear aquamarine waters swayed below a seawall. Beyond, white mounds of drying salt stretched away from the coast. Stone windmills with wooden paddles and triangular canvas sails dotted this meeting of solid and liquid.

"Africa," Pietro pointed. "That way. Carthage."

"Really? How thrilling." I squinted at the horizon. "But I don't see it." Sky, haze, sea—all tints of glittering azure—veiled the vast continent's tip.

"At least you can spot the Egadi islands over there." Everyone pointed west.

"Yes!"

My relatives had put together a special tour starting with an archeological treasure, an intact Phoenician warship pulled up from the drink, now sitting encased in a special tent. Through small plastic peepholes to keep light from damaging the fragile timbers, we peeked in at the ribbed vessel. It had lain in one position just off the shore, preserved in brine since 111 B.C., its own spilled amphorae nearby. It looked so vulnerable on its side but must have been mighty until its final day, the oars powered by slaves lashed with whips while the Romans zeroed in.

"Are we not fortunate to have recovered this one boat? Who knows how many lie under the sea?" Emilia asked in an instructor's tone. Our family was full of teachers.

Her husband led us through the arched portals of the old walled city to a *trattoria*. The antipasto table was laden with so many full platters that it took three long tiers to display them. Roasted eggplant and peppers, quartered artichokes, sliced fennel sprinkled with aniseed, asparagus with grated Reggiano, small potatoes wreathed in rosemary, parsleyed *ceci* beans, marinated celery root, sultana-studded *caponata*, green, purple and black olives, tomatoes crowned with basil leaves, mushrooms glistening in a fine olive oil mist; hard-boiled eggs floating in tomato ragù, whole caramelized onions, baked garlic heads, peperoncini. Hefty rounds of cheeses. *Crostini* and breadsticks. It didn't seem polite to leave them unsampled.

A first course of seafood pasta followed, then a second of roasted monkfish. Pietro's included a sac of eggs, a delicacy which he shared with everyone. I was already breathing shallowly when the blood oranges splashed with warm Marsala zabaglione arrived. The stomach pain was spectacular.

Wedged back into *la macchina* with now zero room to spare, we drove through the center of the old town, vacated in the midday heat. The rolling metal shutters of espresso bars and tobacco stands were drawn down. We roamed the empty baroque streets hunting for the Courthouse where Franca's trial took place—Pietro thought he knew its location. Sunlight seared the high whitewashed facades, and singed the iron balconies. The city was a massive sundial, demarcating shade and light. We became reduced to points amongst lines, planes and polygons in a spare Euclidean square, clinging to the shade. We didn't locate the Court, but we did find a wedding cake tower with an hour clock, day clock, and month clock. Its inscription at the top: Carpe Diem, advice we followed.

Our next destination was Erice on a mountain top. The zigzag ascent took a long while—each switchback knocked me into Maia and each switchforward knocked me into Pina, who both had handles to grip. Pietro had a steering wheel to commandeer and Emilia offered co-pilot encouragement. By the time we rolled into the medieval stone town, the mercury had plunged from the oppressive heat below to a high altitude chill. An opaque fog turned Pina's hair to curls as soon as she stepped from the car. Pietro opened the trunk and distributed folded plastic ponchos. We put them on. They immediately filled with gusts that sailed us forward.

The mist swirled around a bent nun sweeping steps in a convent courtyard. She motioned us over as if she recognized us. She wore nylon stockings rolled up neatly under her knees. Even standing on the stairs, she was at our eye-level—couldn't have been more than three cubits high—and we politely watched her shake clean a doormat and snap off dead geraniums from the terra-cotta pots on each step. Then, her tasks put aside, she wiped her hands on an apron full of holes and, like a faucet turned on, began to dispense gossip in dialect. She'd been waiting for an audience, maybe prayed for one. My cousins stood entranced by her narration, told in a wild and raspy tone. I wished I could understand the words that whistled like wind through the spaces between her teeth. The vows she'd taken long ago could not have included silence.

"Tell us Sister, how many of you reside in the convent now?"

"We are five."

"And your age?"

"Eighty-nine," she straightened up to her full height of four and a half feet, "and I have been doing God's work since I was twelve."

"Bless you, Sister. *Addio*." Emilia pressed some lire notes into her palm.

"God be with you my children," she cackled. "I will pray for each one of you, singularly and as a group."

Maia halted us at a shop selling tapestries with designs unique to Erice. She underscored how ancient the geometric patterns were—elemental red, black and white, or zigzags in blue, green and yellow. "You won't see weaving like this anywhere else."

Pietro dawdled outside at a caffè. He suggested I have one of the town's renowned cannoli. He worried I might be hungry.

"No, no, nothing," I wheezed.

"What about a *gelato*, then?"

I pointed to my midriff and moaned.

"Are you sure?"

"*Tst.*"

"Join me for a coffee?" The man didn't give up. "To stay awake."

"*Non grazie, impossibile.*"

"Catch up with us when you're done," Emilia called from down the street. "Auntie is taking us ahead to the citadel."

I stayed with him while he stirred three packets of sugar into the demitasse (*The Scream, Guernica, The Potato Eaters*), then bolted the whole thing down in one scalding swallow. When we caught up with the others, Maia was mid-lecture.

"... the Elymians built this city of mythical origin, famous the Mediterranean over for its magnificent temple to an ancient fertility goddess. Virgil wrote about it, amongst many others. We know next to nothing about the Elymians. Perhaps they came from Troy. Their language has yet to be deciphered, so they remain 'shrouded in mystery,'" she fluttered her fingers, "but we do know that when the Greeks won the mountain, it became associated with their goddess Aphrodite. Now in Greek mythology, you'll remember the War of the Titans. They battled the old gods for supremacy, that is, the younger generation attempted to dominate, and won. Cronus, in a rage, cut off the genitals of his father Uranus—that's right, I speak frankly—and flung them into the sea. Aphrodite was said to have arisen from the seafoam at the very spot."

"So that's how it went?" Pietro was wiping his glasses again, which were misting over as soon as he cleaned them. "I've never heard it before. She's an encyclopedia on legs, our Maia."

Emilia erupted into laughter. "Auntie, if I taught that version to the third graders, I'd be fired and we'd *have* to immigrate to Australia. *Magari!*"

"Well, my mother likes to go on . . ." Pina confided to me, "but it won't happen. I've heard this for the last fifteen years. She and my dad should just go on a tour there someday. He would kill to see the man-eating sharks at the Great Barrier Reef."

Maia had us marching toward an outcropping of rock on the cliff, to the very spot where the goddess's temple once stood. "None of the original remains—except for these few stones right here underneath the ramp, evidence of their distinctive technique." She ran her hand along them. "The rest were set by the Romans."

The path narrowed and she warned us to pay attention where we stepped. Fine droplets pinged against the plastic ponchos.

"You cannot see it, but the rock wall drops straight down into the sea below."

"Ahh." I peered over the railing into the vapors. Something ineffable whirled around. We all clung to the metal bar and received the goddess's raw force at the sheer edge of her cliff. She suffused everything here: sea, rock, lofty altitude. Knowing her, she had probably called up this nimbus just to amuse herself. I formed a voiceless hymn on the spot to the first goddess, the mother of all the goddesses:

> Up here at your still core
> Timeless
> Fierce and Delicate
> Giving Rise to Life and Life
> Radiant from Seafoam to These Heights
> Please whisper if Franca Lives
> And how to find her.

"Let's put it this way," Pietro said, planted in his immaculate, well-polished tanned leather loafers, "whoever occupied this peak had it made. Prime real estate."

He was standing between a small carpet of bubblegum pink wildflowers and a baby patch of egg-yolk yellow ones, which shivered and vibrated in the wind. The cloud shifted, and suddenly a gigantic steel tower was looming over us. I gasped.

"Impressive isn't it?" he beamed. "Civilian and military communications for Europe, Africa and the Middle East. Since we've been talking about the old gods and goddesses, let's call it a modern version of Mercury."

"But a little sacrilegious here, wouldn't you say?" It was so hideous.

"Well, they picked the highest and the most strategic spot, naturally, just like the ancients did. In Sicily, if we carefully cordoned off every pile of rocks that had at one time meant something, we would be lost. It's progress for us, which we badly need."

I pulled the poncho hood down over my forehead so I didn't have to look at the thing. "Could you say, Pietro, that we're on top of one of the three corners of the island, one foot of the Trinacria, more or less?"

He thought about it. "You could say that, I suppose."

"Wow. So cool."

The tower disappeared into fog and moaned with the wind, sending and receiving a million bits of data. The goddess was deeply mute, but that did not mean she was absent. With any luck she would receive my prayer. The newest, hulking Titan over our heads, transmitting all its info, would not have any capacity to interfere with her—not in her dimension, whatever that dimension might be.

Emilia worried we would get drenched, so we hunched under one umbrella back to the car. We rolled down the mountain with the heater on high; everyone grew quiet. Maia snoozed. I zoned out, happy to take a break from the rigors of speaking.

"Look back at Erice," Pietro advised, smoothly maneuvering

the twists of the road. The cloud had parted and in the gap, the massive profile of the mountain that we'd just stood on was revealed, with the communications tower nothing more than a few lit-up toothpicks.

"We were that far up? Dazzling!"

"If only we had time to take you to San Vito Lo Capo at the turn here, a very charming town blooming with flowers at this time of year. There's too much to show you in one afternoon."

"Oh, I was reading about it the other day. Some big time Mafia Don used to smuggle drugs out of there to the US."

Maia opened her eyes and shook her head. "Where do you find such things?"

"In one of my guidebooks."

"Quick look to your right," Pietro motioned. "There's Segesta." A pearly Greek temple, columns and all, floated above us on a green hill, and then we entered a tunnel, and it vanished from sight.

When we returned to Mondello, Pietro excused himself, and the rest of us climbed the stairs to Sofia's overheated flat. She was seated exactly as last time, and had a tray with a decanter and six liqueur glasses ready. Emilia draped herself across one of the couches like an odalisque and slid her pumps off. "*Ciao*, Mamma."

"Pina, pour some brandy to warm everyone up." Sofia beckoned me to come sit next to her. She fastened both her hands onto mine. "*Erice bello, no?*" Beautiful, Erice.

I nodded vigorously. "And so mysterious."

"Pinetta *mia*, I laundered and pressed all the wedding linens for you. They're in the chest under my bed. Go pull it out. Show the handiwork to our guest."

"*Sì*, Nonna."

I tagged along into the shuttered room and we knelt next to the four-postered wooden bed. When she lifted the lid, the scent of lemon verbena rushed up. She flipped through pillowcases, sheets, tablecloths, hand towels and napkins, every single one embroidered with a precision that almost hurt. I touched a stack of dainty handkerchiefs as translucent as sheets of notepaper. A white rooster had been sewn in the corner of each, with stitches so minute that they could only have been done by daylight with a magnifying glass. I could not fathom the fingers steady enough to thread such a fine needle to perform these stitches, or eyes sharp enough, or patience lasting long enough to complete a single rooster feather. This embroideress, whoever she was, had confined her artistic zeal to a scale so small that the untrained eye could miss it altogether. She had to have been someone used to sitting very still. My elbows creaked at the thought.

"Who did all this work?"

"My grandmother's great-grandmother. I think. Or her grandmother. I'm not sure. Ask Nonna."

"This was her trousseau?"

"I don't know," she shrugged. "I hate to break it to Nonna, but what am I going to do with this fancy stuff from the 1850s? It won't fit any modern *letto matrimoniale*," she used the quaint term for double bed. "Look how delicate these things are. And who has time to launder them, anyway? She wants to hand them down to me—being the only girl in the family—but I'll have to store them away for rare occasions like this when I show them to someone, don't you agree?"

"Yes, it would be awful if they tore, so you have to keep them hidden, yet they're works of art." The thought of all this loveliness buried away—a museum in a chest—filled me with admiration impossible to separate from a sudden sadness deep in my torso. Who was this woman? Who taught her?

"What perfection, though." Pina's fingertips lingered on the finished edges. "Here. Take three handkerchiefs for you and your sisters."

"Really?"

"Take one for your mother too." She counted them out. "But don't let my grandmother know."

I shoved them up my sleeve.

"What's this, Pina, a bed coverlet or a curtain?" I traced the embroidered capital letters A and O centered in a bower of marguerites and tendrils, white on white, with my fingertip. "Alpha and Omega?"

"*Scusa*, cousin. The initials of Anna Orlando, our ancestor."

"Oh of course!" Nonny's mother and Maia's and Sofia's grandmother. A scattering of dainty eyelets surrounded the monogram. If this same design had been used by an architect as a blueprint on that larger scale enjoyed in the outside world, you'd have the exuberant facade of a Liberty building. But women's work, engineered inside and privately, remained unrealized architecture, modestly destined for admiration within the domicile only. Pina crushed the lemon verbena leaves between her palms to release more scent and brought the lid down. We returned to the stifling living room. I sat next to Sofia and took hold of her hand again. "It's a collection of treasures. How could anyone thread a needle as thin as a strand of hair?"

"*Ehh*, they were trained young and they practiced. When they had free moments, they sewed."

"The towels and pillowcases hardly seem to have been used."

"*Ahh*, but they were very much used. It's the quality of the work and the care that was taken that have preserved them. Pina, you'll have to launder them by hand. Don't let your fiancé put them in the washing machine, *capito*?"

"Sure, Nonna."

"Seeing Anna Orlando's initials reminds me to tell you that in San Francisco she worked at her sewing machine out on the sidewalk in front of a tailor's shop on Stockton Street in North Beach. Did you know that? She mended and altered clothing for people on the spot. Our family needed the income. And speaking of her, Nonny used to tell us that Anna, her mother, was once engaged to a boy, but she rejected him and flirted instead with another boy in church. She always told this story with a smile on her face. Did you ever hear it?"

"Yes, I did."

"Can you tell me more?"

"She was fourteen when she was asked to marry the first boy," Sofia answered, "but it's not true that they were engaged. She didn't know him at all."

"Nonny always emphasized that she had rejected the first boy. She must have been a strong girl to do such a thing back then. I mean in those days . . ."

"Oh, she was. She had her eye on Civiletti, whose family sat in the next church bench. And they chose each other with lots of glances back and forth. They married when she was sixteen."

Seeming half-asleep, her arm over her eyes, Emilia spoke muffled from the couch. "What about the other boy she didn't marry?"

Sofia pursed her lips. "*Boh*, I don't know who he was." She took one sip of brandy, then pulled a handkerchief from inside her sleeve to dab her lip. "It was so long ago. What does it matter now?"

Emilia, the odalisque, roused and drew herself up on one elbow. "Mother, I sense you know something."

Sofia folded the handkerchief four times before sliding it back up the sleeve, a precision fold that I had seen Nonny do over the years. We were generations of slide-it-up-your-sleeve females.

"I know that her father and his father owned orange orchards together."

"Yes?" Emilia balanced on her elbow.

Her mother took another bird-like sip.

"And?"

It was swallowed.

"Go on, Mamma."

"By the way, Natalie, they grew other citrus, not just oranges. They grew citrons, lemons, blood oranges, every kind of *agrumi*."

"We don't need to hear about the fruit details right now." Emilia now propped herself on both elbows. "Stay on track."

"Don't rush me, please. A disagreement took place between the two men. The marriage, if it had happened, would have patched their differences up, in the manner of the day."

Pina pulled her thick pullover sweater off. "What sort of disagreement, Nonna?"

"Why are we speaking about such things? We have a visitor from California; this isn't the type of story she wants to hear."

"But I do want to hear it." I patted her hand.

"How about a *Baci* candy, Natalie?"

I'd fallen for this tactic on Good Friday. "Nothing, Sofia, thank you."

"I can tell you know something, Mother." Emilia was sitting upright on the couch now, leaning forward. "Continue."

Sofia looked to Maia. "Actually . . . in fact . . . one did murder the other."

"What?" Our mouths gaped. "Who got murdered?"

"The business partner pulled out a pistol on Anna's father and shot him to death."

Pina gasped. "*O Dio!*"

"No, no," Emilia moaned, leaning forward as if she'd been punched in the belly.

My mouth stayed open. Nothing came out.

"A marriage proposal came to Anna's family the next morning, requesting that she become the bride of the killer's son."

Pina slapped her forehead. "That's crazy!"

"Well yes. The idea was to avoid a vendetta."

"Hold on—why did you never tell me this story before?" Emilia demanded, her eyes huge. "I'm fifty-six. A grown woman."

"I never thought to," Sofia shrugged. "It didn't occur to me."

Maia fiddled with her hearing aid.

Emilia stood up. "It didn't occur to you! Now, I want you to tell us everything and don't leave anything out, so Natalie can hear it too."

"How my back bothers me," Sofia shifted the pillow behind her. "Oh, how it hurts." She could not get comfortable. The old lady heaviness of her living room settled in, suffocating like on the first visit when I wanted to escape and go swimming at the Lido down the street, but I held the pillow for her until she leaned back again and nodded. "When Anna's brother Ciccio heard of the offer, his stomach went into a knot like this . . ." Sofia churned her fists and made a growling sound, "and he was so angry he could not sleep. That is all I know."

"Mother, look at me. In the eyes. What else?"

Sofia did look at Emilia, blinking in her fragile, doll-like way. "*Figghia mia*, all I know is that Ciccio waited for Anna to decide what she was going to do. He was so relieved when she made up her mind."

"Then what happened?" Emilia began to pace under her father's painting of the Mediterranean.

"She took the family *carrozza* hitched to their horse," Maia held imaginary reins in front of her, "rode over to their house and gave them her answer personally."

Emilia stared at Maia. "Auntie, you know this story too, and you've kept it from me!"

"Emilia, calm yourself, come sit by me," Maia patted the space on the settee. "Please."

Instead, Emilia went to the windows and pulled them open. The curtains drifted in. She flapped the lapels of her jacket to cool down. Birds chirped in the garden. We entered a five-way silence. Sofia kept adjusting her pillow and I kept trying to help her. "Please close the windows, darling. We're cold. Natalie's cold."

When Emilia was ready, she pulled herself away from the fresh air and turned to me with a hurt expression. "Do you see, Natalie? I want you to understand something about this island: this is the way Sicilian women are taught to behave. They live their lives keeping the dark truth to themselves, never telling even their own daughters what has happened in the family. They carry around a shame that they die with."

"Who's dead? I'm not dead," Sofia protested. "I'm alive and telling you now. Shame? Who's ashamed?" She glanced around the room. "I'm glad Anna Orlando did it. I applaud her. For a girl who had no power she summoned up real power."

"Why have you hidden it then?"

"I didn't hide it, I just never told you." Sofia squeezed her left hand, her right.

"Which you only did because our visitor brought it up," Emilia sounded indignant, but hurt too.

"Darling, close the window, we're getting a terrible draft."

Maia examined the rug. "Don't blame your mother, Emilia," she murmured levelly.

"I'm telling you, I swear I'll move to Australia where things are different. . . . What was the name of the other family?" she demanded.

"*Che ne so io.*" What do I know about that.

"I have a feeling you know, Mamma. What else don't you know?"

Sofia looked to me. "I don't know what else I can tell you. How can I tell you what I do not know? I know what I heard very long ago when Maia and I were young women. Do you want me to invent details?" she sputtered. "What was told to me I've told you now. Beyond that it's a mystery."

"*Magari*," Emilia groaned. If only. "I can tell you're holding something back. I'm certain of it. Just look at that face!" she said to Pina and me. She was recruiting allies. Sofia squirmed and the pillow fell to the marble floor. I picked it up.

Emilia peeled her jacket off and fanned herself with her hands. "I'm having a hot flash like you would not believe. How this was supposed to neutralize the crime of murder, I cannot imagine."

"Mom, your face is bright red. I'm bringing you some water."

"Yes, Pina, water for everyone, please," Sofia looked relieved for the distraction. "With or without bubbles?" she asked me.

"Bubbles," I blurted.

"Sweetness," Emilia asked Pina, "please put a piece of ice in mine."

We waited for the water silently. The bright-eyed fiancée brought in a tray with glasses and paused before each of us. Emilia gulped all hers down before pressing the rim to her forehead to cool off. She ran the ice cube around her neck.

"Listen to me," Maia commanded in the deep alto she'd used back at City Hall on Good Friday. "I am in no way defending them, but these traditions went back centuries. Things were sometimes resolved this way, like it or not, between families. The man who shot our grandfather wanted no retribution, so he contrived this absurd idea. He thought he could right his wrong."

There it was again—that notion of righting one's wrong by the most twisted means.

"Auntie," Emilia countered, "Did this man have no conscience?" She looked like she had already booked one-way tickets to Down Under in her mind. "Where was the law?" she huffed. "Was there any law?"

Maia's headband had crept forward and she pushed it back. "We don't know if the law was involved or not."

"I'm driven out of my mind by this island! Marriage as truce. A fine merger. Just sweep the little killing under the rug. As if everyone could pretend." Emilia shook her head. "My God, they had to bury their father and deal with this. Why not just combine the funeral and wedding? That way you only have to use the priest once!"

"Stop, Emilia!" Sofia cried out. Her hands were shaking.

"Mom, you've gotta calm down!" Pina poured more water into her glass. "No one is disagreeing with you. Relax."

Emilia would not relax. "What craziness! Shoot the father. Sew the wedding dress. Bake the wedding cake. Ring the church bells!"

"Tie up the confetti in tulle," I added helpfully. A happy occasion, with a hastily stitched pure-white-flag-of-surrender gown to be buttoned into. Vows to choke on. Anna's sovereignty expected to be handed over—at age fourteen! A curtain full of tendrils and daisies embroidered by her own hand, or her mother's, or some other grieving female relative, pulled across the window of her future. Only a dozen eyelets through which to view the world from then on. But Anna didn't buy it.

"Poor family." Emilia was back at the window, her hands braced on the frame, her focus on the fig trees. "You never think these melodramas have visited your own people, your own flesh and blood, and then one day you find out they did."

"And I think I have wedding problems!" joked Pina, studying her engagement ring. We all laughed at that. "I can't wait to tell Dario about this."

"Don't tell him," Sofia begged. "This is for our family's ears only."

"I won't, Nonna." Out of her grandmother's sight, Pina winked at me.

"Well I'm very proud to have descended from someone who possessed her backbone, but I'm still fed up with the shame people had to swallow. We still do, you know, one way or another, as you've just observed," Emilia glared at me, incensed.

I nodded.

Sofia clinked her water glass with her brandy glass to get our attention. "The point is she married who she wanted in the end. She overcame."

Emilia scrutinized the two old ladies for any subtle clues. "Are you both leveling with us? There was no vendetta or anything?"

Sofia spoke. "No. No vendetta. *Basta*."

"But what happened to the citrus business?" Pina asked. "Was there a settlement?"

Maia spread her hands wide and shook her head.

"And you don't know what the feud was about—whether it was business or personal or what?" Emilia persisted.

"No," the sisters answered.

"Was it a crime of passion?"

"We've told you that we do not know more."

"What I wouldn't give to find out the name of that family."

"And what would you do if you knew the name, Mom? Pay them a visit? Go for tea and ask for a slice of citron from our old trees to flavor it with?"

"*Figghia mia*, of course not. I'd simply like to know who they were and if their descendants are still around or if they emigrated or what." Emilia pulled her jacket over her shoulders. "So much has happened in a century. Two World Wars with a Depression in between. We might even pass them on the street, and we'll never know . . ." she trailed off.

"Congratulations, cousin," Pina gushed. "It takes someone from far away to come here with an innocent question that sets off a roman candle."

Maia stood. "Time, *cara*, for us to be getting back."

Emilia came over and hugged me. "Thank you Natalie.

I'm glad the secret is out. It explains more than I can put into words right now."

"*Bohh* . . ." I answered, "it was just something I'd always wondered about. Thank you for taking me on a beautiful tour, for a beautiful lunch. For everything. *Mille Grazie*, Sofia."

On the drive home past the prostitutes' lounge chairs, all of them empty at commute hour, I dared to ask Maia, "What happened to the orchards?"

"The history of this island is such that both the children of a father who is killed and the children of a killer lose." She waited for a green light, the little muscle pulsing in her jaw. Staring at the minute-long red light—an existential joke in the deserted park—I clamped my lips together. To say anything further at this moment might ruin everything. Why didn't she just go through the red light? No one was around.

"They're gone. Both families were ruined." The little muscle in her jaw twitched. Maia stepped on the gas and we flew forward through the red light.

In the elevator at home, she spoke again. "Some secrets are buried to make it tolerable to go on. How would it benefit our children to know where the orange groves were? They'd be reminded every time they drove by."

"So how did our family get back on its feet?" I inspected her face by the light of the dim overhead bulb for any reaction.

"When Anna Orlando married Vincenzo Civiletti, she married into another citrus owning family, and the rest you know."

"Yes."

We hugged goodnight. I closed the bedroom door and leaned against the headboard thinking about Anna Orlando. My mother did not know this story about her own grandmother even though they were always very close. I'd be sure to tell her. It had been whitewashed to the point of near invisibility—white on white.

Chapter XV

The Silent and the Loud

When dawn her peachy fingernails painted, I was already wide awake monitoring the manicure, because I hadn't shaken the image of my teenaged great-grandmother in mourning clothes steering the *carretteddu* over to the murderer's house. Maia said she took the reins herself. From Ciccio? He must have accompanied her. Eyes swollen from crying, urging the horse on in a torn voice, she'd made up her mind instantly. The horse whinnied and stamped at the front door. Without climbing down from the cart, she called out that murderer's name, and when he opened the front door, she looked him straight in the eye and spat out "No!" Then they turned the horse around, home to their mother, the burial and their unsure future.

Gone to pick up final documents at Library.

I scribbled "Gone to pick up final documents at Library" on a scrap of paper, and headed out to the bus stop.

Honoring his word, the substitute librarian had completed the job. I leafed through the headlines and pictures. Bernardo Viola wearing a cap, his wife walking behind Franca to the courtroom. The accused men making faces at the cameras.

"This is all of them," I smiled. "Excellent. *Grazie tanto.* Did you ever hear of this case?"

He was leaning over the counter, looking at them upside down. "Of course. I live in Alcamo."

"You *do*?"

"Yes, I was born there."

"No! Does Franca Viola still live there?"

"Yes she does."

"*Veramente*? Have you met her?"

"I know her husband personally. I walk by his accounting office every evening."

"No!"

"Yes, I do."

"So she married."

"Oh yes. About two years after the trial. We all waited most of the night outside the church for her; I was a little kid. Police had to hold the crowd back. As it turned out none of us saw her. She and the groom had gone into another small church in the neighborhood, to be wed at 5:30 in the morning. Then they went up to Rome that day. The Pope blessed them after their wedding."

"The Pope! Wow. I had no idea. What a stroke of good fortune that you just happen to know her husband. I've come here because I hope to speak with her, to interview her."

"She never gives interviews, I can tell you for a fact. She refuses them all. Excuse me *signorina*, but may I ask why you have this interest in her?"

"It's hard to explain. I've always admired her, from the moment I read about her. Americans don't know this story."

"Admirable she is indeed, *signorina*, but she will not talk," he repeated.

I tried not to let the disappointment on my face show. "I understand. Her life has gone on. For me just now reading the whole story, it's brand new. I would not want to invade her privacy. Again, sir, thank you so much for the photocopies. By the way, do you take the bus or train in to work?"

"*Boh*," he laughed, "neither on your life. I drive in. I've got to report on time when they call at six in the morning with a substitute shift."

"Right, I haven't made it to your city by bus or train yet. Well, again, *Mille grazie*." I carefully rolled up the long sheets inside my satchel and started towards the exit.

"Listen," he called out, "I've been thinking. I'll stop by her husband's office on the way home tonight, and I'll tell him about you, here from America. I cannot promise anything, but maybe if I were to put in a word . . . call me here at the library tomorrow." He printed out his name, Guido F____, and the photocopy desk number on a square of scrap paper. I pressed the slip deeply into my pocket.

"Yes, absolutely I'll call tomorrow. Thank you, Mr. Guido F____!"

Maia tilted her head an inch when I burst in the front door with the news. "He may or may not be able to help you. We'll have to wait and see."

Wait? I didn't want to hear it. I had no more waiting left.

"Listen, what time this afternoon do we see the feminist?" She had gotten it into her head to escort me to the appointment I'd set up. She only wanted to help.

"At three."

"Good. My daughter-in-law has offered to drive us to the meeting. She's heard of this feminist and is very anxious to meet her too."

I nodded. How could I say no? We would be a committee.

THE PROSECUTION MAKES ITS CASE
December 13, 1966

"They will tell you that Franca Viola yielded because she wanted to yield," Prosecutor Professor Alberto Dall'Ora began, "that she was kidnapped because she wanted to run away; that she gave her consent to the elopement, therefore there was no violence.

*They will say she told lies, and they will conclude saying that this
is Sicilian tradition, that these things have always happened here.*

*They say that Franca consented, that she was not opposed to
sexual contact. But it is enough to review the facts to be convinced
that the idea is unfounded. Franca acted under repeated threat.*

*Twelve men came to kidnap her, they shot into the air like
something out of the 'Wild West,' causing her father to fear more
for her life than for her honor. Then Melodia held her without food
for the whole first day in a such a state of depression that even he,
as the girl later told her liberators, began to treat her with some
concern. She was like a small frightened animal in a cage, hungry
and desperate. She was afraid that her father would have shown her
to the door in accordance with a tradition for which a 'dishonored'
daughter either marries or is condemned to shame. Immediately after
her release she told the examiners: 'I yielded after two or three days
because I was afraid he'd never take me back to Alcamo.' Franca
believed that in agreeing to the* paciata, *or peacemaking meeting,
she would be thrown out by her family into the arms of Melodia.
She feared that if she didn't remain silent about the meeting for
a long time afterwards, there would be a new kidnap. She would
wake up only at the end of the tragic episode.*

"Today a kidnap which ends up in marriage harkens back to a
time of hordes, of gangs and of tribes," continued the lawyer. "What
kind of family could be started under these conditions? We ask you
in the moment of sentencing to bear in mind the intimidation of the
mafia, the arrogance of which punishes those who do not succumb.
The mafia is not a club which distributes membership cards. It is not
a club but a spiritual vocation, an attitude of life: when one who
is subjected to it tries to rebel, then the mafia punishes him. We are
asking a just sentence from you. The crimes are clear: kidnap and
presumed rape, according to the provisions decreed by article 519.

"I accepted the task of having the conscience to defend a new
Sicily, this one of Bernardo Viola. That," he turned towards the

defendants' cage, "is, however, an old Sicily, behind the times. When he gets out of prison Filippo Melodia will certainly find reality profoundly different."

Throughout the argument, Melodia watched Dall'Ora without diverting his glance. His face was tense and red, and every now and then he would exhibit a tough guy's grimace. During a break in the trial a reporter asked him if it is right to kidnap a girl to marry her. "No it is not," he answered, "though Franca was in agreement with everything that happened between us. If Franca Viola was the one I knew on December 26th of last year, or the one I knew before, I would be willing to kidnap her again; I do not believe that my countrypeople should have anything to say about it. They knew that Franca and I loved each other and that her father, without justification, opposed us. I have said it a thousand times: I would marry her. I would naturally not marry the Franca of today, full of lies and contradictions, but the Franca I knew who very often took refuge in my arms."

He was asked if he would marry her only to get out of jail. "No! Marrying her like she's reasoning now would be worse than prison for life." Speaking of life in prison he added: "I wouldn't even wish it on Bernardo Viola in spite of everything he is subjecting me to."

During the afternoon session the Honorable Lawyer Ludovico Corrao took the floor: "Does this trial consist solely of a kidnap or of carnal violence? No, it has to do with a much vaster condition, tied to the apparition in Alcamo of a gang of youths who challenged Bernardo Viola, a man who acted believing in the valors of justice, in respect of the laws of the Republic.

"For these youths the idol of love is not love, but possessing the body of a woman. The idol of a man that they cultivate is not a movie star or a sports champion but a mafioso. And this aspiration becomes heightened, this idol has become giant now in Alcamo where it has created a vacuum of power, a vacuum left by the uncle of Filippo Melodia, Vincenzo Rimi."

Why did that name sound familiar? I wandered out onto the terrace, hung my arms over the ledge, lay my cheek on the warm marble and tried to remember where I'd heard it recently. Filumenu the canary was singing in the early afternoon sunshine as if the *scirocco* had never darkened his cage door. Rimi, Rimi. Down below, the tawny cats were sleeping in comma shapes on the cinder blocks. Who was Rimi?

Rimi! The one who commanded a drug empire and committed a zillion murders! I ran in and grabbed my guidebook. An empty Botticelli sugar packet marked the page. The "vacuum of power" Lawyer Corrao referred to must have been during a time when Rimi was serving one of his sentences, because he was released from jail and died at home in 1975, nine years after this trial.

So, when all the witnesses for the defense that first day of the trial couldn't remember anything, they were petrified of a retaliation from him, even if he was in prison. They could so easily have been snuffed out if they'd uttered a single word, and everyone in the courtroom knew it. The presence of his nephew, Filippo Melodia—his *heir apparent*—guaranteed their silence.

I could just picture Rimi the Don outside, sipping espresso in an Alcamo caffè, his pinkie out, his tailored jacket draped over his shoulders. Stooped, a little paunchy, he'd have just been shaved and patted down with Acqua Di Selva cologne by the barber, and the sight of him would terrify any passerby. *Omertà*.

"We are not speaking of mafiosi, certainly"—Corrao continued—"but of the boys who aspire to become them. Melodia had already gained the prestige of a chief, and like all chiefs he believes he has the right to possess the most beautiful girl in the district. So he engaged himself to Franca Viola. Then he was arrested for stealing a motorcycle and found himself facing a man [Bernardo Viola] who rejects him precisely because that man does not want to have anything to do with people like him. Here is the affront.

"*Then he acts in retaliation, to satisfy his offended mafioso pride. There were the threats, the fire in the country house, the grazing on the tomato plants, threatening with a pistol, the letters sent from prison. The criminal plot continues right here in the hall, with obviously intimidated witnesses who remember only what pleases the defendants. It's significant that no one has been willing to testify in favor of the Viola family, which continues to resist. It's very sad to realize that no witness was found to vouch for Bernardo Viola; while everyone saw the accused, which is in their favor, that fateful 26th of December. A mafia vendetta is at the center of this trial.*"

When the judges had already retired, Melodia came out from the cage and faced Corrao with a provocative look. The Alcamo lawyer reacted, yelling, "Who do you threaten, you bandit! You don't scare me."

On December 15, the biggest crowd to date squeezed into the courtroom to hear Public Prosecutor Doctor Giovanni Silvio Coco put forth his requests. This having been his first important trial, his views on the matter were not known to the public.

For the crimes of kidnap, rape, injuries, fire and damages, threats, criminal association, and sequestering of a person, he asked twenty-two years and ten months imprisonment for Melodia; and for all the other defendants, more than one hundred and fifty years collectively.

"We do not lack grounds," he added, "to also hold Melodia responsible for kidnap for reasons of lust rather than with the aim of marriage. But . . . we will not insist. In dubbio pro reo.*"*

My cousin was on the phone with her daughter-in-law Stella, the mother of the redhead kid. I pointed to the line in the article.

"*Scusa*, Maia, I never studied Latin."

She put her hand over the mouthpiece. "It means, 'In doubt in favor of the guilty one.'"

"Marriage contracted under these conditions," Coco said, *"is a farce. It must be considered a positive fact that a girl like Franca Viola has had the courage to refuse the marriage offered to her by her 'seducer'. We hope that there will be other cases like this."*

Suddenly, the joking and arrogance in the cage disappeared. The men remained silent in their places without speaking, visibly shaken. Filippo Melodia stood up and sat down nervously during the penalty requests, his shoulders curved under the burden. He often brought his hand to his face, which was marked by dark circles under the eyes.

"I WILL ENGAGE MY DAUGHTER WITH A GOOD YOUNG MAN"
December 16, 1966

While the prosecutor was asking for the penalties for Filippo Melodia and his accomplices, Bernardo Viola tapped a reporter on the shoulder. "Could you do me a favor? You should write these things down on a sheet of paper because I must take it home."

Viola was seated between the bench of the lawyers and that of the journalists, with all eyes fixed on him. The public, crowded behind the barrier, strained to catch his reactions.

The reporter asked him: "What do you think of the lawyers' requests?"

"If ten more of these would go to jail," Bernardo Viola gestured towards the defendants' cage, "Alcamo would be more peaceful. My daughter does not want him. She submitted only because she was taken by force. The newspapers can say whatever they want. He," he indicated Melodia, who in a moment during a pause in the hearing had lit a cigarette, *"she will never marry. If you would only know how many requests for marriage my daughter receives. Dozens and dozens, and from better men than he. There are even*

doctoral graduates."

He himself had received more than five hundred letters from men who wanted to marry Franca. A day didn't pass when he did not mail four or five letters in response: "Because it's right to thank these people." Everyone wrote words of comfort and encouragement. Franca herself felt a little better for that reason. Two Americans had established a real correspondence by letter with her.

"It's too early to think about it. After the trial I will engage her with a good young man and then she will marry."

Reporter: "But if she does not know him, how will they become engaged?"

"The engagement is made really to get to know each other. If their personalities meet, then the marriage can take place. It's not true that my daughter is afraid of being seen around. It's just that she does not want to let herself be photographed. Otherwise she would be here with me in Court. The other day she said to me, 'If you make the photographers go away, I will come.' But how does one make them go away?"

Reporter: "We've heard that you and your family have been forced to barricade yourselves at home because of threats. If in Alcamo the opinion is against you after the trial, will you leave Sicily?"

"No."

"Did you not tell the captain of the carabinieri *that the brother of one of the defendants and the brother-in-law of Melodia had threatened you with death?"*

"These two—I don't even know them. I went to the captain only because he gave me a ride to Alcamo to save me the price of the bus ride. Write it down, please, write it. What did they have to do with it, these two poor things? They are not the guilty ones."

When the trial resumed, the defense immediately launched a counterattack, the essence of which could be neatly summed up by the headline:

BERNARDO VIOLA WHO WILL NOT CONSENT
TO THE MARRIAGE IS THE MAFIOSO

"There is the Franca Viola of yesterday and the Franca Viola of today," intoned Defense lawyer Ragusa. "The first loved and was loved by Filippo. Why did she change her mind? Did she do it independently? This is," he beat his hand on the table, "what the inquiry must answer. She never had independence and even less so now. Today it is said that she is free from Filippo Melodia; maybe today she is more sequestered than ever. To coerce the will of the girl, to paralyze her impulse towards Filippo, Bernardo Viola responded as 'a man of honor' to the insult."

"Maia? 'A man of honor'?"

"Another expression for a mafioso."

"That's ironic."

"Of course. The lawyer was grabbing at anything. We should think about leaving within the hour."

I returned to my files for whatever more I could complete before we had to go.

"If the mafia exists, it is outside of this courtroom," continued the defense. "The prosecution cannot in all seriousness base the presumption of guilt on the statements of a prostitute [Anna Oddo]. Meanwhile, it is a trial of love. We have offered to you, Franca Viola," he raised his voice, "a bridal veil. In the manner of backward Sicily, as is expected, but we offer it to you. And you have refused it. Melodia acted for love, and now they want him to atone twenty-two years for having been in love with a girl!"

Defense lawyer Pugliese continued in this vein: "For arrogance, for swaggering, Bernardo Viola has destroyed two lives, Filippo's and Franca's, happy that the press backs him up and will make him a hero. Franca had the opportunity to flee many times, especially when the car stopped to let go of the little boy at the communal slaughterhouse. Franca was able to scream for help at that time. However, what did she do? She fainted. This girl fainted too often, every time that she could have saved herself."

Defense lawyer Salvatore Bologna argued: "In a country in which declarations of love are made with the eyes, there is truly a need for officially stamped documents. In certain parts of Sicily where fathers do not permit contact between young people, the kidnap represents a means, certainly disagreeable, but nevertheless real, to overcome the abuses of paternal authority. In the north, say in Milano, Filippo would have invited Franca for a ride in the car and then he would have carried her away without the help of anyone."

The Honorable Rocco Gullo added: "I too, I fight for a new Sicily where there are no violent kidnaps, but where neither are there false reports from the police."

Melodia came very close to crying during lawyer Bellavista's plea: "You justly prepare yourselves to clean up this environment, but it would not be right that Filippo Melodia—just because he is a son of this land which pushed him to commit a crime prompted by the habits of the environment in which he lives—that he must pay in a disproportionate manner."

Defense lawyer Marino: "If even a fragment of the mafia were included in this trial, the attorney general would have intervened. A thousand sacrifices of Franca Viola would not be enough to repair the condemnation of an innocent. Or as the saying goes, Better a guilty one outside, than an innocent inside."

I wanted Maia's take on something. Could Melodia have possibly still hoped for a miracle wedding by this point in the trial? When he abducted her, he of course assumed they would marry. Even if he was just following the time-honored custom that thousands upon thousands of men had taken advantage of over the centuries, could he honestly have believed he had not hurt Franca, his own imagined soon-to-be wife? In his soul did he think he had not done her harm, and that he had endeared himself to her? That she could possibly forgive him, love him and make a life together? A rhetorical question, really. I knew my opinion, but Maia's would have to wait. She was in her bedroom getting dressed. Not that Maia could get into Meodia's head, but she could give me her insight into the mentality of the time.

THE RESOUNDING KIDNAP OF ALCAMO - THE JUDGES ASSEMBLE AT 10:30
December 18, 1966

On the bench, President Albeggiani turned to the accused. "Defendant Melodia, have you anything to add in your defense?"

"Mister President, we've been in jail for a year! A year we've prayed to the Madonna that everything will be fully cleared. We entrust ourselves to your Excellencies! We are in your hands!" Melodia spoke in a strained, tired Italian, his voice breaking: "We have been praying to the Madonna to have complete light and truth." Then he hesitated. "I don't have anything further to say."

At precisely 10:30 a.m. the Court retired to the Council Chambers while amongst the nervous defendants and the public—today even more numerous than in past days—the wait began.

Maia knocked on my door. She had put on a cream colored wool suit. She looked smart, professional. "Stella's waiting downstairs in the car."

"*Un'attimo.*" I grabbed my notebook. "OK. Ready."

At three o'clock we three climbed an eighteenth-century staircase—grand and curving—of a building in the neighborhood of the Teatro Massimo. A woman admitted us into an attic office.

"You have an appointment?" she seemed surprised. "Valeria was supposed to be here this afternoon. Frankly I don't know where she is. You can clear these chairs to sit." They were piled with papers and files, correspondence and mailing envelopes. The woman returned to her task of stamping the inside covers of hundreds of books teetering in tall stacks on the floor around her desk. Stella pulled up a chair, offering help. Pretty soon we had formed an assembly line, leaning piles of stamped books against the wall.

Valeria Ajovalasit strode in and threw down her briefcase. "Hello, hello. I'm sorry to be late. I had to pick up my children last minute. What have we here?" she grinned. "Workers seizing the means of production?"

"This person from California says she has an appointment, Valeria."

I offered my hand. "How do you do. Thank you for taking the time to meet us."

"Please call me '*tu*'. If you speak formally, we won't really be able to communicate. What can I do for you?" She looked penetratingly at me.

"All right, of course, *Tu*," I smiled. "I'm here learning what I can about The Girl From Alcamo Who Said No, and—"

"She thinks she can find Franca Viola," interrupted Stella.

"And I've already told her how unlikely that is," Maia added.

"Do you have any information at all, Valeria? I'm still studying the trial."

"It's quite interesting that you have come to see me today with this request, because we here have ourselves been attempting, through all possible channels, to secure an interview with Franca Viola, right now. I have no current information on her. She has allowed no glimpses of herself or made any statements for twenty years. So it seems as though we—you and I—are even competing with one another," Ajovalasit said with a grin. "However, we have been told *ad infinitum* that she never gives interviews, and so I sincerely wish you good luck in finding her."

Maia asked her something.

"Certainly. The feminist movement is very much stronger in Sicily than anywhere else in the nation."

"Is that so?" I piped up.

"Of course. There is so much more catching up to do here."

The floodgates opened and the smooth, standard Italian we'd been using flipped into the syncopated d's and u's of *dialetto*. Valeria listened intently to the frustrations tumbling out of my relatives' mouths. The three-way discussion expanded to four, like a lively game of doubles, when the other woman came out from behind the desk to join in. Maia half-lectured Ajovalasit and half-unburdened herself. Stella interrupted everyone. Soon they were all talking over each other. I knew just enough to grasp some of the ideas volleyed like endless pingpong balls from an automatic serving machine. If I could grab a minute to flip through my dictionary for an unfamiliar verb, do a quick conjugation in my mind, I could lob it in. But no one can take time out like that in a live conversation, and even so, these four wouldn't have heard me. I began studying the publication posters on the walls. Finally, Valeria turned and gazed steadily at me. "Did you have any other questions?"

"Yes, I do. When did the law change?"

"It took fourteen years after Viola's trial to change the Penal Code in Rome. Nineteen eighty-one, in fact, just seven years ago."

"Very recent. The year my daughter was born," Stella said.

"That's my second granddaughter she's talking about," Maia added.

"I do have another question. What ever happened to all those co-defendants?"

"*Boh*, I don't know. That would take an in-depth study in Alcamo, interviews of descendants, and so on. Someday, maybe, someone will look into it." The feminist stood, extending her hand. "Meanwhile, we shall see which one of us reaches her first. I wish I could be of more help to you. Please take this book as a gift from us, our most recent publication, and thank you for your visit."

As we descended the staircase, my cousins chatted excitedly about how '*in gamba*' she was, how on top of things.

"*Molto in gamba*," I agreed. "I'm glad you both had the opportunity to meet her."

"Too bad your Italian is so limited," Stella said as we reached the street. "She had such interesting things to say. I feel so invigorated, ready to face some of the hardships. I want my girls to think about these things. In fact, I'd like them to meet her one day. May I read the book she gave you when you're done?"

"Take it now, Stella, please. It's too much for me with all my translating."

"Listen," Maia grabbed hold of my arm, "I knew Franca would be unreachable. If this is the end of the road, look how far you've come anyway. This is the achievement."

"What achievement, Maia? I have gotten exactly nowhere." My ears—already warm from listening so hard—were hot and pounding. I had to be alone for a while. "*Scusa*, but I'd like to take a walk and get some fresh air."

"Fresh air, you say?" Stella made a face. "It's just hanging over the city today, *lo smog!*"

"Thank you, Stella, for driving." Kiss, kiss on cheek, cheek. "I will see you back home this evening, Maia."

I had no destination that afternoon beyond a break from speaking to anyone. Stella was right: my Italian was so limited, I loitered outside of it, its intoxicating music—which I adored but sightread very poorly—had just gotten the better of me. Escape into the crowded downtown streets, silence in the midst of all the noise was what I needed.

By late afternoon the city was choking on itself. I trotted along the loud boulevards breathing their strange diesel formula. There was no way to counter the mad exhalation; even the plants were suffocating on their stems. Wisteria hung limply from the sides of buildings. The banana trees' sensitive leaves, which normally picked up the simplest breeze, didn't rustle a single finger in the leaden air. I made headway past hundreds of cars, past a teenaged girl bicycling with a basketful of schoolbooks; a policeman on a podium directing traffic like a symphony conductor, and a lot of good he was doing, too; a bent, white-haired man pushing his wife's wheelchair (she wore a mink coat in this heat); a small truck painted like a Sicilian cart hauling a gorgeous heap of pearl onions; a Tunisian vendor draped in jewelry and beads for sale who beamed a wide grin at me—one thousand kilowatts—maybe because he recognized a fellow *forestiere*. I waved as I rushed forward. A shop owner tracked my gait as if he were a lion and I were a wildebeest separated from the herd. I avoided his pricking glance, but how I would have loved to tell him off in good Sicilian style, my hands speaking for me! Alas, my hands couldn't speak the language either.

I'd made it to the crossroads of I Quattro Canti. Autumn's fountain splashed steadily, unconcerned with the creepy by-products of internal combustion—the black stripes of grime—that stained her wall. I ran my hand through the water to cool the back of my neck. Which way now? I drifted to the front of the convent of Santa Caterina. Maybe today the silent sisters had baked. I took the grand steps two at a time up to the big green door with a half door cut into it. I knocked. It cracked open. An antique nun enrobed in black and white peered out.

"*Suora*, are you selling pastries now?"

She nodded solemnly, her eyes downcast.

"Uhh …" I made a ring of my thumbs and indexes, "something about this size?"

She shut the door. The hallway echoed. Should I have shown her my money? Was there a password I didn't—couldn't possibly—know? Had I blown my one chance at confectionery heaven? How much would it cost me? The famed sweets had become fabled in my mind over the years. I had imagined rare sculpted creations, such as marzipan cherubs lounging on a cumulus cloud of sponge-cake. Or radiant stars of spun sugar. Or thirteen hand-painted almond pastes, figures of the Last Supper, seated at a *zuccotto* torte table.

Minutes passed. A milk-white hand appeared in the opening, sliding forward a square of waxed paper bearing a light-brown cake, a perfect rounded pouf with a rosy-pink dab on top. The pale fingers flashed the price. I placed my bills in the open palm and pranced down the stairs holding my delicacy before me. This fragrant thing looked like, but couldn't possibly be a . . . breast with a meringue nipple pointing straight to the heavens. What on earth?

I bit through the smooth marzipan icing, which gave way to a layer of pistachio filling, sublimely suspended above a tier of sponge. Oh sinful sweet, devoured in church. Whose breast? Something about a pious virgin who refused a suitor's advances and was thrown into a brothel, whose breasts were gruesomely cut off and placed on a plate—*Sant'Agata,* if I remembered correctly. I stopped at this marble step to taste hazelnut filling, that one to savor chocolate, the next to chew for a while, another to swallow. Glorious. I paused at the street portal, looking around, licking the paper and feeling the sugar surge into my bloodstream. There might have been a hint of rum in the icing.

I decided to return to I Quattro Canti. There, I searched the baroque statuary above each corner, wondering which contained the likeness of Sant'Agata whose breast I'd just eaten, but from street level I could not tell who was who. The saints were higher than the four kings who were higher than the four seasons. Using the crossroads as a compass, I spun around until the next direction revealed itself. I crossed the intersection with purpose, smug about using a handful of words so far in my silent moratorium.

Inside the church of San Giuseppe dei Teatini, I dipped my fingertips into the broad brown seashell of holy water clasped by a white marble angel. She hadn't landed yet, her wings were still extended, her feet still above her. She gazed discreetly left, which was the direction I took. One of the chapels, illuminated by a bank of tranquilly burning candles, drew me in. I dug at the bottom of my bag for four five-hundred lire pieces, dropped them in the metal box and selected a taper from a stack, white and pure. The wick caught easily, the flame throbbed, then calmed itself. An all-purpose candle for souls encountering obstacles. I sat nearby watching it pulsate until a full third disappeared into spirit. Slowly, like the dripping wax, calm seeped into my mind. No questions, no answers, no talking, no trying.

I wasn't through with remaining mum and couldn't face getting back on a bus, walking in the door and resuming conversation. Out of the church and back through I Quattro Canti, wandering to the other side of San Domenico Cathedral, I found myself in an alley called the Via Dei Bambinai. I whipped out my mini-dictionary—The Street of the Nursemaids. A tiny woman about my age wearing orthopedic platform shoes leaned against the stoop of her store, as if she were expecting me.

"Wax dolls, *ex votos*, come in and look, *thignorina*," she lisped.

I nodded. I was having an I've-been-here-before-and-know-what-to-do-next sensation. She unlocked the door with a large key at her belt. I'd heard that creaking raspy turn already, in a dream sometime, through gauze and veils.

"A lady like yourself would do well to own a wax baby."

I looked at her confused. "Me? A baby? What about the *ex votos*? What have you got?"

"We have every body part, *thignorina*, for healing the maladies and distresses of humanity. Surely you suffer from some of those." She pulled out boxes of pressed silver hearts and livers, kidneys, gallbladders, brains, stomachs, legs, arms. They glowed in the gloom, these three-inch representations, and I sat intrigued, but nothing yet called out to one of my body parts.

From tissue paper she unwrapped noses, mouths, ears, hair in a flip, knees, fingers, feet both single and by the pair. She kept her eyes on me during this anatomical procession.

"Do you have left hands?"

She stared at me for a long moment. "Absolutely." From a shelf, she located a box and unwrapped more tissues, right hand after silvered right hand saluting as each met the light. I doubted she had any left hands. I knew that they signified something sinister, evidence of the devil or the dreaded *mal'occhio*. The Evil Eye.

"May I?" I touched a packet. She blinked, which I took as an agreement, though she never broke her serious frown, and her hands never stopped. We unwrapped together in silence.

"We lefties make up about ten to fifteen percent of the population."

She didn't respond, and I shouldn't have said anything to incriminate myself.

Finally a slender hand of tapered fingers with carefully neat nails and crimped edges appeared. It could do the beseeching of a southpaw like me.

"I'll take it, and do you have good eyes?"

"We have excellent eyes." She searched through a box labeled "*OCCHI*" and held each crimp-edged mask up for viewing. "They always come in pairs, the right and the left," she said, humoring me.

"Uh-huh," I nodded, "yes."

"They're all identical, *thignorina*."

"I'm looking for an exact pair," I insisted. I found them at last, slightly crossed, with etched brows, cousins to the eyes of the mosaic Gesù Cristo of Monreale and to Santa Lucia's beautiful eyes, so gorgeous that she plucked them out and put them on a plate for her admiring suitor. "Here they are."

"Anything else?"

"*Tst.*" Listen to me, saying no just like a native.

"A baby?" Evidently she had visions of me as a future mother.

"Not this time. Maybe the next." I asked if she had a boxful of high-quality boyfriends somewhere.

"I have many men."

"Guaranteed good quality men?" Green-eyed men?

"All our *ex votos* are of the highest quality."

"For the man, I need a guarantee."

"*Tst.* A heart?"

"*Tst.* I already have a heart, I hope." I waited for her to react to my joke but she did not. Heartache I've had, but I didn't want to get into it with her. Tongues lay nestled on the table. I needed to be able to speak with fluidity.

"And one of these tongues."

We bargained over the price. Of course she knew I was a tourist and tried to charge me an arm and a leg, ha-ha. Second only to pushing in a crowd, haggling was a Mediterranean custom I hated pretending I knew how to do. I set my face in a grimace mirroring hers. We agreed awkwardly, tensely, on a sum. I wouldn't dare tell my cousin how much I'd put on the table. She would have lamented my being cheated in her city and why hadn't I waited till she came along with me in order to get a fair price? I had purchased a sure hand, and eyes with which to clearly see. I bought the language I needed to speak better. The lady quickly wrapped my three items in brown paper and string. Thank you for being exactly the person you are, for awaiting me as I turned the corner. Thank you for understanding my tarnished Italian. Thank you for trying to rip me off—I thoroughly enjoyed it! Thank you for selling me these talismans. Thank you from the bottom of my crimp-edged heart.

I returned through La Vucciria market, stepping on sawdust and fish scale sequins. Smells of overripe greens and of dear departed marine life hung in the air. I took refuge near a stall of big, smoothed, swirled slabs of pink and white nougat, stacked like pieces of quarried marble.

"*Prego.*" A friendly server offered me a morsel of warm hazelnut praline.

"*Grazie.*"

I moved on through the vegetables, attracted to a mound of skinny, violet asparagus. The vendor spread his hands. "Go ahead, try one. Taste for yourself the superior flavor of wild asparagus."

The tender stalk snapped between my teeth. "Mmm," I marveled. "I'll take a half kilo, please." Maia would love them. "And a half kilo of baby artichokes too."

Another haggling over price, another package tied with string. "*Mancino.*"

"Yes, I am left-handed," I smiled, reaching for the packets, "and proud to be so."

"So am I, temptress," he cooed, squeezing my left baby finger for a moment before sliding off it.

My eyebrows flew up in surprise as I looked slightly cross-eyed at him, but no words came. Some *ex votos*, I gathered, worked more quickly than others. On the way home, I slipped the tongue out of the package and rubbed it. A faint tarnish appeared on my fingertips.

Maia asked me to cut a couple of potatoes into cubes on her highly worn wooden board. "Keep going. Smaller, smaller, please. They'll cook more quickly." Meanwhile, she plucked off all the outer leaves of the baby artichokes until the tender, pale green inner leaves appeared. She sliced them thin with her very sharp paring knife. She had two burners going, heating up the olive oil in wide pans with minced garlic thrown into both. When she gave the go-ahead, we took our positions standing over the stove together. I sautéed the cubes, turning them methodically, while into the popping oil of the other pan she laid flat the baby artichoke slices, end to end, crowded in. When the cubes had developed golden crusts, she told me to add the asparagus and poured in a gurgle more of olive oil. After a minute or two, the violet stalks turned green. At the magical moment over the other flame she tossed in a teaspoon of sugar, and a couple of splashes of red wine vinegar. I watched the chokes turn purplish and caramelize. She gave a double shake to both pans and turned off the gas. We helped ourselves from the pans and ate at the little square kitchen table.

"I stumbled upon the Street of the Nursemaids, which reminded me of a story about Nonny I want to tell you. She was second to the youngest of the seven, as you well know. By the time she was born, Anna Orlando had run out of milk and couldn't feed her. So they hired a wet nurse, a Greek woman, who I think wore a big red cross on her uniform. The older kids all teased Nonny that she'd turn out different. They called her *La Muta*, the Silent One. It's true that she hasn't ever been very talkative—she's kept a lot to herself. I would call her character stoic."

"*Interessante*," Maia opened a bottle of beer. "Who told you this?"

"Her older sister, Auntie Paolina," I answered, touching my Trinacria charm, "told my mother. Paolina would talk about things."

"*Beh*, because wet nurses saved lives, the relationship between *allattatrice* and baby was always highly revered here; such a person would have been considered part of the family. Your Nonna might not have made it otherwise. Consider how women of that era made an honest though modest living at this profession, one of very few available to them."

"So I pay homage to that Greek woman, whoever she was," I said. And if she didn't speak the language in the Civiletti household, she might have been *very* quiet, and there's a place for that in this loud world. I bet the Ex Voto lady carried breasts, even a private box with nursing breasts that you had to know to ask to see. Silent milk, I thought. The highly quiet milk of human kindness.

Chapter XVI

The North Coast

I stood twirling with my arms outstretched in the center of a red room with all the windows open. The long curtains billowed luxuriantly, and a lantern flickered on and off. So when I woke up from the dream groggy, displaced, and sticking wet to the sheets, it took me a second. Blood had gushed out.

Oh man, now what would I do? My cycle must have been thrown off by the trans-Atlantic flight, because hadn't I bled only two and a half weeks ago? I peeked out the bedroom door.

Maia looked up from her newspaper. "Good morning, *tesoro*. Have some breakfast. What shall we do today?"

"Uh, well . . ." I stood in my bathrobe, drank the tea she'd made for me, charged with mint this time, and washed down two painkillers to avoid doubling-over cramps. "I've got to call the Librarian." She gestured to the phone which, when I dialed, only rang and rang emptily. I shrugged. "Maybe I'll catch him this afternoon."

She jumped up from her armchair. "In that case, I want to show you part of the north coast. We'll be back by four, you'll see. *Andiamo*."

"Give me a few minutes." I went into the bedroom and surveyed the bloodstain on the pure white European cotton. I couldn't leave it for Primo; he shouldn't have to wash out a woman's blood. The blaze of red would offend him. Mea culpa,

mea maxi pad culpa. I pulled off the fitted bottom along with
the mattress cover, all darkened, and carried them out of my
door to the bathroom.

"But what are you doing, *cara?*"

"I need to wash these out."

"No no, you mustn't do that, you're the guest. Primo will
take care of it. Put them back."

Feeling awkward, but persuaded, reluctantly I did. I dressed
quickly, and left a note on the bundled-up pile on the bed:

> Dear Primo, I'm very, very sorry to inconvenience you.
> These need to be cleaned. Again, I am terribly sorry.

"You look a little pale this morning, *cara*. Feeling under
the weather? I know how that is. We women have all gone
through these things. Why don't you put on that cheerful
yellow blouse of yours?"

I took her advice and put the Boothe garment on.

Minutes later, we sat mired in a monumental traffic jam
along Palermo's waterfront. Only the motor scooters moved
forward, whining between the cars. Weeds sprouted from the
gaping gray walls of once baroque palaces in this devastated
neighborhood.

"What happened here?"

"We don't like to talk about it, because we love America,
but they bombed us in '43. They shot people in the streets from
low flying airplanes, even though Italy had already surrendered."
She cleared her throat. "Some people thought the Americans
were drunk, or crazy from the war. It was a terrible time."

"I'm so sorry."

"The British never targeted us civilians, though. They had
a love affair with us from the previous century. They built villas
here and on the Greek side of the island too. So they dropped

fliers warning people to stay away from the military targets before the bombing started."

I felt ashamed for my country doing this damage after Italy surrendered. "Will it ever be rebuilt?"

"Ehh, eventually . . ." Maia trailed off, stalwart behind the wheel. She carried her wartime losses folded inside: her mother perished here in town because the Nazis confiscated her insulin on these very docks, and her brother was taken by them as a prisoner-of-war to Austria. He made his way back finally, nearly starved to death, appearing at their door looking like a skeleton.

"Look at the nuns," she nodded to our left. A Fiat, packed with five or six teeny sisters, revved. A bundle of jumbo artichokes on long leafy stalks had been strapped to the roof like a bad green hairpiece. "Nuns with artichokes talking theology," my cousin deadpanned. "A good title for a painting."

The driver behind us leaned on his horn. A Saint Christopher medallion dangling from his rear-view mirror swung madly from constant starting and stopping. *San Cristoforo, proteggemi.*

"What does he think we can do about it?" Maia lifted her palms, looking in her mirror. We remained trapped like everyone else by rivers of vehicles and clouds of diesel.

The sisters looked like they were arguing with their hands over something.

"I wonder what they're talking about."

Maia rolled down the window as soon as we came abreast of them again. "Tell us, Sister, we would like to know, what recipe will you use for those beautiful *carciofi*? My cousin visiting from the USA is curious."

The nuns became even more animated, rolled down their windows and waved to me, grinning. I waved back, relieved that they didn't hate all Americans because of the bombing forty-five years ago.

"Fried in olive oil with a flour-and-egg batter, that's what I would do," Maia offered. "Of course, you would want to stuff each with a piece of pecorino beforehand, naturally."

This suggestion was relayed throughout their small car. The driver, barely visible above the dashboard, did not seem pleased, and she sliced the air with her hands.

"Slivered thin, then layered with a fennel *sugo*," came the decree. "Baked slowly. If God grants that we arrive back to the convent in time for lunch," the nun added, "otherwise, it's bread soup again."

"How about roasted with crushed garlic, mint, olive oil and breadcrumbs? Tell them, Maia." I could still taste the Pasquetta feast cooked in the infernal coals.

"*Arrostiti*," Maia shouted to be heard. "*Con aglio, menta, olio d'olive e briciole di pane*. And don't forget to put an anchovy in the center, *ehh*?"

Our recipe-sharing had attracted the attention of other drivers. A man in a business suit from a couple of cars over left his motor running, the black smoke rising from the tail, strolled over and stood fingering the chokes, petting the silvery green leaves. "It would be a shame to do anything but boil them whole because of their excellent size," he declaimed. "That way, you see, they retain all their flavor. If you start pulling off this leaf here and cutting into that leaf there, you will destroy the integrity of the vegetable. And leave as much stalk on as possible. Many people make this error but it's tender inside. Serve them simply, warmed with some garlic and sprinkled with salt and lemon. Imagine the size of their hearts . . ." he paused to observe a moment of reverent silence. "You can't go wrong, Sisters, I assure you."

"Lemon rind in the boiling water?" the spokesnun asked.

"*Beh* . . . this late in the season, I prefer after."

"Why not both?" Maia, the diplomat, suggested. "Is there such a thing as too much lemon?"

"Hey, move it," yelled Saint Christopher, "Go!" The traffic had suddenly opened up.

"*Buon appetito*, Sisters," Maia saluted. "What is your order, by the way?"

"Convent of the Most Precious Blood."

Mmm-hmmm, I thought, exactly so. By the time we made it out of the city, my cousin—brave, pedal-happy chauffeur—seemed energized. I cracked open the window and breathed in. We breezed through groves of aromatic lemon and orange.

"What sweet air," I said, rolling the window all the way down, "and, wow, I've never seen such enormous grapefruits." They tugged their branches toward the ground. My abdomen was tugging downward too—the pills had worked about halfway only.

"Citrons, not grapefruit."

"The slice that you put in the tea every morning! Another way to flavor artichokes, maybe?"

"They are quite bitter. We don't use them for savory cooking, but for sweets. We boil their rinds in sugar water until they have candied. The sweet conquers the bitter."

How Sicilian. In cuisine and in attitude. We sped past old villas. Wisteria laced the shuttered windows.

"Of course, these great homes are in a terrible state of neglect now, but you can imagine them in the eighteenth century." Maia watched the road now and then. "While most Sicilians struggled to eat one meal a day, these aristocrats had so much wealth that they sent their laundry to Paris to be cleaned."

"No! What are you saying? They didn't have it done here?"

"And allow it to be touched by lower class hands? Never." She made a mocking face. "The esteemed reputation of French laundries exists to this day."

"*Incredibile.*" What could I add about the very rich that hadn't been said before? Apropos of laundry, I should have insisted on soaking the sheets in cold water right away, I realized now. How could I do that to poor Primo? I would certainly be taking care of handwashing this lemon silk blouse tonight.

I closed my eyes for a second. My plan of putting nine time zones between Boothe and me wasn't entirely working. I thought about him far too often, mooning over whether he might be thinking about me, musing on whether I had ever genuinely mattered to him. The slipperiness of our yes-and-no relationship included the fact that I hadn't told him before I left that I was done with him, thereby keeping open the possibility that I wasn't.

Resolved: If I prolonged this hopeless relationship when I returned home, I would never forgive myself! What good could come from resuming anything with such a man? I suppose I'd put the Boothe blouse on this morning as a sort of talisman to protect me against my indecision. Paradoxical, I know, yet I put it on as a warning to myself. I put it on as a reminder of all the confusion generated by us both. I put it on so as not to blame him for the indecisive person I seemed to become around him. I put it on so that my next relationship would suffer from none of these miseries.

Resolved: I could still love the blouse, wear the blouse, and refuse the man.

"There it is." Maia jingled her keys.

"Hmm?" My lids flew open and I hid a yawn with my hand.

"Cefalù." She pointed to a bulging granite cliff and a town sheltered at its base. "Named for the hill which, as you can see, looks something like a head, from the Greek 'cephalos'."

Walking roused me. The fuzz in my head started to clear. She was guiding me through the port of a real fishing village doing what it had always done. Moored boats painted bright blue, green and rose, with neat piles of fishnets dripping dry, next to the glossy clear seawater. Six little boys in shorts and sandals shared one fishing rod. We ambled under wrought iron street lamps and passed by arched stone houses pressed together. All balconies gazed waterward, shutters colored lime and orange.

"Thank you Maia, for bringing me here." Spontaneously on this day, to stunning Cefalù after which it was anatomically named. I liked a town with a brain.

I trailed her across a sloping piazza studded with palm trees, and into the tall Norman cathedral to see the tremendous mosaic Christ in the apse. He was so kindly looking, with deep, round, thoughtful eyes that followed us, each one of us at the same time as we wandered through the echoing vault, watching him watching us. He was so welcoming, his outstretched arms forever offering solace and acceptance as we approached him.

Outside on the piazza Maia began to read from her guidebook:

> The Cathedral, a splendid edifice begun by Roger II in 1131, is particularly effective owing to the formidable cliff immediately behind it . . .

But I was distracted. About thirty feet away, a god sat on his motor scooter, hunched over just so. The gold crucifix hanging from his neck dangled in the space between his chest and the odometer. *Dio mio.* He wore a salmony-pink button-down shirt, pegged black pants, salmon-pink socks and black shoes. He was maybe twenty or twenty-one.

> The Facade, a distinctive design by Giovanni Panettera, dates from 1240; it is flanked by two massive towers and enlivened by . . .

He straddled his machine, fiddling a little with the handles, making a show of polishing the chrome, mere gratuitous activity. He was here for one purpose: to be gazed upon, which was impossible not to do, since he had deep-lidded Coptic eyes to sink into, and a Roman profile straight off an old coin of the empire. In addition, he happened to possess the classic physique of The Discus Thrower. *Madonna mia.* So much antiquity wrapped up in one live, throbbing Mediterranean guy.

I wished I could magically slip away for five minutes and hop on the back of his *motorino* and have him drive around the bend, have him stop the engine, lean against a stone wall and kiss his beauteous, beatified eyelids, first one, then the other, then the one, then the other. Just kiss, that's all. A veneration. Then I could rejoin Maia, who would still be reading aloud and wouldn't have noticed my absence, and we would continue on our way discussing Norman architecture.

> The exterior of the south side and transept and of the triple apse is well worth studying.

Well worth studying. A number of women, boys and men, girls, stray cats and tourists were studying him well. The star attraction, the chief entertainment, the major drama of Cefalù, a youthful deity landed in the middle of the piazza, the Pink and Black Adonis. He'd perfected a kind of smoky glance, taking in looks through not only his eyes but his sinews, the black curls of his head, his whole being. I could not tug my eyes away, and when he turned his attention to me for a moment I nearly toppled off my cobblestone. He narrowed his black eyes and flared his nostrils. Help me.

"Hmm," Maia stood firmly planted in her walking shoes, glancing back and forth between Adonis and me. "*Proprio un fusto.*" A real good looker. "Hmmmm." A quarter-smile flitted across her face.

"Nice colors he's wearing," I stammered.

"The colors of his soccer team. But he's got something," she winked.

"Yes, something."

The church bells began to peal. I narrowed my eyes at Pink and Black and lay my own smoldering on thick. He was watching me and everyone all at the same time. Finally, he looked away and the spell broke.

We returned by way of the Autostrada along the coast. I leaned against the window and shut my eyes, still lost in the pull of the Pink and the Black. The car hit a bump in the road, banging my head against the side window. To our right stretched miles of industrial buildings. From two-toned dream to concrete nightmare.

"What is *that*?"

"Termini Imerese. A factory."

"Producing what?"

"Nothing. It has never been used."

"But how can that be? I don't understand. It's lit up like there are people working in there."

"The Mafia was behind the contract to build a factory. They got billions upon billions for the job, but they never intended that the place would function."

"They just took a beautiful piece of coast and destroyed it like this?"

The little muscle worked in her jaw. "That's how they operate."

I gaped at the big blight. "It's as though they set out to build the most hideous structure they could, just to show who's boss."

"People tried to fight it. What more could we do?"

"Nothing, Maia, nothing more."

When we returned home I went straight to the telephone and called the library, just as the substitute Guido F____ told me to do. But there was no answer, so I closed my bedroom door to translate.

THE RESOUNDING KIDNAP
December 18, 1966

Despite predictions that the sentence would be read between 1:00 and 1:30 p.m, the judges remained closed up in council chambers all afternoon. The nervousness of the defendants, their relatives and friends grew with the passage of hours. The overflow crowd milled restlessly in the atrium of the Court.

Toward mid-afternoon the three judges asked for coffee and the delivery boy reported that when he entered the room he saw them writing at the typewriter.

The twelve accused inside the cage formed a circle and spoke in low voices, asking often for cigarettes from the lawyers. One nervously paced back and forth. The bricklayer, Giuseppe Ferro, stayed removed from the others, on edge as always. The relatives were piled up in their corner, sometimes throwing a glance in the direction of their sons and husbands.

Filippo Melodia's father, Vincenzo—hardly noticed during the trial—stood among them. Reporters described him as a man of maybe fifty years, thin with a slightly aquiline nose, and having "the hands of a peasant, of one who works with a hoe, sunburned like someone who reaps grain all day."

"My son is a fine boy, better than any other. Did you hear? The Court said the same thing. He is blameless. They call him a vagabond and a mafioso. But they better stop going on saying these things," he said.

"Did you know that your son had the intention to kidnap Franca Viola?"

"If I had known, I would have split his head."

"Were you in favor of or against the marriage?"

"I would have been happy if they had married, and if they would have been able to do it. She, Franca, was crazy for my son. She still dies for him. Her parents made her change her mind. I tell you the truth, only the truth, believe me." He spoke a halting Italian, which he often abandoned for the hard Alcamese dialect. He talked about the time his son went to Germany, because the whole village goes there for work and he wanted to try too. Then he returned with a little money and bought the white Giulietta car.

"What about the story of the stolen motorcycle, which pushed the Viola family to break the engagement?"

"It was the moto of a friend," he responded excitedly. "He took it to go to his fiancée, but then he returned it. The judges acquitted him."

He said that he was always ready to marry the two young people. "I am sure that if Bernardo Viola changes his mind, she will be happy." He spoke of the shame that came down on his family from the trial.

"But what if they would have kidnapped your daughter? What would you have done?"

"If she had wanted, I would have made her marry."

"And what if she did not want it?"

"I would have had the kidnapper arrested." He excused himself and returned to the hall, anxious to know the fate of his son, who in that moment behind the cage laughingly joked with his friends.

Meanwhile, Franca Viola's father, mother and aunt waited on the other side of the courtroom, while Franca remained at home. Bernardo exchanged some words with the people who were near him. He said that last night Franca had slept poorly. For ten minutes he himself slept deeply, holding his head in his hand.

A telegram arrived in the hall, but he was afraid to open it. He handed it to lawyer Fileccia, who read it to him. It was from the Vice President of the House in Rome, who in the name of the Communist elect expressed its solidarity with Franca Viola. Other gestures of support came from the Communal Council of Alcamo, *and from Parliament, where it was suggested that Bernardo receive a high decoration of the Republic.*

Viola was asked what he thought of this long wait for the judges' decision. He responded with a Sicilian proverb: "Varca chi addimura carica veni." *[A boat that returns late comes back full.]*

One or two times the room was shaken with a tremor, when rumor spread that the Court was preparing to enter. Then at 5:15 p.m. the bell sounded, announcing that the Court would emerge. The hall filled up with more than five hundred people. A cloister-like silence descended. The defendants jumped to their feet, their faces pale, some trembling. Melodia, who during the wait had smiled and joked with the lawyers, hid himself behind one of the carabinieri. *Defendant G. Daidone covered his eyes with his hand. One of the relatives had brought a sheet of paper and a Biro ball-point pen to take notes.*

The three judges of the Court emerged at 5:30 p.m. President Albeggiani read the sentence with a voice muffled by tiredness:

"Eleven years of imprisonment and forty-thousand lire fine for Filippo Melodia. Four years and eight months for V. Melodia and C. Costantino di Benedetto, four years and four months for G. Ferro, I. Lipari, C. Costantino di Giuseppe, V. Varvaro and F. Costantino. Acquitted for insufficient evidence: I. Coppola, G. Daidone, V. Vilardi, G. Brucia and A. Stellino."

Not one tear dropped from the defendants. Their relatives who occupied the section of reserved seats in the hall made no sound. Some shook their heads in a sign of desperation, now resigned. The five acquitted smiled and shook hands with the lawyers who had defended them. Melodia, who for the whole reading of the sentence had remained hidden behind the shoulders of a carabiniere, *did the same too. He had mistakenly believed that he would benefit from two years of reduction, but later it was explained to him that nothing could be done. With the reading ended, the public started to move slowly and quietly toward the exit.*

Within hours everyone was talking on the streets in Alcamo: clusters of people in front of newsstands, bars full of customers sipping aperitivi. *Only after the sentencing did the townsfolk publicly line up with the Violas. At the "Calipso Bar" on Alcamo's main street, where the kidnappers planned the raid on the Viola house, regulars recalled how Melodia used to sit down, opening his jacket to show everybody that he had a pistol under his belt.*[†]

The Roman newspaper, Corriere della Sera, *referring to Bernardo Viola's comment during the seven-hour wait for the verdict, editorialized: "The boat came back late, but the load was not as heavy as one might have thought."*

The evening the trial ended, Mr. Viola was glimpsed in front of his house, loading a suitcase onto a rented "2100" with a hired driver.

"Enough with journalists, now I am tired. I don't want to say anything more."

His wife rushed up to give him a strong hand. They left with an unidentified relative for Palermo to deliver a gift to lawyer Ludovico Corrao, a tablecloth embroidered by Franca. She was not with her parents. They said she was at home with the flu, but she may not even have been in Alcamo. Rather, she may have been in hiding with relatives near Palermo.

Bernardo Viola was asked, "Do the years seem few to you?"

"For me," he responded, "they can even be thrown out tomorrow. The important thing is that they leave me in peace."

Might as well make a day of it and call the mayor too, I figured. I listened to the lonely sound of his phone ringing into infinity.

"Mayor Ludovico Corrao speaking."

[†] Author's note: see Appendix, page 343 for comments made by locals and Palemitani.

"Really? Oh my! How do you do, sir? What a pleasant surprise. How remarkable that you have answered personally. I've taken the liberty of phoning because you are the mayor of Alcamo, and as it turns out, one of Franca Viola's lawyers as well which is quite a coincidence, since I have come from America to find her, and—"

"Yes?"

"Would you be able to, that is, could you possibly help me to secure an interview with Franca Viola?"

"She absolutely won't speak to anyone," he stated as if he had repeated it frequently over the years. "I'm sure you can understand that. She treasures her privacy and does not wish it disturbed."

Emotion caught in my throat. "I do understand. Please sir, if you would, tell her that many years later she still continues to inspire me. Certainly I'm not alone in that sentiment."

"I will give her that message the next time I speak with her." His tone—very courteous, polite and thoughtful—only drove home the impossibility more.

"Can you tell me what her life was like after the trial ended? Did she leave your city?"

"She remained here in Alcamo. Her family did not leave."

"Were they safe?"

"The police kept a guard in front of their house for several months after the trial, because there was a concern. When Franca and her mother attended daily Mass, they were followed at a close distance by uniformed officers for protection. And the *carabinieri* accompanied her father to his plot of land."

"I see. Sir, I deeply appreciate your time. And your public stand during the trial inspires me too. I have been learning about it from the newspapers of the time."

"Thank you, but the courage was all hers and her family's."

"*Grazie.*"

"*Grazie, Lei*. You are most welcome. And safe journey to you."

I hung up and hung my head. Franca would never talk. I had to let go of the idea. I was the one stuck in 1966.

Maia's voice boomed from her armchair, "It's enough that you've gotten as far as you have."

"And even if you go no further, you will have accomplished something," I grumbled under my breath and scampered into the bedroom. The mattress crunched with crisp, clean sheets, the spread smoothed like taut marzipan icing across the surface by talented, lovable Primo—cook, baker, rug-shaker, bed-maker, blood-cleaner-upper, Persephone mythoanalyst.

I slipped into the bathroom and turned on the bidet. It spouted multi-plumed jets of water, like the *Fontana di Vergogna* in the Cathedral Piazza, all over the front of my yellow Boothe blouse. I had to laugh. "So there you have it."

Everyone here who questioned my interest in pursuing Franca's story—they knew something I had all along resisted accepting. Maybe I had to stop. I was straining the island's privacy, insulting her fierce Medusan heart, defying the ancient ravines and folds of Monte Pellegrino and the great height of Erice to have ever imagined otherwise. The librarian said it was impossible. So did the feminist. Now the mayor confirmed the same thing. I adjusted the handles. The bowl filled with pulsing warm water.

Chapter XVII

Ruins, Bureaucrats

"Vasheengtone, Ahhdams, Jeffersone, Monrro-eh, Madeesone, Queenchee Ahhdams . . ." a voice was filtering into my room.

"Madeesone before Monrro-eh," Maia interrupted. "When is the test?"

"Tomorrow," groaned Costanza, another granddaughter.

"All right, *tesoro*. From the beginning again."

I listened at the doorjamb in my nightgown, impressed that Italian high school students learned all forty United States chief executives by heart. We never did. I didn't dare walk out until the drill ended because I would have failed in an excruciating way.

"Good morning, Costanza, no school today?"

"We're on strike," she smiled bashfully.

"What for?"

"I don't know," she paused for a moment. "Better conditions."

"Rather vague." Maia shook her head. "And for the fourth time this year."

"It's only one day, Nonna, and it was the teachers' idea."

"*Basta*. Enough of this fiasco. I'm taking Natalie to visit La Zisa, La Cuba, and La Cubula," Maia informed us, folding her newspaper.

"Friends of yours?" I was teasing her; I'd noticed them on the city map.

"You could say that. I haven't seen them myself for years. All three require a certain effort to locate, because they are hidden away. You will find them quite fascinating. I have to say it again: I feel so young, rediscovering my own city with you here."

"If you don't mind my phoning the librarian first, just in case."

I gave up after the twentieth ring. Maybe he was on strike too. Anyway, I was pretending not to care anymore. Now that the search had come to a halt, I was free to sightsee like the next tourist, and to take care of the urgent business of mailing Evelyn's package to Agrigento. I would do it this afternoon.

The trial had vindicated Franca for the public to see, but Arcangela had been granted no such reprieve. She had put her own self on trial and had found herself guilty. She expected neither forgiveness nor understanding. By trying to solve her terrible dilemma alone within the mores of her time, she tragically miscalculated, taking the only route she thought available, with no tolerance to the right and no mercy to the left. I would no longer delay reuniting her with her photos. I had been carrying her family around in my satchel. Arcangela needed her daughter back.

"Costanza, why don't you come along with us?" I asked.

"Nah, I've gotta study."

"I should hope so," Maia said. "Being on strike isn't the same as having a day off. You have your year-end exams to think about." She pulled her jacket on. "We'll review the presidents this afternoon, *va bene?*"

"Sure. Oh Natalie, is it true that in the US you can just walk into a store to buy a pair of Timberland shoes without putting your name on a waiting list?"

"Your sister asked me the same question. It's so funny because we Americans covet Italian footwear. Write down your shoe sizes for me and I'll be sure to find out."

"*Oh-kay*. Bye," Costanza waved, "Bye, grownups!"

The section of town we drove through was bleak post-war modern, but that didn't keep Maia from entering into a trance about what once was.

"Believe me, these buildings are worth the search, being remnants of a tremendous twelfth-century pleasure park between the old city and the Golden Shell," Maia raised her voice, dodging traffic as if she were driving a bumper car. "These were the fantasy realms of the Arabo-Norman kings, where elaborate gardens and fountains, man-made lakes and pavilions covered the expanse, where exotic imported beasts roamed, where the royals luxuriated."

We wound through harsh urban streets without a branch or blade of green anywhere. Maia turned into a sagging neighborhood of stone sheds and small vegetable plots guarded by a few retired dogs, roosters, and the top half of a crucified scarecrow.

"La Zisa. There it is," she yanked up the brake smartly and threw her door open. "As lovely as I remember it." The Moorish building rose lyrically from a palomino-colored field, its central arch soaring, its upper windows open to the morning air. Signs posted everywhere prohibited entrance.

"It's always in a state of restoration," Maia explained as we walked toward it. "*Scusi*," she used her commanding-yet-polite-I-am-a-Palermo-senior-citizen-tone in addressing a workman. "We'd like to look for five minutes, if you would be so kind."

"Sorry," he yelled back, "we're constructing a scaffold."

"Typical," Maia muttered. "We'll just stand inside for a minute, on the opposite end, away from all the work," she called out. "All we want to do is see the light stream through the open windows." To me she added, "The walls are said to have a beautiful apricot glow when the sun strikes them."

"Oooh, apricot," I gushed.

"Something could fall," he shouted.

"He's right about that. An empire for example." She proceeded gamely. "We have a visitor here all the way from California. Surely you don't want to turn her away."

"Come back in ten years."

"This is not a laughing matter, my good man. You've been restoring and restoring. Why can't the public, who pays your wages, see the progress?"

He shrugged and walked away.

"Notice the line where the pond once was."

I slid my sunglasses down and squinted. "Maybe I see *something*. I'm not certain though."

"The entire park was filled with coursing waters and reflecting pools. *Ehhh*, poets sang its praises," Maia's eyes half-closed at the faraway thought. "My husband and I used to picnic here, before we had our boys. Well, let's push ahead. We have the two other buildings to find, so that you can get an idea of the immensity of the park."

We drove through more gray slums stamped with impossibility. Everywhere, packs of young children mingled with older kids on the wasted streets.

"The poverty breaks my heart. Some who come here from the country regret the move, but then they cannot go back to a place they know full well is worse. Their villages are bleeding. What are we to do about our great problems, I ask you?"

I was seriously wishing I could formulate an answer when we merged into a thoroughfare solid with vehicles. Maia searched for parking in the chaos. She finally became so fed up—"*Boh!*"—that she pulled into a red zone and turned off the ignition. A bartender in the Caffè Nettuno leaned out his window. "*Signora*, you might get towed," he warned her.

Maia brushed aside the thought. "I doubt anything will happen. We'll only be here a few minutes."

We trudged up the crazy-cacaphonous boulevard to a military compound, Caserma Tuköry, where we sought formal permission to see La Cuba. The guard, a rifle-carrying boy of twenty or so, scowled with an exaggerated authority that made me want to laugh out loud, especially since he had powdered sugar all over his lips. An incriminating, partly-eaten *brioche* lay on a plate on his desk. He confiscated my passport and Maia's retirement card. Another grim teenaged soldier was summoned to lead us alongside barracks to a narrow passageway. He fixed his ramrod legs into the dirt. "Here it is." A pastel apricot stone wall faced us.

"*This* was the pleasure *pavilion?*"

"We're standing where the lagoon surrounded it. We see here one side of the cube-shaped palace."

Impatiently, the guard pushed a pebble around with his boot. "There's much more."

"I'll say!" Maia retorted.

"But you are not permitted to see it," he added.

"Notice, Natalie, the similarity to La Zisa's massive stone-work at ground level. La Cuba stands several stories high. The barracks obscure all dimension. But can you imagine the sultans dallying with their consorts here in the shade, can you imagine zebras and peacocks roaming the grounds?"

"Yes, yes I can, because you paint a vivid picture." I couldn't, but she had worked so hard to get me here.

"Someday the public will see it completely restored."

The guard kept a suspicious eye trained on us and a suspicious ear tuned in.

"At ease, young man, we're leaving now. Onward to La Cubula." Maia wanted me to be drenched in nothing less than the full twelfth-century experience. We hit the street again. I kept up with her determined pace. Her walking shoes clicked briskly along the pavement.

The caffè proprietor ran toward us on bowed legs, waving his arms, leaning sideways at a dangerous angle. His eyes were frantic. "*Signora*, I warned you, I told you that this might happen!" He actually wept as he moaned, "I told you so, but you wouldn't listen to me, and now this."

My cousin, the color drained from her face, mutely stared at the empty red zone, but the man was undone. Customers in the bar poured out onto the sidewalk like an opera chorus, crowding around to hear his riveting reenactment. He described the police, the gruesome rattle of the chain, the hooks being applied, the terrible scraping of the bumper along the street, the sparks flying. He danced around the sidewalk like a jerky Sicilian marionette, lunging, pacing, halting, miming, sobbing, arguing, not with Maia but at life's cruelty. I pinched my lips together hard and commanded myself, do not crack a smile, I'm warning you, Natalie. Someone handed him a handkerchief. He dried his face, then began again, holding his head in his hands, wailing, "Oh me!" He pointed to the space where the car had been. The crowd wordlessly studied the void left behind.

I wanted to say something helpful to Maia other than I'm sorry, but I couldn't think of what it was. If it weren't for my presence in Palermo, my cousin wouldn't be hyperdriving all over the city to hunt down this vanished garden and that closed-up ruin. She wouldn't be parking in forbidden zones. She'd be at home reading the paper. The fault rested with me. Mea maxissima culpa.

The man was still at it. This would never happen back home. Americans don't run out to witness the aftermath of a towing. My eyes stayed fixed on the red paint. How the poor guy must have carried on during the actual impoundment. Now he sat on the curb, fanning himself while the murmuring crowd slowly returned indoors.

I tagged after Maia into the caffè. "Let's go get your car wherever they've taken it."

She waved away that idea with her hand, disappearing into a wooden phone booth. I paced up and down the length of the counter past gleaming brass fixtures and a row of *gelati* in their trays—*cocco, caramella, zabaglione, pistacchio, kiwi, cassata, nocciola.* There were *biscotti* and cookies too, fashioned into pianos, drums, violins and harps, treble clefs and six-teenth-notes. I was a distracting and expensive influence on my cousin, who was wearing herself out watching over me. Her taut voice threaded from the booth. She emerged insisting that we take a cab home.

"What a pity that you cannot now see La Cubula. It is truly lovely. To pick up the car, we must first go to a magistrate and pay the fine, then procure permission to retrieve the vehicle from a separate office, which will issue us the right papers to present at the car-storage facility. Too close to lunchtime now, as all the offices will close for three hours. There's nothing to do but go home and eat. Three different places all over the city I have to go." She held up three fingers. "It will take the rest of the day."

"Aye-yi-yi." I slapped my forehead. "What bureaucracy. It could undo a person."

"It does, all the time. My son will handle this," she stated with certainty. "Sons are good at this kind of thing. Would you like an espresso and one of these *biscotti*?"

That did it! I was weighing on her, even though she had insisted daily I could stay as long as I wanted. I had to leave. The taxi pulled up. I looked back one last time at Mr. Caffè Thespian, crumpled on a tall stool, a cigarette dangling life-lessly between his lips, a vacant gaze on his face. He felt so much. So much!

Our cabdriver did his best to advance in the midday jam. I kept an eye on Maia, who looked out the window distractedly, her mind on the recent loss. Our driver decided to maneuver crosswise over to the first intersection, so we were treated to yells, honks, and gestures I had not yet seen around town. He sang throughout, cheerful as a cherub, eyeing me in the rear-view. I eyed him back.

"Maia, let me take you to lunch. It's Primo's day off, right?"

"Better to eat at home."

"Well then, let me cook you something Chinese. Do you have soy sauce and ginger?"

"At my neighborhood store they sell a few foods of the Orient."

Finally I'd hit on something helpful.

"There's my car," she shrieked. Ahead by half a block the nose of her white Fiat bobbed in the metallic sea.

"*Permesso, signora*, I shall chase it down for you," the cabbie offered, and up on the sidewalk we went. He caught sight of me in his mirror and winked. After several imaginative moves, we came alongside the tow truck.

"*Permesso.* I will ask him to unhook your car. For a small fee."

I gaped at Maia, astounded. Go ahead, she gestured, if you can. But he couldn't, judging from the heated interchange in dialect. The towman was devoted to the rules of the city. No bribes today, and away we were escorted, her car pulled elsewhere.

Maia and I fought over who would pay. I pushed the money into the cabbie's hand, and as she turned toward the lobby he said, "*Signorina*, it has been an incomparable pleasure transporting international cargo such as yourself." He kissed my hand and took off.

"Okay, you go in and put your feet up. I'll be back in a jiff. We'll be ready to eat in no time."

How many times had I carried Evelyn's package along, intending to mail it? This was another of those times. Lunch took priority. At the neighborhood grocery down the street, the shopkeeper climbed a stepladder under the import section high up on a corner shelf. He pulled down a bottle of soy sauce wearing a sticky layer of dust, and an opaque packet of candied ginger. Reaching way back he found a mottled can of black bean sauce. The small package of dried mushrooms imported from Torino were porcini, not woodears or oysters or black, but it was the spirit of the thing I was after. From the vegetable display I gathered broccoli rabe, mustard greens, carrots and eggplant—oh, and a small hot green pepper. Spicy Szechuan/Sicilian style, with a kick. I wanted to make her a meal that would transport her far away from the city she loved, which indifferently issued her a penalty. The municipality that stole her car away when she had only gone to admire imprisoned pieces of its long history. Which had the nerve to confiscate her identification card when they should know who she was—a civic treasure.

I picked up a tetrahedron package of ultra-pasteurized milk for the cats and stopped at the fourth floor to give it to the Professor. I rang his bell, hoping to tell him that I'd spoken to the prosecutor at the trial whose name began with C as he had remembered, who was now Alcamo's Mayor Ludovico Corrao, but he must have been teaching a class. I left the carton on the marble threshold of his door.

Maia, her granddaughter and I ate out on the terrace. They went on about the rare pleasure of tasting Chinese-style vegetables in a sweet and hot ginger sauce. When the presidential roll call began unfurling again, I excused myself to wash the dishes and pans. What a relief to do a basic domestic chore after all the care lavished on me these last nearly three weeks. There were no more newspaper articles to pore over. The work was done. The hot water warming up my hands, the steam rising calmly from the washbasin, put me into a kind of a surrendered stupor. Through it I heard, "Gahrr-fee-ehlde, Art-urrrh, Clayvaylande, Arreesohn, Clayvaylande again, MmKeenlayee ..." I decided this was my moment to dial the librarian, while they were both outside on the terrace. It was possibly now or probably never. The phone rang fifteen times.

"Photocopy department . . . *Ahhhh*, *signorina*, I'm relieved that you've called. I spoke with Franca's husband last night. I told him you've come all the way from California and have a sincere interest in her story. He went home to ask her whether she'd be willing to talk. *Signorina*, she has agreed. You are to call at their home next Wednesday at one in the afternoon, at mealtime."

I let out a shriek. "This is good news, amazing news, Mr. Guido. It's unbelievable!"

"Yes, you are a very lucky person. I would do exactly as they requested, if I were you. Do not call before next Wednesday," he stressed.

"Yes, of course."

"Here's the phone number."

I grabbed a pen and scribbled it on my right palm. "How can I thank you, sir?"

"It's nothing, really. Nothing."

"On the contrary, sir—it's everything. You've helped. You are so kind. You've opened the door." He had plucked me a golden apple but acted as though he'd done nothing more than issue a library card.

"Don't mention it."

"If I may ask one other question: whatever became of Filippo Melodia?"

"Well, *signorina*, after he was released from prison he was killed."

"No," I gasped, "what happened?"

"During an argument with another thug, he was shot to death."

"Oh!" My stomach clenched. "That's a shock."

"*Ehh*, he who starts out bad, finishes bad. Good luck," he

signed off. "I hope our island has treated you well."

"It has, and you have treated me stupendously well. *Ciao ciao.*" It must have been the white candle lit the day before yesterday in San Giuseppe dei Teatini that did it, the all-purpose one employed during my temporary vow of silence.

But this news about Melodia's violent end was far from ding-dong-the-witch-is-dead. All I felt was sad. Sad that the tradition had ever taken hold, sad that people had ever thought it was normal, sad that this beautiful island—plundered, violated, invaded from without and from within—had retained such a weird notion of honor for so many centuries. Sad for the pain caused all the way around.

"Frahn-kleen Delahnoh Row-ow-seh-vel-te, who uniquely served for four consecutive terms of office . . ."

"So sorry to disrupt your recitation, Costanza," I blurted, throwing my arms around Maia. "The Alcamo librarian really did what he promised. She'll talk to me on Wednesday. Can you believe it?"

"I am pleased," she answered quietly, a small smile on her lips. "However, when you call Franca Viola next week, you must ask at the outset if there are any conditions."

"Conditions?"

"Meaning do they expect payment for your interview? You wouldn't want any misunderstanding on that score."

"I didn't know such a thing existed. I will, when the time comes."

"Who's this Franca Viola?" Costanza asked.

"Now that question I can answer," I beamed.

Chapter XVIII

Planning the Getaway

"Rest? I always rest! Why don't you stay?" Maia had saturated all her geranium pots on the veranda. We stood in a big puddle while Filumenu chirped raucously. The golden morning beckoned. "We have so much more to visit right here. The Palazzo Abatellis and the Puppet Museum and the cathedral, not to mention the Casa Professa and the Palatine Chapel. The *Stucchi* too. You must see the fine stucco work of the Baroque in all their glory."

I didn't reveal my plan to rent a car, which would allow me to hang out in Alcamo for a couple of days, familiarizing myself with the setting and conversing with locals. Reluctantly, Maia drove me (her son had brought the car back last night) to her long-time travel agency. The chain-smoking agent had translucent white skin, the better to offset her Titian orange lipstick and matching fingernails. Maia inquired after her mother.

"She's still recuperating from the operation, *Signora* Santilli, three months later. Every day I remind her it was only a spleen, that it could have been worse. She just cries more."

"Tell her I'll be calling her tomorrow."

"I will, and enough on that subject. *Dimmi gioia, dimmi?*" she asked me in a husky low voice. Tell me exactly what you need, joyous thing.

"I'd like to rent a car for a few days. Nothing fancy. The most economical you've got."

"When?"

"Tomorrow."

She shook her head, dragging deeply on the Titian-tinted filter. "At such short notice, I doubt I can find one. Let me confer with my colleague." The lovely Titian had to brace herself with two more puffs before picking up the phone. The consultation was so seductive sounding, that if the colleague had any sense he would have offered up his own car for me on the spot. "We have no vehicles of any type available for you."

"Nothing at all?"

"Not a single one, neither luxury, nor touring, nor economy. We are completely devoid of them this week. Next week we'll have plenty."

"You see?" Maia faced me, a hint of triumph in her tone.

"Truly, I would find one for you if I could. I'm so sorry." Another sexy pull on the cigarette. "Let me show you our packaged tour options." She took out a glossy brochure from her desk drawer. On the cover a glamorous couple kissed before a Greek temple at sunset.

I sank low into the vinyl chair. A pre-digested Sicily—ugh. "It's not my style. How about a *motorino*? I'm sure I could figure out how to ride one, with a helmet."

"The insurance is sky-high for a *forestiere*. No, do not even consider it. You won't be sorry," the agent said soothingly, tapping the itinerary on the brochure with her pencil eraser. "The Mini three-day excursion gives you quite a taste, considering, and it includes Piazza Armerina."

"Does it go through Alcamo?"

Maia shot me a look.

"No, it doesn't."

"Which tour goes through Alcamo?"

"None."

"But that's where I want to go."

"I'm sorry. I can't help you there. With the strike going on, connections are sporadic, at best. You'd have to take a taxi from Trapani."

"Which will cost you a small fortune," Maia jumped in. She was not going to be driving me to Alcamo, that was certain. It could jinx my interview. And I was not going to be asking her to. Yesterday we'd both reached our limit for tooling around anywhere in her little white Fiat. And it was true that I had always wanted to see Piazza Armerina.

"Now, you wish to travel first class, I assume?"

Maia nodded vigorously.

"No, no, second class." I chewed my lip. One pair of determined Maian eyes intent on securely escorted travel for me, and another made-up set intent on a sale bore into me. "What is the total cost second class with surcharges and everything?"

"As you wish." She pulled out her Olivetti calculator, did her addition—tic tic tic—and tore the inch-long receipt off with an expert zip.

I tried to delay the inevitable. "But how will I get back to Palermo? I've got to return by Wednesday, no matter what."

"You can take a train from Messina or bus from Catania, whichever you prefer."

"There aren't any strikes happening that will keep me from returning by either?"

"Not on that run."

"But one could start."

"*Tst*. Not likely with the tourist season underway."

Man oh man. I was in it deep now, yet I knew I had to get out of Palermo and leave Maia alone. She needed a break. I needed a break. My head nodded and my hand accepted the pen, committing a signature to paper in slow motion. Both women were exultant about my safe and sensible decision. There lay my name on the CIT— Compagnia Italiana Turistica—contract: inky, quivering, final.

Of all the lunches Primo had made, the *pasta colle sarde* was the most extravagant and exotic. It tasted something like sweet and sour curry, but the synthesis of flavors took it way beyond the curry dimension.

"I asked Primo to prepare it for you since you're leaving tomorrow."

He bowed. "It is the signature dish of our city. The sardines must be flaked for best flavor. Do you know, *signora*, we used to catch sardines in the harbor, as kids? We tied our own nets out of pieces of string."

"*Bravo*, resourceful Primo. Well done."

"But there's more than just sardines in here," I said.

"Yes, currants, pinenuts, wild fennel flower. Have more, *signorina*," he urged, his laden spoon hovering over my plate. "You won't find home-cooking on the tour."

"I can't manage another bite, which is sad because it's so delicious."

The spoon descended.

"Oh, Primo," I protested. It was hopeless.

"Natalie, he will accompany you downtown to the bank when you exchange your traveler's checks."

"That's completely unnecessary, Maia. I'll go on my own." I cleaned the plate with a crust of bread.

"*Signorina*, do you want your purse grabbed? Do you want to be knocked to the ground?" Primo untied his apron, neatly rolled it up and placed it on the lower shelf of the serving cart. "I'm ready to leave whenever you are."

"But first I've got to get to the post office."

"We have plenty of stamps here," Maia said.

"But this package from a friend of mine has to be sent insured to Agrigento."

"I thought you had taken care of that already. Why mail it from here when you will be in Agrigento by tomorrow evening?"

"I will?" Oh boy. I had not paid close enough attention to the itinerary.

"It stands a much better chance of arriving there if you send it from there," she reasoned.

"Of course."

On the bus Primo surprised me by speaking English. "Why didn't you tell me all this time?"

"I do not speak it in front of *La Signora* Maia, that would be disrespecting, isn't it? My father taught me. He lived in America. At New York. Brukleen. He save money over there for many years but he always intending to come back in Sicily. Since you have a curiosity on marriage I will tell you about him. You see, his mommy and his daddy had arranged a union for him to a cousin, and so he came home for the matrimony."

"To your mother."

"No, no, I am to explain. When he and that cousin met, he say to his parents, 'Mother and Father, I cannot marry the girl. We will not make a good life together, it cannot be.' And so he made the plans to marry a girl who he like, with which he make special visit in the house of her parents. This is my mother. And so, you see, the day comes when he goes to the church to be wedded. Well, I must tell you what took place when they stood before the priest. You see, the relatives, the cousins of the girl who had been refused, they come running in to the church," he covered his mouth with his hand, "and suddenly they throw the black paint onto the white wedding dress of the bride. Oh yes to blacken her name. To make justice for their family in front of everyone. Black, very black wet paint all over the white dress, isn't it?"

I nodded.

"Ahh, *signorina*, every word, she is true. *Completamente vero* true. And so, do you know what then happened?"

"No."

"My mother, the bride, she stand exactly in place, before the altar, before the priest, before the Father, the Son and the Holy Spirit. And so do my father. *Poi*, while they remain *perfettamente* still, without moving the muscles, my mother's family they run, run like a train home. And they take the white cloth. And the scissors. And the thread. And they run back into the church, and the priest, he had in the meanwhile stop the ceremony. *E allora*, while all the peoples sit and pray and cry, my mother's family surround the bride, and out of the dress cut all the black part, and they sew in the new white part. And my mother, she stand without breath. And then, when the dress is pure once more and white, then the priest continue to make them married. And they were. And here I am," Primo heaved a sigh, bringing his right hand over his heart. "I swear it."

"Holy moly. Did they leave your parents alone after that?"

"Always they give the disgracing looks, whenever they pass in the neighborhood. But they believe to throw the paint in front of all the people, and before the eyes of God, is to receive honor back again, isn't it? I tell this to teach you Sicilian reasoning in those old fashion times. On a land like this one, if you think you will lose something, you defend it. You may not have another opportunity in your life. *Capisci?*"

"*Capisco.*"

"But now the descendants of all the families do not care what happen in the past and play soccer together and go have *gelati* afterward . . . And my parents had always happiness in their marriage. Here's our stop."

Primo and I trudged toward *Il Banco di Santo Spirito*. He pulled me toward its sliding glass door. We passed through three sets of them into a glass-walled antechamber. A security guard on the other side demanded that we hold up our ID cards to the window. When he buzzed us through he interrogated me:

"What is the nature of your visit to the bank? How much in traveler's checks do you intend to exchange? How long do you plan to remain in Sicily? How long have you already been here? Do you like Palermo? Where did you learn to speak Italian? Were both of your parents Italian? Where are they now?"

He ushered us to an empty desk where we sat for ten minutes. No one showed up. The guard returned. "I don't know where he's gone. Give him a little time."

We waited twenty more while various bank people stood around smoking. Eventually the officer arrived, all smiles, shook our hands and asked to examine my traveler's checks. He turned on his desk lamp, held them under the light, flipped them over to study the colored ink pattern on the reverse.

"Do I begin signing now?"

"No, you do that at the cashier's window. But, *prego*, first you need to fill out these forms." Four pages of name, age, sex, local address, local phone number, passport number, intended length of stay and signature. Separate form for the amount I wanted exchanged—in triplicate, since there was no carbon paper. Primo sat placidly by.

Once the officer duly notated, stamped and blessed this paperwork, he directed us to the cashier's window. I joined a clique of customers standing behind a red line painted on the floor. I received overt, shameless, curious stares.

"How will I know when it's my turn?" I whispered to Primo perched on a bench a few feet away. "There's no order."

"Push. Don't let anyone get in your way."

The other Mediterranean habit besides haggling I couldn't pull off. Not that we had a cashier to push for, the booth being empty. What gives with this crazy bank? And Primo willingly subjected himself to this ordeal when he could be home crushing oregano into salsa, ironing, beating rugs, or chatting with Maia instead?

"I think we should leave now. I could buy money at some exchange bureau. At least we won't lose the afternoon standing around."

"No!" Primo looked scandalized.

A uniformed man approached, causing an excited buzz within the group. He stood ten feet away and threw a fistful of metal medallions at us. The men around me went haywire, lunging for the pieces clattering to the floor. I looked to Primo. "What's going on?"

"Quick, quick, grab one," he cried, making a scooping motion, "hurry."

I bent down to snatch up a tag that had rolled next to my shoe. "235" was imprinted on it, which I relayed to Primo. The disk thrower retreated behind the cashier's window.

"*Finalmente,*" I sighed to the man next to me.

"Don't be so sure. Look at him."

The cashier had placed a Dagwood-sized hero sandwich on the counter. He removed his jacket, unfolded a white cloth napkin, tucked it under his chin, held one end of the bursting *panino* to his mouth and started to eat. The crowd stirred.

"*Disgraziato!*"

"He's having lunch!"

"That does it, Primo. We're leaving. I'll pay more somewhere else. I don't intend to spend my last day in Palermo watching a clerk eat on the job."

He held up his hands in prayer, imploring, "*Pazienza.*"

The cashier chewed, swallowed, selected a tag out of a pile next to his elbow and said into a microphone, "*Settantatre.*"

"Seventy-three?" I turned to Primo. He shrugged.

After lucky seventy-three transacted his business, the cashier took another big bite, picked another tag and announced "*Dodici.*"

Twelve. We weren't even in numerical order. I walked

over to Primo. "*Andiamo*," I bristled. "Let's go find something else. Honestly, I don't care if they charge me a big fee. It'd be worth it."

"You won't find one open now. They keep irregular hours. Then you'll just have to come back here. Stay put," he held up his palms. "It's better."

After a mini eon passed I heard, "*Duecento trentacinque*."

"That's me." I stepped up to the window. The cashier spoke into the grill-like mouthpiece fixed within the glass partition, but I could barely hear him.

"It worked a second ago," a voice behind me pointed out.

"Do I sign now?" I pushed all the papers into the drawer. He read them and said something. "Sir, I can't hear you."

He reached over to jiggle the microphone. "You would like two hundred and fifty American dollars, exchanged, *Signorina?*" blared his voice.

Oh that's just great. The exact amount I planned to walk out of the bank with had now become public information to the gathering of attentive men behind me, actually to the entire Consortium of the Bank of the Holy Spirit. Primo teetered on the edge of the bench, his eyes bugging.

"*Sì*," I mouthed, keeping my head still.

After studying and stapling the sheets, the cashier pushed his sandwich to the side and gestured that I could begin signing my traveler's checks, patiently watching each signature. He then counted out multi-colored fifty thousand lire notes, fanning them across the counter like an oversized hand of cards. He switched to ten thousands and five thousands, tallying aloud in a singsong. I glanced behind and noticed customers' lips counting silently along with his. Mortified, Primo took in the scene from his bench without blinking. The line painted on the floor meant nothing—this had developed into a group concern. The cashier stumbled over a bill, losing count. A voice behind me called out, "No. That was two *hundred* eighty-five thousand . . ."

The cashier wiped his mouth on the napkin still under his chin and began again. This time everyone including me counted out loud. When the cashier plunked down the last 500 lire piece, the man at my back tapped me on the shoulder reassuringly, "He got it right." The others nodded.

Primo sprang to his feet. Everyone congratulated me as I pushed the money into the depths of my bag. Everyone knew I was from a place called Bare-klee. Everyone knew I was not married. We'd been through something important together. I waved. They did the same. *Ciao ciao ciao.*

Primo took my elbow. "*Ehh*, that was a breeze. I've seen it take two to three hours. Hold your purse close in front of you with both hands." His eyes darted around as he steered me out of the building and briskly back to the bus stop. He wouldn't hear of only seeing me safely onto the bus. He ushered me all the way back to Maia's. When we passed the Politeama he mentioned that he and his friends sometimes received free tickets from an acquaintance who worked in the box office, with the instructions to enjoy the arias and clap loudly. Wishing me "*Buon viaggio*," he turned right around on his heel to catch the bus one more time today.

A young woman in blue jeans, denim jacket and Team-Bear-Lahnnd shoes was waiting at the elevator. "*Buona Sera*. A university professor lives in this building. Do you happen to know which floor?"

"There's a Political Science professor on the fourth."

"I have some books to return to him."

We entered the lift together. Her Nina Ricci perfume filled the available space.

"I'll get off with you and show you which apartment." We rang his bell to no avail so she left the stack of books at the door. "There's a chance he might be feeding the cats in the lot downstairs. I'll ride back with you to show you." But he was not to be seen.

"Thank you, *signora. Addio.*"

"*Addio, signorina.*"

The elevator was filled with her lingering scent. When I let myself in Maia was asleep in her armchair, feet propped up on the ottoman, glasses slid down, the *Giornale* in her lap. I tiptoed through the living room and let myself out onto the terrace. I'd be in the provinces starting tomorrow. Jeez, including Agrigento. It's got to have changed since then, I told the skyline of Palermo. You did.

"Everything set for your trip now?" Maia joined me at the ledge.

"Everything." I leaned over for a parting glimpse of my intended. He wasn't down there. I had hoped for one more green-eyed dose before leaving tomorrow.

"I'm so glad you will see more of the island again."

"Me too."

Chapter XIX

Bilingual Bus Ride

"Do not neglect to go see the Bronzes in Reggio di Calabria. I know it's not part of the planned itinerary, but you have one extra day on the Greek side of the island. You won't be disappointed, I promise you." Maia embraced me. "The Philosopher too, who's in the same room. Make sure you pay attention to him."

"Will do. *Arrivederci!*" I climbed the steps of the much-too-fancy, oversized Mercedes bus with smoked-glass windows, nodded hello to my fellow voyagers and continued straight back to the rear. The Pullman gunned westward out of the city with Germanic efficiency.

"Upon your left please to notice underneath the mountain the city of Alcamo," our young guide Carla informed us over a crackly address system. "Renowned for its excellent white wines and productive agriculture."

"And for the brave family Viola," I added, my voice drowned out by the noisy engine vibrating under the seat. A pang hit of once again bypassing her town. She was up there somewhere in the ample spread of white buildings. She had agreed to talk on Wednesday, only five days from today. What a miracle.

"Please to notice upon our left the Santuario della Madonna and the many people climbing to the shrine of Our Lady." Hundreds coursed up a hillside carrying something white in their hands. "They are giving their thanks and to make prayers on this Day of Liberation by the Allied Forces."

We breezed to a nearby stop. "Now, Greek temples aren't found only in Greece as you will see. Some describe Segesta as the best preserved temple anywhere, though it was never completed, for motives which remain unknown." Forty cameras began to click. "When you hear this claxon," she signaled to the driver who tapped out his personalized horn code, "your time is completed, so please to return then at once."

Carla verbally directed us up the path; she stayed on the bus. Slow bumblebees weighed down with yellow pollen bump-landed onto red poppies, burgundy sweet peas, violet thistles and lupines. Their weight pulled the flowers over, but that didn't stop them from getting what they needed at each bloom. The sunlight refracted on their fuzzy bodies in glints of rainbow iridescence. The sun seemed to power them.

We climbed the giant steps of the temple and slipped through the limestone columns. No ceiling at all, just a classic frame for the frisky clouds that bopped along overhead. One black bird with fine white wingtips and shoulders flitted between the pocked colonnades and out where the roof had never been; then a whole fleet of white-and-blacks rose and dove. The bees floated around at blimp speed. Their muffled buzzing and the delicate breeze felt like gifts. The temple couldn't be more Greek. Our driver honked. Ah well, we'd sort of had enough time. Back to the Pullman.

We entered a tunnel and came to a sudden halt inside because the roof of the bus had gotten wedged into the ceiling. By the light of the coach's lime-fluorescent bulbs, our driver tugged at his flat steering wheel. The engine under my loins roared with effort.

"Please to move yourselves upon the right side," Carla motioned, her copper hair glinting under the greenish lamp. "Please everyone, to assist." We did. "Now everyone to lean.

Please to jump at count of three: *Uno, Due, Tre.*" We jumped. With a grinding, furious acceleration, the driver pulled loose, we cheered and drove out into the light.

The spring morning carried us, suspended, through tinted fields. Geraniums, jasmine, wild *finocchio* spilled from stone walls onto the road. Stripes of undiluted new green clover flickered between the grapevine rows. Hills of lavender quivered in the fresh lemony sunshine. Flowering peach and almond trees, agave and prickly pear, the citrus groves that Carla called "the premier crop of this island" and sentinel cypresses: these all made me bounce with giddiness on top of the mighty motor.

"Slow down," someone called out. "Not so fast. It's too beautiful. Can we enjoy it please, if it's all the same to you?"

Carla either didn't hear the question or ignored it. "Now, the name Selinunte comes from an ancient Greek word Selinon, meaning wild celery. We believe earthquakes broke down the temples you will shortly see. Please to take twenty-five minutes for walking, and do enjoy the areas of greatest interest. Now I will silence myself. Please to begin." An enormous, quiet plain of ruins lay splayed before us.

"What?" a Chicagoan turned to her husband. "To cover all this ground on our own? They've gotta be joking."

"Seven temples—four near, three far—equals three minutes per temple not including running time," he calculated. "Let's get going."

We lurched out of the bus, hurtling towards the spilled city. My companions took off gamely in athletic shoes (American) or leather footwear (Italian), and me (the blend) in blue polka-dotted canvas. Shoulder-high wildflowers leaned into the narrow footpath, a red and yellow welcome. The bulbous faces of echinacea daisies looked like they were watching.

Cataclysm had shattered Selinunte out of existence. The whole thing was a jumble. I trotted as far as Temple C, nearly swallowed up by purple borage and yellow broom. Flocks of black and white birds winged around, and a definitely ribbed, celery-type plant poked through, resembling to scale an Ionic column. I climbed the fluted ribs of the nearest tipped pillar, and walked barefoot the length of one long groove. A purposeful ladybug proceeded in the same direction on the warm limestone.

"You're adorable," I told it.

The horn sounded.

"*Boh.*" I stayed put on the pillar until the tourists came galloping back from their race, winded and red-cheeked. One of them, a black-haired Roman, extended a hand to help me down.

We stopped for lunch at a seaport village. Americans were seated with Americans, Italians with Italians for ease of communication. I introduced myself to four retired nurses from Cincinnati, but there wasn't room at their table. Carla directed me to sit with Marge and Lloyd from the Midwest. Lloyd reached for the breadbasket.

"Now honey, if we touch that we'll be charged for it. The CIT manual and Michelin said so. Do we really want bread right now? Let's think this through."

"Leave the gun. Take the cannoli," Lloyd wheezed dramatically.

"Excuse me?"

"Honey, please. Don't get started. Natalie won't sit with us again if you do." She glanced at me.

The *piatto secondo* was composed of three fried orange fish with brilliant orange eyes to match their scales, gazing resignedly up at us. I could not eat something so cute and pushed the plate towards them. "All yours, Lloyd and Marge. I'm not that hungry."

After lunch, we were herded into the street, then waited near the shore while Carla and the driver attempted to turn the big Benz around at the edge of the village. Turquoise water slapped against the slim rocky beach where children squealed and fishermen hollered musically—Arabic inflected—back and forth. Half way to the horizon, past the combers, sprays of water were erupting.

"Say, is that the Mafia?" asked a hopeful American attired in a yachting-style jacket and cap.

"Where?" Lloyd craned his neck. "Where?"

The black-haired Roman turned to me. "Tell him it's fishing by dynamite. When you blow up the sea, the fish float to the surface. It's the lazy way to do it."

"Is it legal?"

"*Boh*, legal, illegal," he chortled, "they do it anyway. No police patrol out there. Or so I have read."

"He sleeps with the fishes," said Lloyd brightly.

Marge quickly pulled me aside. "My husband has been obsessed with *The Godfather* since it hit the screen. Please forgive him. He's been dreaming of Sicily for a decade and a half. Realizing this trip is one of the high points in his life."

"That's cool, but will you get to Corleone?"

"There's the rub. He was too wary of us striking out on our own with a rented car. He wants to get close, but not too close. It's more like the *idea* of Mafia. Do you know what I mean?"

"Yeah."

Summoned by the horn, we piled into the bus and picked up speed.

We passed turnoffs with the voluptuous names of hill towns—Salemi, Menfi—and of harbor towns—Sciacca, Eraclea Minoa, and Porto Empedocle. Minoans blown by eastern winds in pursuit of Hercules, the testosteronic, ego-driven, overly muscled He-man, rowing his own barque from Greece on one of his twelve macho labors; Empedocles—the great poet-philosopher-healer. Next time maybe, with a rental car.

Along the southern coast the sea glinted so brightly that it looked like milk. Carla alerted us to the birthplace of Luigi Pirandello in a village called Caos, then disconnected her microphone and sat down. We sped past his very small house on the edge of the sea, past the single, gusted pine tree where his ashes lay. The vast wrinkled skin of the Mediterranean beyond emphasized its isolation. Perfect for a writer.

"Stop!" the Roman cried. "We must see it. *Six Characters In Search of An Author. Henry the Fourth*! One of the finest Italian writers of this century, yet we don't even slow down in respect, let alone stop," he lamented. "And I have saved so long for this trip."

The bus driver heard his plea and made a turn so that we could drive slowly by the house again. Carla dozed through this maneuver.

"To think that he looked out upon that slanting tree and perhaps derived inspiration from it. How lonely the life of the writer whose words spread so far." The Roman had a sympathetic audience whose eyes remained locked on the poignant sight until the bus rolled on.

"Are you a writer?" I asked him.

"No, I am a reader. I have been reading all my life."

Carla had perked up. "Onward to the great Acropolis of Agrigento."

We were disgorged onto a hot pathway and hastily turned over to an elderly man wearing a straw hat, tank undershirt, bermuda shorts, socks and sandals, all white. He pointed theatrically with his cane to a tremendous gnarly-rooted tree.

"Welcome to Akragas, ancient Greek for Agrigento. It is said," he intoned in a smoky voice he could have blown rings with, "that this very olive was planted by the priestesses of Juno three thousand years ago. Ladies and gentlemen, the grand tree still bears fruit."

"Can we taste 'em?" Lloyd spoke up in a spontaneous departure from his Godfather gig.

"You Americans always ask the same question," the man wagged his finger. "Apparently you remain ignorant of the fact that they are out of season, but even if they were in, you would regret putting one in your mouth, for the fruit straight off the branch is very bitter. *Amarissimo.* Olives must be cured properly over time. One must have patience. Take note, *Americani.* Let us begin. I have a great deal to show you."

He limped up the incline to Juno's temple, paused to convert his cane to a fold-down seat, fanned himself with the hat, and lectured, leaving no fallen capital or piece of pediment unexamined. Seduced by his noble baritone, Marge and I hovered close and listened to him reconstruct the many missing parts of Juno's special sanctum in both languages.

"He's a juicy kind of scholar," Marge said to me.

"Juicy?" He had overheard. "What is juicy? This term I do not know."

"It means alive, *vivace*, full of color, not dry. It's a compliment, sir."

"*Signorina*, are you from the Kingdom United?"

"From the States United."

"You speak your Italian well."

"Oh no, but let me tell you that your English, sir, is excellent."

"You flatter me. Perhaps I may call upon you to translate if the need arises?"

"Well," I demurred, "very unlikely, but I'll try."

"Excellent. Onward to the Temple of Concordia, people."

"I feel transported to another realm!" Marge rhapsodized while we clomped along the ancient avenue. "I feel like we're in Greece in Sicily! He's putting it all together for us. Carla sure could take a lesson from him."

"Yeah, he's good."

"Madam, let me clarify something." The guide had been listening. "This land *was* Greece—a key part of Magna Graecia. *Signorina*, will you make sure she understands this point? Tell her in English."

"You just did, sir, very clearly."

Marge was lapping up his personal care. "I love this guy!"

"Yeah, me too. Before him, I was getting ready to demand a refund and hitchhike home to Palermo."

"But you would have missed *this*! "

"Wow." An unbroken temple shimmered before us in the afternoon's white heat, a great presence. The fluted columns stood, in double rows, seared to their marrows by the sun. Ionic energy pulsed straight from them into my bones. I lost track of what our guide was saying. Something really big happened in this valley, and the pillars had kept the memory warm over a long dimension of time. This temple was telling the truth. Something about light and peace. Something about how to keep both peace and light. Something way beyond words and thoughts. An emotion.

The guide was finishing up at the Temple of Olympian Zeus, the largest Doric edifice ever known, whose stones had been erected by Carthaginian prisoners and shaken down over centuries by quakes. He explained that the huge figure of the giant—*Il Gigante*—lying stretched out along the ground was a reproduction of one of thirty-eight colossi, set between pillars, which had once shouldered the epistyle of the massive structure. The rest of the giants were no more—they'd been broken up and hauled away long ago. "Let me clarify that the one remaining giant, or *Telamon*, is safely preserved in our museum. I repeat, this is a copy."

"Honey, can you believe the size of this guy?" Marge raved to Lloyd. "To think he took up only one third the full height of the temple! The whole thing must have been absolutely immense."

"He's been hit by a thunderbolt," Lloyd replied.

The giant did look a little flattened.

"*Signorina?*"

"Yes, *dimmi*," I smiled. At your service.

"I need your help on a certain point." The Americans clustered close. "Do you know what a *'fallo'* is?"

Startled, I nodded.

"Would you be so kind as to translate for your countrymen and countrywomen please?" He smirked.

I stared at him. Had he really never learned the word? "Phallus, folks."

"Thank you," he bowed. "I wasn't sure if you would know. You're not married, am I correct? Since you wear no wedding ring," he simpered, "I thought you might not be familiar."

"Are you kidding? Don't worry your pretty little head, sir. I'm well acquainted with the ubiquitous organ."

The group tittered nervously.

"But if you really want to impress with your command of American English, you can't do better than 'weenie'."

One of the nurses said, "Oh for Pete's sake, it's only anatomy."

"Right. Exactly. It's the *way* he asked. He wanted to put me on the spot in front of all of you. He was smirking."

"What is smirk?" he smirked.

I headed down to the giant's feet and kicked at the gravel. Maybe I should have laughed off his pointed goading, but I couldn't. Why I let the sexy travel agent and Maia talk me into this tour I did not know. If only I had just pulled a Trinacrian-Medusa and flown, run, slithered or crawled to Alcamo by myself, I could have absorbed Franca's environs for three whole days. I could have sprung for a taxi. What a dope I was.

"Natalie," Marge approached, "he sent me over to bring you back. I think he feels bad."

"I don't care. He *should* feel bad. I've lost interest. I'm jogging down the path to check out the Sanctuary of the Chthonic

Deities, whoever they are. Wanna come?" And thanks to an extra brochure that the Titian beauty had included in my CIT itinerary packet, we pieced together that the excavated shrines to early Earth Goddesses—one circular, one square—yielded hundreds of buried votive female figurines the size of hands, whose archeological significance had not yet been determined.

As briskly as the guide could hobble, we were returned to the parking lot. "*Arrivederla, signorina*. The pleasure has been mine," he bowed. "Enjoy your trip."

I bowed back with no words. It certainly hasn't been mine. A disappointing, disillusioning encounter. We loaded onto the bus and coasted out of the park, passing our guide tottering down the road, relying heavily on his cane. He had exhausted himself, it seemed. I looked back through the rear window. An undulating heat mirage swallowed him up.

In order of importance we were dropped off at our accommodations—first class to a fancy hotel splashed with bougainvillea; second class to the Hotel Jolly, a moderne box plunked in the middle of a green field. As I made my way down the aisle, two girls remaining on the bus with other Italians seemed flabbergasted: "You're not third class?"

"It's an unfortunate error made by the travel agency," I lied, feeling guilty.

At the Jolly, a blue pool sloshed with swimmers, ringed by cypresses and truly tanned sun-worshippers in bikinis. Beyond the valley soon to dry up, I saw the city where the too short, too clinging, too pink sundress worn by an American teenager that summer of the moonwalk had whipped up the population in the piazza. The suddenness with which they fell upon her like a swarm of angry bees, their screeching and outrage at her bare arms. Then deliverance by the Black Hand. It had all happened just up there.

The cavernous dining room brimmed with two hundred German conventioneers reflected in the mirrored walls *ein*, *zwei, dri, fir, fünft* times. I wandered back to my room after the steam table meal and fiddled with the television knobs. I checked out the little refrigerator, a chilled altar to international business expense accounts and second-class wallets aspiring to first, stocked with Galliano, Campari, Cynar, Stolichnaya, Johnny Walker Black and three-sided bars of dark Toblerone chocolate. I stepped out onto a shallow balcony to watch the sun drop into the hills.

Swallows were swarming the pool now that the people had left, skimming the surface, dipping their beaks in the water and swooping up into the balconies of the hotel to add mud to their nests. The inner corner of my balcony overhang had its very own mud house and one hard-working swallow. Back and forth without rest they all flew until dusk closed in. The pool was still illumined, perfect for an evening dip.

I stepped into the swimsuit. But first, Evelyn's package for Arcangela. At the front desk the concierge had no stamps, and informed me that though I could buy them in town at a *tabacchi* or a bar, it would be much wiser to bypass the post and make the delivery myself.

So it had come to this. I had to go up there, after all these years.

I asked her to call for a taxi. I rushed to my room, pulled a stretchy black widow dress over my swimsuit, took my wad of lire notes, put on the wedding ring, and filled the mini orange water pistol which I'd packed for unimaginable situations like this, just in case.

I held out the package for the cabdriver to read the address.

"Sure, not a problem." On this island there seemed to be one setting: racing speed. Whizzing past limestone *tufa* houses, he had me flying into his seatback each time he braked, and tipping over every time he turned a bend.

"No taxis allowed in the piazza. I'll leave you off here."

"But how will I find the address in the dark?"

"Check over there at the bar." He pointed to the far end of the large square.

I couldn't tell if this was the same piazza of the Black Hand or not. "Please, please do not abandon me."

"I'll be right here waiting with the meter running, keeping an eye out. In fact, I'll put the headlights on for you." He lit a cigarette.

"Promise?"

"I take good care of my clientele. Ask anyone."

Light streamed through the bar's plastic strip curtain. I tried to slide unnoticed through the green strands. Capped heads turned in my direction as the heavy dangles trailed over my shoulders and thwacked back into place. Chatter ceased. I approached the barman, who looked me over, from my shoes all the way up. The card game stopped.

"Good evening. An espresso please, decaffeinated if you have it."

"We have it." He tapped ground coffee into the holder and drew the lever down. The powerful hiss of steam made me jump. I knew I was being stared at. I put one foot up on the rail, and casually leaned an elbow on the counter. Too posed. I straightened and let my arms hang. Too regimental. I hid my hands in the pockets. One was wet from the leaking water pistol. Forty years ago Arcangela watched her daughter die in forbidden childbirth here. Nineteen years ago my family could not walk across the piazza, which might have been this one. Were these the men, or the relatives and sons of the men who had whistled sssss to alert everyone back then? I could not believe I had brought myself back to the city I'd vowed never to set foot in.

He slid a baby cup over. "*Senza caffeina.*"

"Thank you, sir." I poured sugar in and stirred the sludge around.

"Left-handed," he said.

"Yes, *mancino*," I answered. I tipped the demitasse with my pinkie lifted, and drained the hot syrup down, the way everyone drinks it. Ow. I asked for a glass of water. I really did not belong in this bar. The slaps of cards against a table top began again.

"Um, I'm trying to deliver something to a resident in the neighborhood." I handed over the package printed with Arcangela's name and address. "Can you direct me?" He glanced at the exuberantly scrawled American-style writing and then at me. "You are a *forestiere*. Where do you come from?"

"From faraway. From the USA. San Francisco."

"Are you related to her?" He wiped the already shining counter.

"No. A friend of mine in California is a cousin of her cousin. Do you know her, by any chance?"

He glanced over at the card players. These wayward photos that Evelyn pressed on me were entrusted to her for safekeeping in this town decades ago. Did some of them know the terrible story? "*Ehhh*," he replied, with the slightest shrug of his shoulder. Could mean yes, could mean no.

I polished off the sweetened sediment by scraping it with the weensy spoon.

"And so what do I owe you, sir?" An ornate gift box of Gianduia pralines illustrated with lacy Spanish fans was on display next to the cash register. "I'll take these *cioccolatini* also, please." I left the change he made and turned to leave. A buzz rose before I passed through the curtain.

"Who is she?" I heard someone ask.

The barman had trailed me through the strips. He raised his hand and pointed. "To the left of the corner building, as you face it," he said quietly.

"*Grazie*." I checked to make sure the cab was waiting with its lights on, then hurried along, though I did slow down at a restaurant glowing with light and filled with diners, wondering if it could possibly have been the place the Black Hand had taken us. I found myself stopping to read the menu, inviting after the oh so Jolly cafeteria plate of nude pasta. Down at the bottom were *Dolci* and *Gelati* Specials. This could have been the place. This could have been the piazza. Or it may not have. I wondered whether the Black Hand still ruled here, or if he had passed the baton to a new Doctor of Soap. I wondered if the women with their brooms were still around. I wondered if they'd be willing to talk to another woman in black, even if she was a foreigner. I wondered if we would have the kind of warm rapport Sicilians are so good at as long as they don't feel invaded or offended. I even wondered if Arcangela might have heard the hissing through her shutters, and seen our family trying to deal with the confrontation the summer of the moonwalk. If this was even the piazza.

I heard scuffling and spun around. Six or seven men from the bar had been following me, I now realized.

"*Ciao!*" I called out. "*Buona sera.*"

They did not answer. They simply stared. I shrugged to mask my fear and dismay, turned away and continued toward the house to the left of the corner building. I pulled the bell at the front door. A dog barked once. What if she wasn't home or did not answer? I couldn't just leave the package out here. I pulled the bell again. The men now stood behind me, though at a certain polite distance.

Faintly, through the thick door, I heard, "*Aspett', aspett', un'attimo,*" then a command, "*Stai zitto,*" be quiet, and then an eyehole in the door slid open. "*Chi è?*" rasped a muted voice.

I thought it might be a housekeeper. I leaned in close so the men couldn't hear every word. "Please excuse the disturbance. I have a delivery for the lady of the house."

"Who are you?"

"I'm an emissary, a courier, delivering an envelope from America."

"*Aspett'*." Locks slid back, the door eased, light poured out. A bent woman and a small, slender dog peered at me. She held the collar of the fawn-like creature which hyper-sniffed at her side. "I cannot see you well. I cannot hear you well either. Please speak up: who are you?"

It had to be Arcangela herself. My heart skipped a beat or two. "*Cara signora*, I do not mean to alarm you in any way tonight. I was asked to return some photographs to you, via your cousin Maria via Evelina Gualtiero in California, my close friend. She was told that you wanted them. Here they are."

The dog whimpered from way down in its compact torso. Its triangular ears stood up straight at the whispering of the men behind me, who maintained their distance.

She opened the door wider. "I've been waiting." Her voice sounded so brittle and dry. "Please come inside."

"Certainly, for a moment." I stepped into the vestibule and handed her the package.

Her hands looked arthritic. It took her quite a while to wriggle out a photo. I resisted the impulse to help her. This was her moment. She held the image inches from her face. "Ahh!" she let out a strangled cry and stroked it with her fingers.

My eyes filled, imagining her teenaged daughter bleeding to death upstairs so many years ago, and the desperate *fidanzato* Roberto crying and pounding on this door, and the neighbors hearing everything but having to pretend they didn't.

"They have come back to me at last. My darlings. They were to be married. They were to be husband and wife. They were to have a child."

I nodded, but didn't know if I should say anything. Wasn't it best to be discreet? Was I supposed to pretend I didn't know, just like everyone else had pretended that night and long afterwards? I wanted to be respectful. "Evelina who visited you many years ago said all the photos are here. She has also written you a letter, which you will find in the envelope."

The old dog watched me with concerned eyes the same toffee color as his coat.

"But you are an angel. What is your name?"

"Natalia."

"Whose daughter are you? Who are your family?" The hound started to lick the back of my hand. "Tell me who your mother is."

"My mother is Dora. Evelina's good friend."

"Do you have a daughter?"

"No I don't."

"A son?"

"No."

"Are you married?"

"I'm not."

The dog started to strain toward the sounds behind me. What did these men intend? They were close enough to have heard nearly everything. Maybe they knew about this woman, maybe not. Maybe they felt protective of her, or maybe they wanted a glimpse of the old lady, *la vecchietta*. Maybe *I* was the focus, stirring things up, and they, unofficially patrolling the piazza, the guardians of the square, were only concerned with making sure I did not cause a problem. Maybe they kept a watchful eye out for any neighbor here. Or did they have some absolute interest in this particular woman? It could have been innocent curiosity. I just did not know.

Arcangela seemed unaware that the group hovered behind me and I wasn't going to tell her. I wanted nothing to disturb this reunion. She deserved privacy. She might have been one of the last people alive to have had to bear the burden of the old mores around here, of having to make her fatal decision to protect her family's honor. A dilemma that I myself, born in a different era and place, would never have been thrust into. She brought up the tail-end of all that, and she was still here. I wondered how she had managed.

She lay the package on her stand and patted it. "You're sent from God to return my treasures to me," she said, taking my hands. "*O, che mani freddi!*" What cold hands you have!

I didn't realize. Cold from all the unknowns since the cab dropped me off at this benighted square. I could feel her bent fingers warming me up. "It's my complete pleasure to be able to bring them to you personally, *Signora* Arcangela." I saw a crystal of a tear appear in her eye and meander down her face. I could not cry in front of her. I stooped and petted the dog on his head, trying to control my emotion with everything I had.

"Come upstairs, have some tea with me."

I glanced over at the cab's diluted-yellow lights blinking at the far end of the piazza. Was he signalling that time was up? Here I was face-to-face with the real person, the real story, an embodiment of heartbreak beyond imagining, the true Sicilian tragedy, asking me in, while the men behind me monitored everything.

"I wish I could. I'm so very sorry, but I must catch a ride back to my hotel. These sweets are for you, with love from Evelina." I handed her the Gianduija praline box.

"I am so grateful to her."

"*Addio, Signora* Arcangela. *Buona Notte.*"

"I am so grateful to *you*. For being here. *Addio, tesoro, addio.* Bless you. Give a strong embrace to Evelina."

"Most definitely." I backed away waving, allowing the tears when I knew she couldn't see them.

Now for the men. "Excuse me." I brushed past them, angling towards where the cab had been flashing its lights. But where the hell had it gone? "As you may have seen," I called over my shoulder, superstrolling, with my voice cracking, "an envelope was hand-delivered. Did you want to ask me something about it?" Their shoes scraped the stones, the whole bunch in a pack shadowing me. What were they planning to do? I increased my superpace and they matched it. I really did not want to have to make a run for it. My dignity, after all. But finally, faintly, I could make out the cab in profile. "Well, good night then. My taxi is waiting for me."

A light hand on my arm startled me. "You didn't tell her who you really are," the man admonished. "You didn't tell her your last name."

"You're right!" I spun around, gasping at my breach of etiquette. The last thing I wanted to do was insult her. "I didn't think it was important. I just came to do someone a favor. To complete something."

He touched his cap. "You need to identify yourself, who your people are. Your father's name is Roberto, yes?"

"Oh no, not at all. It's not like that. I'm not related."

His face fell. "How disappointing. I so wished you were his daughter." The men surrounded me.

"Ahh. That's why you've been following?"

"Does your friend in California know where Roberto went?"

"She knew what happened to him here, but nothing more."

"There's never been a single word from him." The man's leather jacket gleamed in the street lamplight.

"How awful." I looked him in the eyes. "Not a one?"

"No one knew where he went. The United States? Argentina? Australia? Roberto was my good friend. It breaks me up to this day. Look at me, a grandfather already."

"Such a tragedy. To never hear, to wonder, to fear the worst . . . I am sorry."

He spread his hands and sighed, the gesture of Southern resignation. "After he left, his family emigrated too. They refused to remain here."

"I see. What a total loss."

"To all of us. He would have made such a good medical doctor for the neighborhood, after the war."

I had an idea. "*Senti*, I can have my friend back home make a copy of the engagement photo for you, if you'd like."

He looked up at the sky. Tears brimmed in his eyes. Then he looked at me and nodded silently. What an evening for weeping.

"All right. Do you have something to write with by any chance, a Biro? I didn't bring anything with me."

Someone produced a pen. The man spelled out his name and address which I wrote on my right palm in black ballpoint. We shook hands, then all the right hands of the group were extended to be shaken. My God. What a place. I checked my palm to make sure the information hadn't rubbed away.

"I should have shaken hands first, but it's still legible," I assured them.

They laughed politely, and the tension of our encounter gave way to the bond like the one long-separated blood relatives have. The whole entourage now accompanied me to the taxi.

"Everything taken care of, Miss?" The cabdriver held the door open. "Very sorry, but you took a long time and my battery was running down. I had to turn the lights off."

"All done. Good night, gentlemen."

The group called out "*Buon Viaggio*," patted the cab roof, and we sped out of town and down to the valley. I memorized the name and address of Roberto's friend. Back at the Jolly, I went straight to the pool, pulled off the dress and jumped into the deep end.

So the task was completed. After my swim, the ink was still readable on my palm. I copied it into a notebook. I switched the television on, and found a documentary about the great Italian author, Alberto Moravia. What he could do with a story like this! I broke open the seal on a junior Cynar and toasted both Arcangela and Evelyn. The artichoke liqueur was almost undrinkable, murky, sweetened and ultra-bitter, really more of a medicine than anything to savor. A *digestivo*, an *aperitivo*, but mostly for right now, a dram. I capped the little bottle for when I really needed it, shoved it in my purse and fell across the bed.

Chapter XX

Onward

O n the road early. Half-awake, I greeted Lloyd and Marge, who had planted themselves in the front seat, and proceeded to the rear of the bus, where I slumped. Carla entreated us to admire the miles of citrus orchards along the coast. The glossy green leaves caught the sunlight. Her hypnotic mantra *'agrumi, agrumi'* over the loudspeaker lulled me into half-sleep. We veered inland toward the central hills, bound this morning for Piazza Armerina, called by some the greatest tiled Roman floor ever unearthed.

"Now Mussolini ordered to plant the many eucalypticuses lining the roads. He believed the tree not to need water and thus planned a forest over the island. Perhaps you will agree how this particular project of *Il Duce* did not make a big success." Birds flashed through the branches of the squat, misshapen trees.

"None of his projects made a success!" retorted the Roman. He received a burst of applause.

Three of the nurses from Cincinnati came up the aisle toward me with a favor to ask. They couldn't follow half of Carla's English, between her accent and her grammatical errors.

"I mean, do we have to hear her butcher our language at every turn? I mean, 'eucalypticuses'? Really? It's almost funny. I have to laugh."

One of her friends mimed holding her ears, while the third asked, "Shall I bother to go tell her this time that she's not saying it right?"

Her friends just shook their heads. They all turned to me and pleaded, would I go explain to her what a hard time they were having? Would I be willing to correct her when I heard mistakes? I suggested they hound her mercilessly; if she pretended not to understand their complaint I would translate it for her. After the phallus fiasco at the temples yesterday I had had it with the role of go-between.

I felt in my coat pocket—still damp from the faulty water pistol—for a postcard and a pen compliments of Jolly, and wrote:

Dearest Ev, Photos unexpectedly hand-delivered to Arcangela—tearful but appreciative & still hanging in there. Her faithful companion a bow-wow dell'Etna. I want one! Please make another copy of engagement picture for an old friend of Roberto. Will explain.

Yours XOXO N

If I'd had more room I would have written how not ending up mailing the package from Palermo gave me this unexpected chance to have a reckoning with Agrigento, which I would never have attempted otherwise. *That* particular go-between assignment had succeeded.

The sign read *Villa Imperiale di Casale*. Extruded from the bus, we were hurried along a stone pathway into a glen of vineyards and olive trees. Rectangles of Plexiglas on the ground covered excavated pits, half-buried rooms still shallowly breathing moisture. We passed through the atrium portals of the villa, a membrane: at our feet a Roman world appeared, begat of colored stones brought from the far frontiers of the ancient empire, mortared to the ground, bit by square bit.

"Master tilers of Arabic Africa and Rome devised this rich polychrome palette." Carla was functioning as a guide this morning and her new repeat term was *"policromia"*—multi-colored.

A yellow-robed emperor raised his hand in greeting. Enter, he beckoned, looking up at us. Coptic-eyed minions offered towels and pillows and ointments for the baths to be taken in either the Frigidarium or Tepidarium or Calidarium, as you pleased. We did not tread on these treasures, but on the metal platforms suspended over them, gazing down on the continuous stone carpet that flowed room to room without thresholds.

A zoo stretched ahead in the Great Corridor; all the known animals and many imaginary ones—feathered griffins and phoenixes—on the move. Roped rhinos and bridled tigers and tethered, bucking bulls, oh my. At their sides, in tunics, keepers guided them, all migrating in the same direction, to the city where all roads led? For the benefit of Roman citizenry. Four high-stepping horses pulled a chariot to that great center of the world.

Hunting scenes unfolded. Spears thrust into the lion's heart. Wild boar spilling mosaic blood. Oxen yoked. Stags herded into a mesh trap. A netted boar borne upside-down between two hunters, a dog snapping at his forehead, looked distraught, poor beast, and still somewhat alive—his eye wide open while his fate closes in. Hare carried by the hind feet. One man grappling a bird as big as he. Another gripping an antelope by the horns, steering it up the gangplank of a sea vessel. The animal kingdom captured for Roman glory to be paraded at the Circus Maximus. Yet prey occasionally turned on predator: a griffin guarding a caged and worried man between its wide paws and a speared lion pouncing on a soldier.

And so, suddenly out of the quiet admiration we'd been enjoying, did screaming school kids overtake our tour from behind, pouncing on us. Within seconds navy-sweatered legions of them jammed the narrow catwalks. Carla shouted and pointed for us to move to the side. Impossible. I glimpsed Lloyd trying to direct the swarm, his voice buried in the roaring flash flood dressed in uniform. Kids shoved on, whooping the battle cry of youth triumphant. I got hold of the metal rail by one hand before my espadrilles lifted off the grating. The walkway swayed, threatening to collapse and spill us all into the hunt. They were having a blast squashing themselves together in a joyous adolescent swoon. We stayed pinned to the rails for who knows how long until, just as quickly as it came, the wild, gleeful child-wave surged forward and carried us along with it right out the exit gate. It was a five-ticket, deafening ride.

"Has anyone been hurt?" Carla looked us over anxiously.

"I lost my lens cap."

"What in God's name is wrong with these Italian teen-agers?" The nautically dressed lawyer smoothed his ascot and repositioned his cap. His wife shook her head and checked her quilted Chanel purse.

The protest started. "What about the Bikini Girls?"

"We didn't see them."

Carla fretted, studied her notes, looked at her watch. "Only four minutes left."

"But we paid good money to come all this way. We want to see the Bikini Room and we want to see the Erotic Cubicle!"

"Bikini, Carla, Bikini!"

"I do apologize," she held up the orange card that we were expected to follow, lemming-like. "We've lost our allotted time. The restaurant demands us to eat lunch now. I am so very sorry."

"Oh hell's bells," Marge fumed. She and Lloyd tried to reenter the rotating gate, but the seated guard would not consider it.

"*Senso unico*," he barked flatly.

"What did he say?"

"That it's one way."

He showed us that he could not unlock the contraption.

"But we were forced out." Lloyd pulled himself up to his full midwestern height and loomed over the bored young man. "Do you know who I am? I'm Moe Green."

"Natalie," Marge pushed me in front of her, "you tell him in Italian."

That he's Moe Green? "Sir, you don't know what just happened to us. We were accosted by that mob of kids, nearly trampled and then we were forced out, exited against our will. We didn't get to see the Bikini Girls!"

He counseled us to go around to the front and try to enter again. We three took off. Our defeated fellows were already trailing the orange card back down the road toward the restaurant. We trotted past the school buses loading up their hysterical cargoes, took a left and slithered in behind a French group just entering the atrium. This time the sounds of the fountain plinking in the central courtyard and the refined whispers of well-heeled Parisians were all we heard inside the villa. *Ç'est magnifique, ça! Ç'est si jolie.*

Imagining this place at dusk, or better, by moonlight, with the scent of grass drifting from the low hills and the murmur of lost Romans rising from beneath, I thought about going AWOL. Marge and Lloyd could return to the tour if they wanted, and the bus could go without me; locked in for the night, I'd wander from room to room, tickle a tiger, rest on a bench, bathe in the tiled spa waters, lie down on a mosaic towel, then tour the whole place over again without shoes to feel the mosaics underfoot.

Marge and Lloyd had drifted out of the Peristyle. I raced after them towards the missed rooms. We'd only seen a fraction! Chamber after chamber of sporting children playing with birds and gathering flowers and fruits. Cupids hauling a fishnet through zigzag waves out of which leapt dolphins with eyebrows—one big fun sea-life bash. Then the mythological scenes: Orpheus enchanting the animals, or was it the other way around? A gorgeous blue woman whose hair radiated in coils, cradled an elephant tusk in one arm and a tree trunk in the other. She held court with a baby elephant and a tigress bowing at her feet like favored pets, and a phoenix in a flaming nest admiring her big bold beauty. Thick gold gleamed around her neck.

"Who is *she*?" Lloyd and I asked at the same time.

"She," Marge read from her CIT brochure, a special gift from Carla, "is Sheba, Queen of Sheba, and no slouch in the flesh department, either."

The ten bikini girls were not lounging around deepening their tans. They were athletes playing ball, clasping dumb-bells, racing and throwing the discus. One was crowned with a laurel victory wreath. The two-piece bathing suits were strapless—very fifties-style—but the bodies themselves were oddly proportioned, with ultra long torsos and shortened legs. Had the mosaicists never seen women without veils?

Here was my main man Ulysses, with a smirk, getting the Cyclops blotto on a bowlful of homemade wine. The hulking giant had three eyes instead of one but still couldn't see the trick being played on him, maybe because all three eyes looked crossed.

Onward to the "erotic scene cubicle," which was framed within a perfect garland—yet quite faint after the build-up we'd been given, we all agreed. A woman and man embraced, a fruit basket balanced on her hip. Her garment, loosened down her back, revealed buttocks like a ripe winter pear.

"Where have you been?" our tour mates demanded envi-ously as they made room for us on the bench at the end of the long banquet table.

"Searching for the lens-cap." Lloyd plunked it on the tablecloth.

"Seeing what we came to see," Marge answered.

"Bathing in art," I added.

"We didn't save you much pasta." The family-style stainless steel bowl was sent toward us.

"You shove in all your sausages and your meatballs," was Lloyd's answer. Marge rolled her eyes, but he made me laugh with his amazingly quick and appropriate Godfather quote.

Sometime in the afternoon our bus pierced Siracusa's outer clutter and confusion, and set us second-classers down at the Grand Hotel Villa Politi for the night. A smiling, always-pre-occupied Carla handed out small paper slips:

WARNING. Several bag snatching incidents recently took place all over the town. Our guests are warned TO BE CAREFUL.

I parted the gauze curtain in my somber nineteenth-century room. Below, a ledge crowned with bougainvillea and tufted with greenery led to caverns that descended into a deep pit. I lifted the receiver of a heavy black phone from World War II with a thick, straight, cloth-covered cord.

"*Pronto*, front desk."

"Could you tell me about these caves on the grounds?"

"They are limestone quarries."

"They're not catacombs, are they?"

"No, but seven thousand Athenian prisoners were held down there until they starved to death in 413 BC."

"Thank you." Yikes. Fill the orange gun, leave valuables and purse in the hotel safe and get the hell out of here.

The sun shone high. I crossed a broad intersection where cars madly circled a monument to those lost at war. Men huddled at the base throwing cards. One spotted me and nudged the others.

"*Salve,*" I called out. "Greek Theatre this way?" They nodded and waved me on. I must have covered about half a mile without finding anyone to ask more directions from, when a young man came toward me, squinting against the blinding late afternoon light. Or was he scowling? I steadied the water pistol inside the pocket, just in case . . . "Excuse me, which way to the Greek Theatre, please?"

His answer was an elbow slammed into my upper arm full force. I stumbled, the breath shoved out, the water pistol emptied into my jacket. He kept going, his shadow trailing him. Why, I swallowed. Why? Why did you do that to me? I stood there swaying, unable to move. Someone tugged at my shoulder. I flinched.

"*Venga, venga,*" an old lady gestured. "Come along with me."

She took hold of my other arm and walked me into a church. She pointed to a statue of the Madonna, patted me on the back, then joined the other old women kneeling in the front. They looked like bats in a fold of a safe cave, their heads black-wrapped, shoulders black-furled. All the old ladies of the south in perpetual mourning did not notice me plastered against the back as they droned:

> *Ave Maria piena di grazie*
> *Sei benedetta fra le donne*
> *Benedetta il frutto del tuo seno Gesù*
> *Santa Maria madre di Dio*
> *Prega per noi peccatori*
> *Adesso e nell'ora*
> *Della nostra morte.*

Pray for us sinners now and in the hour of our death. Sequestered from the world just outside the walls, they were pleading endlessly for redemption and safety on its behalf. Pressed down with gravity, they chanted directly to the Holy Mother

Full of Grace. If not Her, who? Daily they brought the weight they had borne for the length of their long lives to church and laid it at the feet of the Queen of Heaven. Daily they petitioned for mercy while the world proceeded outside with its card games, its unemployment, its travails, its urge to combust. Its Elbow Jabbing. The serenity of the chapel soothed me a little bit, just enough to inch out the church door; the harsh sun bore down indifferently and the hostile young man was gone.

Having abandoned the search for the Greek Theatre, I heaved myself across the hotel bed face down, shoes on. The spread smelled of disinfectant and mustiness. I turned to my side and watched the walls, the color of drying blood, until the eight p.m. dinner service.

"Natalie!" Marge and Lloyd called from their table at the far end of the faded but graceful dining room that might have been a ballroom once. "Come join us."

I faked a cheery smile and sat down in my rumpled clothes. The scent from small vases of freesias with purple and saffron throats at each table tempted me out of my dark mood. I sniffed a flower, then sneezed.

"Try the veal. It's the best in the city."

"But I'm trying to eat vegetari . . . oh . . . oh yeah, good one, Lloyd. You got me there, haha, from Godfather One." I planned to remain in the company of my midwestern friends from here on in.

"Did you know that Winston Churchill used to vacation here?" Marge's hair was damp from a shower. She looked fresh and glowing in a dressy peach colored blouse and wrap-around travel skirt. "Guess what? We got the room he used to stay in. Imagine that? When we wake up tomorrow, we'll have the very same view of the sea that he had waking up. Picture him, right here having breakfast, smoking a cigar, reading the *London Times*. Isn't that the neatest thing?"

"Ah, lucky you!" I got the Starving Athenian Prisoner room.

"You look like you just woke up with a horse head in your bed."

"Yeah, I don't feel too good." My arm was still smarting.

"Honey, for crying out loud, she does not and don't say things like that, and especially not while we're eating. Natalie, we took the most marvelous walk to the Greek Theatre. You must go see it."

A waiter materialized and slid a bowl of *minestra* onto my placemat.

"Were people friendly?" my voice sounded like a frayed thread winding out of somebody else's throat.

"Gosh, yes, very helpful. We pointed on the map, did our best, and they walked us there. We love the Sicilians. They're so warm."

The waiter stood patiently at Lloyd's side.

"Natalie, tell me *again* how you say ice cream."

"*Gelato.*"

"*Por favor,* I mean *per favore, una gelato.*"

"*Che tipo?*" the waiter asked me.

"Lloyd, what flavor?"

"Chock-o-la-to."

"Make that two," Marge gave the victory sign.

"Are you enjoying your brief visit to our city?" the waiter asked me.

"Well . . ."

"Have you seen the Greek Theatre?"

"I didn't make it all the way there."

"Perhaps I might show it to you when I am off work this evening at twenty-two hundred hours thirty? It is very beautiful, illuminated by moonlight. It is very old and very splendid."

"Oh no, I don't think so." I displayed my Crackerjack ring.

"Well then, perhaps you would prefer to come dancing with me down at the Discoteca Fandango?"

"Thank you, but it's nearly time to turn in."

He bowed and disappeared.

"Did you get married this afternoon, Natalie?"

"And may their first child be a masculine child."

"It's just to throw people off."

"He's making you an offer you—"

"Honey, I've been waiting for this. I knew it was coming. Where's the camcorder? So now you finally get to say it. Well done, Lloyd. Let's order champagne. Are you happy?" She pinched her husband's cheek affectionately. Lloyd wore a satisfied look that no one, not even a super freaked-out tourist-target, could resist.

"But I do refuse, politely. I have to."

Ice cream arrived for them; for me a green salad dotted with black olives.

"But he seems harmless," Marge grabbed my arm.

"Ow, I got hurt."

"Oh, sorry."

"You didn't know. Someone elbowed me kinda hard a coupla hours ago."

"Need some aspirin?" She whipped out a flat metal travel pillbox and shook four pills into the bowl of my dessert spoon. "He's not half-bad looking. Go enjoy yourself at the amphitheatre. Take a chance. You're on vacation. What's wrong with a little flirting? Italy is the world capital of romance. Do it while you can. I would. You're an attractive woman. He's cute as can be."

"He seems sincere enough, but I can't know." I swallowed two aspirin, and put the other two into my pocket.

"What harm could come of it?"

I shook my head. She was traveling couple class, I was traveling single female class. We were in the same hotel, same tour, different universes.

"Too risky. If you'll both excuse me, I'm taking this salad and a stalk of freesia to my room now. I have a hot date with seven thousand dead Athenians."

"What do you mean, dear? What are you talking about?"

"Never mind, a private joke. See you bright and early tomorrow."

Chapter XXI

Wet Scirocco

And so the next morning it proceeded, our tour. We were handed over to the local Siracusan guide who mumbled in both languages equally. He didn't respond when asked to speak more slowly and clearly. He cared a great deal that his bow tie was straight and that his suspenders didn't slip, leaving one pant leg longer than the other; continually readjusted, they did not hold. A caricature of a character in search of symmetry who had no business being employed by CIT.

Beautiful Greek theatre? Finally. Roman amphitheatre? Check. Sprinting its egg-shaped length in one minute, we paused to peer into the melancholy gladiators' pit. Dionysius' Ear, the tall, cool cavern with acoustics known to convey whispers in brilliant clarity for hundreds of feet? Some ancient named Dioscuros wrote about how a tyrannical Emperor So and So eavesdropped on the political prisoners kept inside and thus squelched rebellion. We were allotted two whispered words each, three seconds to listen for their echo, and herded out. By ten, the mercury had expanded to 35 degrees Centigrade, and a widower walked right up to me on the street and asked for my hand in marriage since he always had dreamed of seeing America before his earthly days ended.

Beat the Clock had us trotting along the streets towards the Ortygia, the promontory of ancient Siracusa. He halted at a lovely fountain of Arethusa who was, word spread through the group because we couldn't hear him, some very exalted handmaiden or priestess to Diana. The spouting fresh water apparently traveled underground from some central inland lake whose name no one could make out, but also, the ancients believed, from some river in Greece, a physically impossible feat but an intriguing myth. Wild papyrus plants flourished in the bubbling water, as did glinting silvery fish. We requested a minute in front of this rippling oasis where Virgil, Ovid and Shelley had once taken breathers and notes, but our guide pivoted on his heel and took off.

"He must let us draw the water from the well," panted Lloyd dejectedly.

"Someone grab that man by the suspenders and don't let go," barked the nautically dressed lawyer, striding off after him. Everyone loping along wanted to kill him. We teemed with solidarity, all three classes, cursing and puffing to keep up.

We chased him into the *Duomo*, cool as a wine cellar and dark enough that we bunched up on top of each other. The interior was slow to reveal itself, like a darkroom photo image emerging in its bath, and what a gift. A Greek temple to Athena had been reborn as a Christian church by walling in the spaces between the Doric columns. Iron grillwork like black lace filled the arches, added in some later century. This surprise, this brilliant place cast a spell over our vexed group. The two Italian girls lit a candle in a side chapel the color of spun honey, then knelt on the inlaid floor and prayed. Lloyd was inspired to tally the number of candelabras that hung like queenly pendants. Maybe our guide's mad dash had been intended to provide us as many minutes inside this sanctum of three thousand years as could be borrowed from the itinerary; if so, he was forgiven. He had deposited us inside peaceable walls. The cathedral's stone acoustics swallowed up most of his few words but this fact I caught: the Greeks had built upon a site already sacred to earlier people. Religions and ages were united here, a monument to continuity.

"Thirty centuries," Marge raised her palms. "It makes my heart ache, it's so glorious, and I'm not religious, I'm Unitarian. Think of the masons and ironsmiths," her voice caught, "and sculptors and all the ones who did the grunt work who over the span of time gave their highest best to this *Duomo*, for people in the future they would never know. They left it to us. They wanted us to understand."

"And we do."

Ecstasus interruptus: our pal was already departing through the splendid Baroque portal. We poured out into the sunshine after him, but he had vanished without saying goodbye. Carla was over on the shady side of the piazza, holding up the stupid little orange card. The grumbling recommenced. Even the long-suffering quartet of Cincinnatians was up in arms. "We feel cheated by CIT, and that's a pun, but we mean it!"

Mutiny! Carla was pelted with complaints as our group, cruelly yanked away from magnificence, tromped back to the bus. She nodded, distracted. She had heard it all before. "If you had signed up for the weeklong package, you could have stayed inside longer. I regret that there's never enough time on tour to savor our unique heritage," she said with fleeting sympathy. She conducted a head count as we entered the idling bus. I plunked down with Marge in the front row, pissed.

"Two Americans are missing," Carla whispered to the driver.

"I'll never in my life be able to duplicate what I felt in that place," Marge teared up.

I stood. "Well then let's run back there right now."

"OK, let's!"

"Ladies, where are you going?" the bus driver called out.

"If we see the missing people we'll turn back. We don't want to just sit here." We trotted the distance and stood in the portal again.

"Yes," Marge sighed, "Yes! I'm drinking it all in. My eyes are cameras. I'm absorbing this forever."

I said nothing, not wanting to ruin the spell, the mood in the air.

When we returned to the bus, we joined the group which grew more and more distraught each minute given up at the cathedral, as a half hour more ticked by. Carla paced. The bus driver stood outside smoking. When the missing duo showed up, they claimed to have been separated from the group in the confusion of the Ortygia, yet they carried bulging plastic shopping bags imprinted *Enchanting Memories Of Siracusa*. No one would look at or talk to them.

"Don't tell me you're innocent because it insults my intelligence," Lloyd announced loudly from the front seat. I heard him from the rear of the bus.

Nearing the outskirts of the city, Carla may have been bribed to stop at a bank so that one of the rich Americans (ruling class alive and well after all) who had spent all his cash, could exchange more traveler's checks. We waited, burning diesel, for three-quarters of an hour. I funneled my fury into writing postcards.

"If it were clear we would to see Mount Etna, Europe's tallest and most active volcano," Carla prattled. Dimpled clouds concealed the summit. "Her mouth was believed to be the entrance to the Inferno, to the underworld. On a happier notation, a thousand years ago, the very first ice creams—*gelati*— were made by the Arabs. They had previously introduced the crop of the sugar cane to the island. When they scaled to the top of the peak to collect ice and carry it all the way down to mix with the beautiful fruits of our island, *gelato* was born."

A vast emerald slope swept down to the Ionian Sea. As we skimmed along Etna's flank the color simply deepened. She was pure Sicilian power, that mountain, the immense geological fact, the primal goddess who with one lava hiccup could wipe out entire villages. Human beings were zilch to her. Was she spitting and hissing up there? We couldn't see.

The green idyll ended when the smokestacks appeared, piling yellow-black folds of pollution into the low-hanging cloud. A whole petrochemical city of tanks, piping and valves filled our scenic windows. I worked my way up the aisle. Two of the nurses distracted themselves with a magnetized miniature chess game. Marge and Lloyd stared dully out the window. I leaned over their seat backs. "Can you believe this refinery?"

Marge shuddered. "Sort of Rube Goldberg, I'd say, minus any humor."

For a minute Lloyd was quoteless. Finally he came up with, "It's only business, Sonny, nothing personal."

I gave them a meaningful look. "Mafia. That's all I can say."

"But," Marge's eyes widened, "we've asked Carla repeatedly and she says there's no such thing anymore."

"Ha," I snorted, "I'm afraid so."

Carla stirred from a catnap in her seat across the aisle. "*Signorina* Galli, please to take your seat. Our rules require all passengers to sit always when the Pullman is in motion."

"Sure, Carla, *subito*." I returned to the rear. The endless monster thing stretched on. Poor Sicily. I lay across the length of the back seat, covered my eyes with my arm and let out a howl that probably no one heard.

"Are you noticing the unique black lava rock used in recent construction? Are you wondering why? Because throughout history, magma has flowed all the way down to Catania, bringing building materials directly, courtesy of many eruptions." We plowed through bleak, black blocks of housing. Everywhere everything was black, from the sky to the shadows, until we penetrated the eighteenth-century center of the city—stately, light-colored and full of domes.

"Please to notice the fountain. Please also, the black lava elephant and the significant Egyptian obelisk on his small back. The little proud animal symbolizes Catania's noble tie to Africa. The animal may be prehistoric, if not Roman." The creature with tusks like curved icicles thrust his long trunk forward. I blew him a kiss. We blasted out of the center of the old town.

The fog thickened as our bus strained to climb the hill to Taormina. None of the famous panoramas of enchanting villas and the infinite Ionian horizon could be seen. We pulled into a small square.

"Galli, Natalia, your Mini Tour concludes here. Please to move forward at this time."

"You're leaving so soon?" The nurses looked up from their game boards.

"Bye bye." I squeezed along the aisle, shaking hands.

Marge pressed a slip of paper into my palm. "If you ever come to Chicago."

"Thank you, of course, if I do." We hugged.

"*Ciao*, Natalie, *ciao*."

"Any parting advice, Lloyd?"

"Watch out for the kids when you're backing out."

"Yes, always Godfather," I bowed. "You are so committed! I kiss your hand, Godfather."

I watched the big bus maneuver out of the small terminal. Arms waved behind the smoky glass. I waved back, a tear falling. It was over.

Sale! Specials!—proclaimed signs in tourist shop windows—Further Reductions! I stood in front of a trinkets shop, suddenly free and on my own.

"Nobody buys during the *scirocco*," complained a shopkeeper in a heavy sweater. She nodded at the scads of German tourists filling the Corso Umberto.

"This you call a *scirocco*?"

"A humid one. It brings terrible grit which I must constantly sweep. You might consider buying a kerchief to cover your nose.

It's not healthy to breathe in the air, you know. Most tourists don't realize this, especially the Germans and Australians."

She had an inventory bursting with masks of comedy and tragedy made from papier-mâché, ceramic or metal, as big as shields suitable for hanging in one's baronial manor, and as compact as cufflinks. She had tragicomic key-rings, bottle openers, ashtrays, tee-shirts with smiling on the front and crying on the back, and sports bras with *commedia* on the right side and *tragedia* on the left. Sumptuous, gilded gift candy boxes were decorated with Venetian *Carnevale* and *Commedia dell'Arte* masks.

I fingered a tragic pen and comic pencil set with an added neutral eraser. Boothe would love this—I found myself missing him again and wishing I wasn't here alone. I thought of buying it to bring back to him, but dispatched that idea.

"Have some pure mountain water," the woman held a glass out to me. "Even though the day is cold, one should drink."

"It's sweet tasting. Thank you." I held up an intertwined blown-glass cruet set for oil and vinegar, with hand-painted stoppers, smiling and sad.

"Which would you put the vinegar in, *signora*?"

"*Beh*, vinegar can hardly be thought of as happy, and conversely, olive oil is no tragedy, but filling them is up to the individual customer. Those are handpainted by nuns. Shall I wrap the purchase for you?"

"Glass breaks so easily, and I have a long way to go. I need to get settled before I carry around anything more. You'll be open later?"

"Yes until 20:00 hours. Come back. Do come back. Perhaps you knit? I recommend these knitting needles—take a look at the faces on the knobs."

Yep. Embossed masks—grin, frown—on the tips.

"*Signora*, I never could learn how to knit, because I'm a *mancino* and everyone who tried to teach me was right-handed, but I can crochet. Do you sell crochet hooks?" I could make the Prof a fashionable, narrow tie, pale green to go with all his sweaters, in my spare time before Wednesday.

"Miss, how would a single item fit in with the theme of my shop?"

"I see your point. Is there a yarn store in town?"

"Yes, but she's closed until 1800 hours."

"I'll swing by later, then, if I have a chance. I hope the sun shows up for you."

Taormina had many designer shops. Elegance was everywhere. The Dolceria window displayed marzipan apricots, black figs, little watermelon slices, grape clusters, lemons, ripe red and green prickly pears, stalks of *finocchio* and baby eggplants. Plates of pasta with peas, ravioli, drumsticks, shish-kebabs and fried potatoes sat expectantly, luxuriantly, on veined marble shelves. Sweet almond paste, all thanks to the Arabic invasion a thousand years ago. Bless those sweet-toothed Moors!

I wandered the length of the Corso, but not being a shopper I grew tired of looking at things. Who needed more things? I needed an experience, a connection. Too early to find a *pensione*, even though the dark sky felt like dusk. Way too chilly for the beach, sadly. An arrow pointed to the *Santuario Madonna della Rocca*. I hid my suitcase behind a pink oleander hedge and took the stone steps upwards, hundreds of them. Prickly pear leaned in, waiting for a chance to impale anyone who strayed from the center of the steps. The climb chewed at my calves, but if I stopped, I would have wanted to quit, so I kept pumping left, right, left, right.

At the top of the stairs I couldn't see my hands, the *scirocco* mist was that close. What was I doing here alone and teetering on the side of a cliff trapped in a heavy gray cloud? A pointy-eared something with fur brushed against my bare ankle. I jumped backwards a full foot.

"Whoa!" I shrieked, spinning around. "Get away." I swung my satchel back and forth, my heart thumping. It could be a fox. Rabid. A rat. It could be a weasel, if the island had them. The steep plummet was right here hidden by the cloud. No railing. I didn't know which way to inch.

"Yeow!" The creature yelped.

"You better be only a cat," I yelled.

"Mwow."

The drizzle surged and then ebbed. "Rrrow." In the crotch of a tree a few feet away, a gaunt feline sniffed the air. Huge yellow eyes. Skinny, chewed-up tail dangling like an old cloth-covered electric cord.

"Oh phew, only a kitty. C'mere darling."

It wouldn't budge. I deliberately waded away from it through scratchy grass toward a stone wall to lean against. The animal watched me from the narrow trunk. His markings gave him a permanently stunned look. I dug out a dried pizza crust, broke it into pieces and threw them toward him. Belly on the ground, he crept forward. When he got up the nerve to nibble, his ribs pumped like bellows. The whole body shuddered when he swallowed. I broke open a package of crackers and made a trail. He followed it. By accident I crinkled the wrapper and he sprang backwards with fright. I didn't move again until he returned to the crumbs. This took minutes. When he'd eaten everything, he licked the dirt, darkening his muzzle, then rolled over, ecstatically rubbing his back on the ground and purring.

I heard a strange flapping of wings above—so did the cat, whose triangle ears swiveled. He stared up wide-eyed at the opaque shroud of *scirocco*. The mist wheeled around, closed in, but at an unexpected moment opened enough for me to see the height to which the stone wall rose. The cat's pupils tightened. He was looking straight up the wall, transfixed by whatever it was on top.

A hollow, poignant wingstroke slapped the air. Whoever it was had a giant span, the wave long and undulant from shoulder to feathertip. We were being watched, I sensed, but by what—a golden eagle? Did it come to grab the cat with its talons and fly off? This I would not allow. The cat crawled nearer to me. I had to protect him, but he wouldn't let me hold him. I stood over him, and we listened together, suspended in a long wait.

A funny nibbling sound began, as though the bird was preening and aligning the feathers on its wings. Then with long, deep slaps that made the vapor swirl, the winged thing flew off. I scrambled to follow the sound and the cat scampered with me, but the wingbeats died away quickly, like the last of an echo. I had a feeling that the bird was soaring way above, still observing us with keen vision.

I now stood next to a low building made of rough stone, its wrought iron gate padlocked. The sanctuary of our Lady of the Rock! Red and gold glass votives flickered inside. The now familiar exhalation of warmed wax—breath of the spirit—blended with the damp cool air. No one human seemed to be near. The kitty jumped confidently between the slender iron rails and pranced through the shrine as if he were at home, leaping up onto the altar, sniffing the lace cloth, rubbing against the Madonna's robes.

"I can't follow you in, little thing. Come back here." But I had no more food to lure him with. He left me like the great bird did. *Ciao ciao* you straggly meow. It was time to go back down, time to find a place to stay.

The town was packed with strolling Germans, and I kept half an eye out for the yarn place because the Professor was on my mind. When wedding bells rang in the Piazza Domenico, a crowd massed around the ancient horse fountain, anticipating the first glimpse of the white and black dyad in the church portal. A *gelato* vendor took advantage of the gathering to sell from his cart.

"Artichoke ice cream? You've got to be kidding. Of course I'll try it." What a cool way to eat a green vegetable. Two food groups in one. Bitter, creamy, not too sweet. Dinner.

When the couple appeared, we cheered and applauded. The anointed pair couldn't be older than twenty. Salt and grains of wheat were thrown on them.

I found the yarn store just off the main drag. One skein of seagreen merino and a crochet hook later, I booked in to the Pensione Ticino where hiking up four flights of stairs to my "roof room with an Etna view, continental breakfast included" was nothing after the mountain climb. I checked several times in case an orange lava flash from Etna burned through the clouds, but no luck.

Early tomorrow I would be aiming for the toe of the mainland and the two bronze statues over there, per Maia's suggestion. What cost art? I washed my black dress in the sink, wrung it out and hung it on the doorknob to dry. I drank delicious mountain water from the tap. Squeezing between wind-dried sheets, I pulled up the blanket and, punching the pillow so that I could lie with an eye trained directly at the window, hopeful for some red-hot action from Her Magnificent Eminence, I succumbed to sleep in the arms of Morpheus.

Chapter XXII

Scylla and Charybdis

The next morning I climbed into the clammy recesses of the still damp dress. Yeesh, it would have to do. Today I was for sure a southern Italian widow, hair twisted into a knot, no more polka dotted shoes and, of course, the wedding ring on.

The express bus passed through little coastal towns that seemed deserted. An occasional swing of plastic bead curtains suggested that someone had already entered a *salumeria* or just emptied a dust pan before we rolled through. The port city of Messina pulsed, however, with more than enough humanity. I trudged into the ferry terminal, *La Stazione Maritima*, a looming Fascist-era monolith, to find that the hourly *traghetto* to Reggio di Calabria would soon be loading. I made sure to check with two different clerks about the train time to Palermo tomorrow, confirming that no strike of any sort was happening, before laying down my diminishing lire notes to buy a roundtrip ferry ticket for the city across the strait.

Locals were already shuffling aboard. At the railing I dangled my arms over, looking down into see-through navy blue-violet water, the remarkable color I remembered from our first crossing the year of the moonwalk. With a fierce horn blast we bumped off the dock, chugging the waters into a lacy white froth. Hilly Messina at the easternmost corner of the island gradually grew smaller. We glided through purple, that rare color which Homer sang of as wine-dark. Faint breezes taunted the nautical flags. The water had a glassy sheen without any ruffling to it. Long, thin clouds lay splayed across the sky.

A ferryman wearing a hat with a pompon the color of a clown nose affixed his eyes on me. My attempt at a smile only deepened his stare. Where were my clown shoes when I really needed them? I looked away at the placid strait.

"You know," I said in English to the horizon, "a person wearing a fuzzy red bozo ball on his head really has no business looking *me* up and down." I casually checked if he was still pinning me with his look. He was, so I focused on a rust spot where the hull met the royal purple water, and out of the edge of my eye saw him exhale scrolls of cigarette smoke through his nostrils.

Raindrops started pelting at an angle, big ones that splattered into ovals on the deck, blowing from the east. Shipmate Pompon strutted in a wide arc, carrying a bucket. He neared me and upended the pail, spilling plastic bottles and *gelato* wrappers over the side.

"But it won't disintegrate," I sputtered.

"So what? It sinks to the bottom."

"The sea life will suffer from that stuff."

"Really?" He shrugged his shoulders.

I watched the garbage spread in the bruised water and mingle with the wake. Yes, really. Poor sea.

His stare was unnerving me. I kick-rolled my luggage into the cabin and he followed. I saw myself reflected in the window—flyaway hair loosed from its knot. Talk about clown looks. No wonder he'd been staring. Who did I think I'd been fooling with this widow get-up? I sat down, repinned my hair, located the green yarn and started to crochet the Professor's tie. The merino, soft and soothing, slipped along my fingers. I was sure the color would complement his wife's beautiful sweaters. I looked up—an old woman in a gray dotted dress was watching me. I forced myself to smile daintily at her. She narrowed her eyes to slits and spat at my feet, then turned away in disgust. I gaped at her, stunned. I was a solo voyager, a foreigner unattached to family or husband, a threat, a renegade, a dangerous female on the loose. The spitting woman was merely doing her duty warding off the evil eye—me.

I shoved the yarn into the satchel and hauled my suitcase back out to the deck while lurching swells began to rock the ferry and rain flew sideways. What an easy mark I was, alone on the wine-dark *mare*. I had no one to come to my aid, no protective Maia fretting. She hadn't wanted this for me; she warned me to take the Deluxe Tour, but no, I had to be independent, stubborn and cheap.

Somewhere on both sides of this very strait lurked the famed she-monsters Scylla and Charybdis, who devoured all of Odysseus's crew and reduced his ship to splinters, leaving him piteously dangling from an olive branch over the coursing whirlpool that took everyone and everything else down. I'd just sink like one of his minor crewmen when the monsters so ordained it, a footnote, unnoticed. The waters would swallow me up along with the trash and smooth over. Woe is *io*.

For the rest of the crossing I kept my eyes glued on Reggio until boom, we landed. I waited for everyone to disembark, then took hold of my straps and made for the ramp. Pompon stood at the top holding an umbrella in a classic circus pose.

I tried to grin. "C'mon Charon, give me a break." His stare did not lessen and no glimmer of pleasantry flickered in his eyes. I continued down to the mainland and dragged my luggage along the quay, each cobblestone a slippery crisis. My stupid valise careened sideways and landed splat in a puddle. I rearranged the satchel and purse straps to crisscross my chest for balance—X marks the spot—and looked for assistance from anyone. No taxis or buses anywhere. All the other passengers had rapidly vanished. How had they managed it?

A little car pulled up. "Hey! Do you need a ride?"

"No thanks. I need a cab."

"Do you see any? I don't. I'll take you."

I squinted through the downpour. He had a beard, unusual in Italy, maybe a kindly scholastic type.

"Where do you need to go?" he asked politely. "I'll take you there."

"*Scusi*, where are the buses and taxis?"

"None to be had at this time of day. I will do it. Hop in."

"Only if we go straight to the museum. I will pay you for the ride, agreed?"

"No charge." He opened his trunk for my suitcase.

I hesitated. This was not smart, but then again, a deserted terminal at siesta and the heavy rain. "That's all right. I'll hold it in front with me," I rotated my wedding ring to full-frontal diamond. We shot along the slick maritime boulevard.

"My name is Valentino."

You're kidding. "How do you do?" I gave him a business-like nod, didn't say my name and thought, I've just made a mistake.

"Where are you from?"

"The United—"

"Are you married?"

Here it came. "Of course. Yes, I am." The loose ring kept slipping but I straightened it and displayed it for him.

"Me too. I'm married also. With two children. A girl and a boy."

I stiffened. "Congratulations."

"Yes, I love my beautiful children."

"How nice. Is the *museo* up here?" I pointed to some civic-sized buildings.

"Soon, not quite. Here they are." He flipped down his visor, showing a photo of two toddlers.

"Sweet. Precious. Your wife and you must be very proud."
I emphasized the word *sposa*.

"Where's your husband?"

"He's in Rome doing research." My left thumb hooked itself around the satchel strapped across my chest. "I'm on my way to meet him."

"Why aren't you together?"

"Because I've been doing my own research."

"Your husband lets you go off by yourself?"

"Lets me?" Never mind I'd fabricated a husband. "I have my own work to do."

"I read that eighty-nine percent of American men are less than average sized."

Here we go. "I wouldn't know."

"Yes, and seventy-five percent of American men have sexual affairs."

"I have no idea." I eyed the door handle. "Don't believe everything in print."

"What do you think about these things I have read?"

"I don't think a thing about them. They do not concern me."

"Yes, I've heard that most American men are very small, unlike Italian men."

"If you're trying to impress me with the hugeness of your masculinity, I'm not interested." My fingertips blanched pressing into the metal dashboard. "I am happily married."

"Everyone knows that Italian men are so much better at making love." His speed around a corner made the tires squeal.

"Please slow down. I want to get out now."

"Why? This isn't the *museo*."

"Stop the car." My right thumb had the door pull primed.

"Don't worry. Stay calm." A traffic light turned red. "What are you doing?"

I pulled the handle. "I'm getting out." The door pressed shut against my shoulder as he sped through the red light. "Stop! Let me out."

We were now on an overpass. Everything tilted at loony angles: the roadway, the distant buildings, and horribly, my elbow into his from centrifugal force.

"Take me back!" My voice raised itself.

He dodged cars, honking and swearing.

"What are you doing?!"

Saliva caked at the corner of his mouth, a sweat stigmata popped out on his brow.

"Slow down!"

He floored the pedal. Why did I get in? What an idiot! Mea maxissima culpa. Next time he braked, I would throw the door open. I would do it. I had to do it. I had to. I'd jump.

"You're crazy. People know where I am. The *carabinieri* will hunt you down if you harm me in any way."

We were off the overpass back on city streets, slaloming, shooting through intersections as if inside a video game. At least the authorities would inform Maia and Primo of the details. They'd be told I was trying to escape when I got smeared all over the asphalt. Eventually, my cousin would run into the green-eyed professor in the lobby and would tell him what happened. He would be saddened. Life is so unfair, he'd remind Maia. "*Ehh,*" she'd agree.

"You know, we Italian men like to talk to American girls because we've heard they are sexually uninhibited, because we think we can get them into bed."

"You can't, you can't!" I yelled. "You are a goddamned idiot!"

"More than fifty percent of us succeed."

"*Basta* with your damned statistics, *imbecile*! You are one hundred percent wrong." It was maybe foolhardy, but I decided to yank his emergency brake. We bucked along the street until he pried my hand off and shoved it angrily away. "Just because you've heard something doesn't mean it's true. Just because you think something doesn't mean it will happen!"

He scraped the car to a stop, my suitcase wedged between me and the dashboard, my forehead up against the windshield. A cottonish quiet filled my ears.

"You can get out now," he moaned.

"*Disgraziato*," said a cool ventriloquist voice, mine. "*Cretino mascalzone stupido son of a stupidello!* How dare you!" I flung open the door, pushing the suitcase out first, peeled myself free and stumbled to my feet.

"I didn't mean to hurt you," he groaned. "I did what I promised. I brought you to the museum."

"A thousand thanks. Here's my tip." I reached into my pocket to grab the change from the ferry ticket sale to throw at him. The water pistol fit right in my palm. At last. I aimed and squeezed the trigger—two tablespoons of pure Taormina mountain water arced delicately onto his maroon leather jacket and dripped down to his trousers. Wordless, he zoomed away like a giant fly.

"*Signorina*? Please release your *bagaglio*." A guard at the entrance was trying to free the suitcase handle from my fist. "You must leave your belongings here. You may only take your purse with you."

"I've come to see the Bronzi," I said through chattering teeth. My heart pounded so loudly he had to be hearing the thumps.

"That's fine, but you're bleeding."

"Am I?" I felt my forehead.

He produced a first aid box. "Please," he urged a square of gauze and a strip of tape on me, "let me direct you towards the W.C."

"*Va bene.*" In the bathroom I washed the small trickle of blood off my forehead and pressed on the small cut at my hairline before bandaging it. I fished out the two aspirin Marge had given me in Siracusa and swallowed them with a gulp of water.

The museum hummed with tranquility. A safe haven. I descended the staircase gripping the rail and slid onto a bench behind a throng. The sounds of Japanese and of Romance languages filled the large chamber. My neck had hardened into a solid column of tension. I thought, maybe I'll just lie down for a minute. No one will notice. No one will mind.

I felt a tap on my shoulder. "It is forbidden to repose anywhere in the National Museum," said a guard.

I propped myself up. One, two, three milky eyes gazed into eternity over the heads of admirers who had traveled here from their sundry lands. I waited at the back until all the groups drifted out of the room. I had plenty of time since I wasn't going anywhere, not until the museum closed, or until I stopped shaking, anyway.

Two nude green men of gentle, heroic aspect were looking forward; somehow they knew I had blown in. The long-haired one with a headband and plangent eyes (Statue A) was poised to take a step. The short-haired one who wore an Attic cap (Statue B) lacked a left eye. We all stared together, me at them and them into space. I carefully rose from the bench to read the cards at their feet:

> *Figure virile, nude, stante*
> Circa 5th century B.C.
> Length: two meters
> Weight: approximately 250 kilograms
> Lips, nipples, eyebrows: copper
> Teeth: silver
> Eyelashes: silver
> Eyes: ivory and limestone

Fascinating information but big mistake for me to have stood up. My head began to throb. I minced my way back to the bench to lie down again. The guard could poke me awake next time he popped his head into the gallery, but until then I'd just ... recover by reclining here and looking ... sideways at A and ... at ... B. ...

Sleeping or in a daze, I felt only mild surprise when the magnificent statues began to communicate through their lips of copper and their eyes of ivory and limestone:

At a distant epoch we possessed weapons and shields, A & B confided, *but we needed them no more and the wine-dark saltwater seized them. Freed of such implements, we breathed peaceful deep watery drafts, easily so. Ticklish sea horses played in our beards. Dolphins winked at us as they skimmed by.*

"Is that so?" I murmured from the comfort of my cool stone bench. "Sounds kinda fun."

Golden Greece gave way to Imperial Rome. Those tremendous empires rose and fell. Crusaders, Venetians, Greco-Albanians in commerce and combat, in discovery and evasion, sailed over us. No one knew we lay there. We housed sea mollusks along our proud lengths of torso, arm, leg, neck, they continued in their sometimes archaic manner. *Between our toes they nestled. Cruel men and kind men lived out their mortal spans. Giving birth and dying giving birth, women pushed full civilizations into this world. Waves of children to adulthood grew, to old age and drifted through the veil of death.*

"Just like that, huh?" I had them all to myself in the room.

We rested in sand and rock throughout those times. We heard the cries of the leviathan. We sang back to the great beasts and the small. We learned mysteries of plankton, whispered fluently by the tiniest of creatures. Sea crones communed with us. Time marked twenty-four centuries. It mattered not.

We shocked a diver one daybreak who thought he had found drowned fishermen. Much bubbling commotion! In the year you humans call 1971 sacking and shackles around our feet and necks were fastened. We breathed air again, reawakened to the realm of full light. Mortals massaged us, smoothed and oiled our salt-pocked skin, eased away barnacles and sea urchins.

Human hands and minds fashioned us; fate made us plunge into the depths; human sinew and labor hoisted and restored us. We admire the strong force that is human persistence. Now we live here in a house of time. We are revered. Mortals of many tongues flock daily to us.

"Yeah, I too have flocked."

A: *From some great distance, over an expanse of oceans and lands.*

N: "A young civilization that calls itself California. A hard to explain place."

B: *With a purpose in your heart, we surmise.*

N: "Yes, to know more of the three-cornered isle from which my motherline sprang, and to question a brave woman there. And to meet you, which was all my cousin Maia's idea; otherwise I'd be snorkeling in Taormina and crocheting an *alta moda* pale green tie."

A: *Mighty Thrinakria, the island of the world's delight, the Sun. The joy of man. And has this woman answered you?*

N: "Not yet. We have a phone date set up Wednesday, if I return alive."

They blinked their silver lashes. They appeared amused by me.

A: *Alive? You're in the presence of two unalive statues, so stop with the melodrama.*

N: "I'm a brash and clueless mess, getting myself into hot water, plus I'm neurotic and impatient."

B: *Neur-what?*

N: "It's a Greek word, but never mind. Messed up. Lost."

A & B: *Lost forever also seemed we, and a brother separated.*

N: "Weren't you lying near each other under the sand?"

A & B: *Yes, a family were we.*

Their lashes flickered again, and I divined that they had communicated underwater this way until the barnacles encrusted their lids.

N: "You kept each other going, right? And you awe visitors now. You're heroic and strong and made of bronze. I'm freaked out and made of squishy human protoplasm. I bleed, as you can see. Your headband, Statue A, looks just like how my headache feels. The aspirin has hardly made a dent."

A: *Only the dead feel no pain. Relish your life.*

N: "Relish being jabbed with an angry elbow by an enraged young man? Relish being spat at by an old lady with archaic attitudes? Relish being taken for a ride by a jerk? What do I get to relish next?"

B: *We acknowledge these adversities. Pay them little mind. When you ignore ignorant thinking, you elevate your understanding.*

N: "That's easy for you to say, warrior guys. I'd feel safer out there if I had you as bodyguards."

Nearby, a presence cleared his throat. I felt a tad more alert, and slowly bent an elbow to prop my head on my hand. Still woozy, I eased myself up from the bench and took my time crossing the room to read his sign:

> *The Philosopher*
> Head, male, bearded, identity unknown
> Circa 5th century BC Bronze
> Eye: glass enamel

"So *you're* the old Philosopher. Maia told me to pay attention to you, too."

—*Welcome.*

"Maia venerates you. She's wise also."

—*Yes, she is.*

"She knew the impediments to my travels. I needed protection, though I foolishly bucked against it and voyaged recklessly. What looked like smothering and needless old lady worry turned out to be reasonable and thoughtful concern. What looked like limitation has sometimes proved to be a type of freedom. I thought I could push against the barriers here, but I cannot. She has seen so much, as you have."

—*Do not waste breath in self-criticism. Curiosity opens closed portals.*

"And provokes some people."

—*Thus it has ever been.*

"Just an hour past, I was detained against my will. Abducted, sort of. He terrified me."

—*The terror was short-lived, was it not? A quick trip to the underworld, a quick return. You used your wits and found your way here.*

"Fortunately, he did drop me off in front. It could have been worse. But what if he's out there, waiting to get me again when the museum doors close? He knows I'm in here. I may have wrecked the brake system on his chariot."

—*I can assure you that tribulation is done. Move forward on your way. One sandal in front of the other.*

"I don't want to leave this room."

—*Yet at dusk you living souls must retreat. Every evening is thus.*

"But I'm petrified I won't have safe passage back out of this strange land."

—*You* are *petrified? Ha Ha. Hey green guys, did you hear that one?*

Statue A: *Heh.*

Statue B: *Heh.*

"Hah, I see what you mean."

—Listen, remember the strength of your great-grandmother.

"I haven't forgotten. Anna Orlando wasn't a *forestiere*, though. I don't know my way around this province or understand its customs. I cannot speak this dialect. I know not a soul here."

—*Contemplate how strange her own world appeared to her, how she had to guide herself ahead as if through a dark wood, without assurance of any safe outcome. For a girl with no power, she summoned up real power.*

"I've heard that expression before, somewhere. You're right, Phil. My travails are nothing compared to hers. Just maybe I have a few drops of her blood in my veins," I allowed.

—*I think so. Here's a notion for you: the admirer, upon entering our chamber, is inclined, out of innate curiosity, to perceive something heroic in the two Bronzes, which amplifies her own soul, so that upon leaving she possesses something magnified within herself, perhaps a resolve newly recognized, with which she mistakenly thinks she did not enter.*

"All I know is, I entered for some respite, for comforting."

—*Excellent. So I propose to you that heroism does not seek praise or glory, for its essence is internal; whether it inspires others is not its principal purpose. Heroism exists no matter whether adulation is heaped on it or public condemnation rains down upon it.*

"But you and these green men were fashioned to inspire us, no?"

—*Without a doubt we were. Ergo, when you return to Panormus to consult that brave young woman,* he paused to cogitate as philosophers do, *accept that she may not assent to being recorded on stone tablets for posterity or for adulation.*

"Franca—you know about her!"

—*I do. And the many other Francas who go by other names in other places in other times.*

"I have this terrible feeling you're telling me I won't be able to interview her."

—*I make no such prediction. I'm not a seer, just a simple philosopher.*

The loudspeaker announced closing time.

"Oh no, now I'm going to panic again. Can you offer any final advice?"

—*You carry a talisman around your neck. Do you know what it means?*

"My Trinacria." I felt for it through my widow outfit's conservative neckline.

—*She—you may call her Medusa, or Juno, or Hecate, or Aphrodite, or Proserpina, or Demeter, or Hygeia, or Teiresias if you want to get really complex, or you may call her nothing at all—has the capacity to soar with wings above this earth, to stride with muscled calves upon it, to go deep as a winding snake into its depths, as needed, when needed, sowing seeds. Brilliance that she is, she has the capacity to choose which action to take when. Beautiful—though branded as ugly, and supposedly tricked and killed by arrogant youth who knew too little and were cowed by her potency—she is always amongst us, as powerful as ever.*

"Philosopher, you are one hell of a guy."

—*I came from a mother too, you know.*

"Of course you did. I sure hope there's a postcard of you I can buy upstairs."

—*Carry a calm impartiality with you when you walk outside. You may wrap it around you as a cloak whenever you choose.*

"Ah," I hitched my purse over my shoulder, "that helps."

—*Continue to inquire, dear woman, a most noble human pursuit.*

"Thank you."

—*Don't mention it.*

I circled the room, clinging to the cool peace of the sanctuary of my three men, wanting their bronze strength to rub off, sealing a pact that would allow me to draw from their words whenever needed. Their form of heroism remained perfectly still. Curators had given them labels, but not names—their identities might never be completely known. They belonged to everyone. They belonged to me.

I climbed the stairs to street level to face the present, to once more traverse three-dimensional Reggio, back to real humans and unpredictability.

Chapter XXIII

Rescued

The kind custodian at the front desk placed the suitcase into my hand, helped me put the satchel over my shoulder and ushered me toward the exit. He was very sorry not to know of any hotel or *pensione* to recommend, but fervently wished me *Buon viaggio*. Outside, I checked around for the hell car, just in case, but it was long gone. I approached a woman at the bus stop.

"Pardon, will this bus take me towards any *alberghi*?"

She motioned me away. "That one won't." Another followed, clogged with people. "Neither will that. Get on the one coming down the street behind it."

I shoved along with others spackling themselves into the backdoor.

"I'm looking for an inexpensive hotel," I announced to all with fake bravura. "Can anyone direct me?" My bandaged third eye elicited quick glances and silence. I tugged at my impartiality cloak. "Rooms to rent?" No one answered though we were sardined together. Bronze power, bronze power, I chanted internally. "Does anyone here speak Italian, please?" Not a single sardine reacted. I squelched tears before they formed. My face heated up. I would not succumb. I had to keep going.

"Of course I do." A man squeezed forward, grinning quizzically. "What else would we speak? What is the matter, miss?"

"Hotel," I swallowed hard. "Economical. Modest, but clean."

"I'll help you find one," he smiled, "I will."

"*Grazie tanto.*"

"I see that you are hurt. Are you in pain? I am a pharmacist."

"Oh . . ." I felt for the bandage, "I don't know. I don't think so."

Someone in the helping professions who has compassion for a lost and upset person. Maybe he could provide me with a mild sedative to calm my nerves. Just a dram.

"Why have you stopped in Reggio?"

"To see the statues in the museum."

"You have come solely for them?"

"They were worth it."

"Is that so? It's funny, I've never gone inside. They say there's a third one, you know. They found three warriors in the sea."

"You're kidding. Where is it? In a museum up north?"

"No," answered a teenage girl whose breast pocket hanky was tickling my nose, "in the living room of a mafioso, so we hear."

"Wow." The third brother lying at the sea bottom. They had alluded to him. Statue C? I bet *he'd* have some interesting things to say.

"*Scusa*, we leave here. I'll take that suitcase. After you." The smiling guy carefully edged people out of our way. He laughed at the task of pushing and pulling my luggage through the rear door. I stood at the curb and watched as if from a distance. "We go this way."

"You can put it down and roll it."

"I don't mind carrying it. It's light, very light." *Legerissima.*

We turned a corner. Three *albergo* signs on one block. "Oh what a relief. Thank you for your help. I don't want to impose on you any more."

"I'm not leaving until we find you a room." He took the worn, carpeted stairs two at a time and rang the bell.

A *padrone* appeared. "Double bed?" *Letto matrimoniale.*

"No, no," I waved my hands quickly, "single. *Sola.* Just me."

"*Passaporto.*"

I dug it out and handed it to him. "I'd like to see the room first, please."

The windowless cubicle could be had for sixty thousand lire, despondent decor complimentary.

"No thank you."

The pharmacist gave me a puzzled look.

"Moldy," I whispered. "Bad. No air."

"Let's go over to the next one," he laughed. What did he find so amusing? The second *albergo* had no vacancy; the third did.

"This looks good, and a better price," he beamed.

A closet crypt, I thought, a ripoff. I'll have another anxiety attack in there. I shook my head.

"Listen, I know someone who runs a rooming house, clean and inexpensive. I mean this sincerely. I'll take you there. My brother's car is just down the street."

"Uhhh, no car. I'll walk."

"Too far." He grinned, hugging my suitcase to his chest.

"I'll take a cab then."

He laughed doubtfully. "Try finding one around here. My brother is in that cinema right there. See the marquee?"

Because and only because *Casablanca* was playing, I tagged after him. Someone sat reading a newspaper in the ticket booth. The two spoke a dialect even less understandable than Sicilian. The brother-person seemed hesitant to hand over his keys. "You better add some gas," he grumbled.

"Sure," the pharmacist trilled, putting my suitcase into the trunk of one of the teensiest autos ever designed. I started to protest, then remembered the Bronze pep talk about endurance. We didn't cover more than a kilometer when the car gasped and died in the middle of the boulevard.

"Don't worry. Stay inside while I go get gas. Be right back." He dashed off.

Oh glory. The sickening transit of rush hour shot by, shaking the car in its wake. Even if I wanted to exit this lesser tin can, I couldn't survive to the curb. For the second time today I braced for a crash. Then I thought about crocheting to pass the time until the collision. I pulled out the beginnings of the tie, not sure that merino had been such a wise choice. But the color couldn't have been better! I heard shouts, felt jostling. Half a dozen young men had closed in.

"This isn't my *macchina*," I yelled. "Don't steal it. Or me. *No benzina!*"

"*Uno, due, tre!*"

"What are you doing!" I was aloft. "Where are you taking the car?"

"To the side of the road. *Complimenti, bella!*" They set the car down, blew kisses to me, slapped each other on the back laughing, and moved on.

The guy came running with a wide-mouthed glass jar splashing gasoline over the rim.

"*Brava.* You moved the car out of the way, strong American girl."

"I didn't do anything. Whatever you do," I warned, "do not light a cigarette, please!"

"What?" he warbled. "Can't hear you." He poured some fuel into the tank, the rest dribbled down the side. "Hand me that newspaper, will you?" The headline read *Cher Wins Oscar for Best Actress*. He rolled it into a funnel, whistling, then inserted it and poured the rose-colored liquid into the makeshift cone. Vapors wavered around his head like a halo-in-training. He threw the darkened newsprint to the street and lit a cigarette. *Madre di Dio*, if we make it there without igniting.

"Ready," he grinned, jumping in, smelling of gasoline. "Let's go!" We convulsed forward. "What are you making there?"

"A tie for my husband."

"The color looks like the sea near Scilla. Listen Natalia, you are welcome to stay at my apartment."

"How do you know my name?" I demanded.

"When you showed your passport at the first hotel. You could have my room. I mean that sincerely."

"I need to rent a room."

"I don't mean it the way it sounds. Sincerely, I don't. I truly mean that you are welcome to stay at the home of me and my brother. You can stay for as long as you're in Reggio."

"That's a generous offer and I thank you, but no."

"As you wish. But I offer it sincerely." He pulled up to a one-story cinder-block near the waterfront. Rooms To Let. He brought my suitcase in and greeted the proprietor, who led me down a linoleum hall. Clean and monastic, the room possessed a window and a sink. Palm fronds rubbed at the glass.

"Twenty-four thousand lire. Payable now."

"Excellent. I'll take it. Couldn't be better." My shoulders dropped a few inches. I pulled off the bandage and rinsed my face in the sink. When I returned to the lobby to pay, the man who brought me was gone.

"But I wanted to thank him. He went completely out of his way to help. Oh, no. I didn't even learn his name."

"Mimmo. Domenico."

I ran out. He was trying to start the car. "Mimmo Domenico," I yelled, "don't leave yet. Thank you so much."

"Success in finding a room for you is thanks enough."

"Will you join me for dinner?"

"But," he hesitated, "I'm not hungry."

"Well I'm starving. Please come. I invite you."

"No, I cannot."

"You don't want to offend me by refusing my invitation now, do you?"

"*Beh . . .*"

We walked via a broad promenade along the waterfront. Not a bad-looking city. In fact, handsome with palm trees and iron street lamps holding three lanterns in one. Then we took a side street. He paused in front of the Pizzeria Lirica, which was packed. I took one look inside and cracked up. Standard American pizza parlor with red and white checked tablecloths, dripping candles in Chianti bottles, posters of Sorrento and Capri faded to shades of blue, blue and blue. Hilarious.

"Do you not like it?"

"Yes, perfect. It reminds me of home, that's all. Do you see any empty seats?" Young couples, all charged up with springtime, had taken over the joint. We threaded through to the back and were squeezed in at the end of a long table. Candlelight glistened in the fake grapes on an arbor overhead, their plastic leaves rustled at the breath of a rotating ceiling fan. I poured mineral water into our glasses and ordered two pizzas.

"Two?" he looked worried.

"You're hungry, aren't you, after that walk?"

"A little." He chewed his mustache.

The radio blared so loud, I had to shout to be heard, "Tell me about the pharmacy."

"I attended school, got a very good job, but I'm not employed currently. I was laid off three years ago." He looked down. "My compensation ran out last year." He shrugged resignedly, in that southern Italian way. This city, gracefully landscaped along the water and boasting renowned antiquities who give free advice, was steeped in distress just like the rest of the south. "On May Day we will rally, we workers. We won't be left out anymore. My brother and me and all our friends will march together," he hollered over the noise. "You should see it. Why don't you stay for the rally?"

A white blob flew from out of the top of his head and returned, like a yo-yo. Then a larger one did.

I cracked up. "I'm not making fun of May Day. I believe in May Day. Workers of the World, Unite! A thing coming out from behind your head is what made laugh."

He turned around. The chef flung dough towards the ceiling.

"A pizza is a thing of fantasy, of caprice, of the imagination," Mimmo Domenico mused loudly. "*I* almost got work in a pizzeria last year. There's an art to throwing them. You have to fling from the elbow, then the wrist. And you have to make sure not to tire out the dough, or it becomes tough. Then you work under pressure to top it quickly and slide it into the oven. Pizza makes people happy."

The fire-roasted, sliced artichoke hearts with pesto and mozzarella fantasy arrived, with thin crust blistered crisp.

"Yes it does. I'm happy!" I grabbed a piece.

Mimmo kept his hands under the table. I pushed the pan toward him.

"Please eat."

He cautiously helped himself. "It's good." He ate hungrily. Conversation was becoming exhausting in all the clatter. The mushroom and anchovy pizza pie came.

"Why don't you stay a few days, till May Day, mmm? I want to show you all of Reggio and Scilla."

"You mean the monster?" I yelled. "I think I already met the monster."

"What monster?" he shouted back. "I'm talking about the beach. You could relax in the sand."

"I'd love to see Scilla up close, really stare her in the face, but I cannot. Tomorrow morning I return to Sicily."

"To meet your husband?" The ring was working.

"To go back to Palermo for an appointment."

A white circle spun up out of his black hair, like a thought, but didn't come down.

"Maybe you should apply for work here. The guy just lost his dough."

Mimmo turned to look. "Where'd it go?" he laughed.

"It's rotating on the ceiling fan."

The white-hatted tosser stood underneath, his mouth open. The corny Italian pop music went dead and every plastic grape stopped swinging. Conversations faltered table to table. Lovers tore their eyes off each other, then looked up and started pointing and giggling. A ladder was brought. Italians make the most of these crises, really milking them.

Mimmo jumped up. "I'll get it!" Before anyone could beat him, he climbed, gathered together the yeasty mass stretched out across the paddles, and handed it down gingerly, as if it could be salvaged for chef's surprise. "Give me a towel while I'm up here and I'll clean the fan for you."

He received bravos and slaps on the back when he descended, and a half liter of *vino bianco* and two glasses were brought over.

"They should give you a job on the spot, Mimmo, I'm serious."

"It's only right to lend a hand when needed."

"If only everyone lived by that rule." We clinked wineglasses. "Eat up," I coaxed him. "I'm done."

"Your husband's lucky."

"Oh please." I sipped from my glass, flustered.

"*Sei squisitissima, Natalia, veramente.*" You are most exquisite, really. What a brilliant word. The superlative form. All those s's, the way they spilled from his tongue. Pure silver, the most sublime word yet in Italian, the language of love. Our eyes caught. "I mean it sincerely."

"Thank you for going out of your way today. You saved me."

"It was nothing. You were in need."

The bill was set at his elbow, but I retrieved it. "I told you, my treat." He glanced around when I paid. No one was watching, yet everyone applauded when he got up to leave.

A balmy evening had taken hold. We strolled back along the Lungomare, ideal for viewing twinkling Messina across the freshly polished sea. The palm trees held the liquid pastel afterlight of dusk. He pointed southwest. "Look. Etna."

"At last!" Orange and devilish, the great summit was flashing her fiery grin. "In order to see her I had to leave the island."

"You know, I've never been over there."

"Across the water? Why not?"

"I don't know," he shrugged.

"It's not too far away. You should go someday. Take the ferry to Messina and see your sister city."

The sky was darkening theatrically. Etna's mouth was blurting the latest mysteries from inside, casting a ruby floodlight on the clouds.

"Once, if you can believe it, I saw her blowing out smoke rings."

"No! You're joking. You're not joking?"

"That was a long time ago, *gioia*."

"Imagine. What I wouldn't give to see that."

He grabbed me suddenly and lifted me up. "*Sei legerissima! Veramente.*" You are the lightest, really.

"You said that about my suitcase. Now I have proof that I can't believe you."

"Oh, believe me, you should." He put me down but held me by the elbows and a look. This was the moment that squadrons of women came here to feel, and then breathlessly write home about: the dreamy eve, the romantic language in the ear, the *squisitissimas* and *legerissimas*, the perfect brochure setting, the helpful volcano backdrop, the guy.

"I'd better turn in."

"So soon?"

"I've got to be at the morning ferry."

We walked to the rooming house and stood outside the door, the manager watching from the front desk a few feet away.

"Golden dreams," he whispered and kissed my banged-up forehead. *Sogni d'oro*, another beautiful expression.

"Goodnight, Mimmo. Thank you again."

In my roomette I pulled the cord on the bare bulb and lay down on the squawking mattress. The springs shrieked at every slight movement. Turning on my side I found a hangout between five protruding coils. The bed gripped me in its metallic embrace. He was really very sweet, that Domenico Mimmo. A champ at beautiful expressions. I fell into a slumber, golden, and scalloped around the edges.

Chapter XXIV

Will She Speak?

When dawn her rosy knuckles cracked, I was already standing at the front desk, asking the manager to phone for a taxi. He nodded to the gasoline-streaked car outside. Mimmo sat on the hood.

"Oh!" I pulled the wobbling suitcase outside into the daybreak.

Mimmo galloped over. "I'll take you to the boat," he smiled.

"But you shouldn't have troubled yourself. What about your brother?"

"He didn't mind. I took the initiative. I did."

"You've been sleeping out here?"

"It was nothing."

"You really shouldn't have, honestly."

"Do I upset you?"

"No, you surprise me is all."

"You wish a coffee and a *cornetto*, yes?"

"No."

"Andiamo!"

We were at the ferry soon enough. People streamed up the gangway, carrying loaded sacks and boxes of produce, steering bicycles and motos.

"This place was deserted when I arrived yesterday."

"*Sì*, but this is work time. Lucky them. I wish I had their trouble to get up early every morning and commute by ferry to work."

"Why don't you cross the Strait with me?"

"*Ehhh, purtroppo* . . ." he backed away a step, laughing self-consciously.

"As my guest, though I won't have any time to linger in Messina. My train leaves right away."

"I cannot accept."

"Sure you can, Mimmo, you don't have to be anywhere else, do you?"

"I've never set foot on any boat."

"Today's the day then."

He glanced left and right while I bought his roundtrip ticket, but bounded up the gangplank like a kid on a holiday and used the suitcase to push ahead to the prow. At the railing, he began waving to people on the dock.

"Friends?"

"No, *gioia*, but I've always imagined doing this."

The ferry horn made me jump but Mimmo laughed at it. Truly, the man was gifted that way. We shoved off the big toenail of the continent and began the glide through sparkling, tidy waves. The sky had been cleansed to a sheen. Etna was blue-flanked and puffing. The maritime flags snapped friskily in the morning breeze. We had a front row view of everything. Awash with the thrill of returning to Palermo today, I smiled into the churning white foam way below. My phone appointment was a mere six hours away. I couldn't get over the miracle of it.

"What do you think so far, Mimmo?"

"Where's Reggio?" he joked. He was watching his city diminish to a dot. "Every street, every quarter I know. They make up my world. And now they disappear from view. My brother won't believe where I've gone today. It is a profound thing to move along on top of water."

"It really is, especially violet-purple velvet water, so calm this morning."

Mimmo clutched his stomach suddenly, looking queasy.

"Are you feeling okay?"

"No, I'm not. Is *this* motion sickness? We used to fill pre-scriptions at the pharmacy. I never knew . . . what they were . . . talking about . . . and now . . ."

In the fourteen and a half hours since we'd met, I had yet to see him subdued.

"I have just the remedy!" I pulled out my tiny bottle of Cynar. "Take a little sip of this and keep your eyes on the horizon."

"Are you sure?"

"And take some deep breaths."

"Okay."

"You'll be all right, Mimmo."

"Will I?"

"Yes. Maybe have another small sip."

"Umm . . ."

"Don't forget to inhale and exhale."

"Whatever you say, *gioia*." He gripped the railing and gulped air.

Oh dear. I gingerly patted his back.

"*Guarda!* Dolphins!" At least five—hard to say exactly— had popped up through the creamy fizz under us, then shot forward like quicksilver and held their positions as if leading the boat, skimming between the water and the air, having a blast. "I can't believe it. I've never seen them up close before . . ." Mimmo trailed off, hanging his arm over the railing, amused by their antics. The man even waved to them with both hands.

"Hey, neighbor, what brings you aboard?" Yesterday's fer-ryman, festooned with his memorable pompon, had appeared at Mimmo's side.

"*Ciao*, Carmine, *come stai?*"

I turned my back to them. They chatted away while I imagined Maia driving us to Alcamo this afternoon, finding Franca's door, knocking on it, seeing her face, shaking her hand, us being invited into her living room. Or maybe she preferred the meeting held in a caffè, so as to protect the anonymity of her home. That was more likely. I just hoped I wouldn't dissolve in tears when I saw her in person.

We were nearing Messina's port. The moment the engines slowed, the dolphins veered off to the left.

"Don't go, don't go," Mimmo pleaded, but they were dematerializing into the swells.

"They'll probably ride back with you. Keep the Cynar in case you need it. Little sips, remember."

We landed with a jolt and the jostling began. Mimmo put his hand on my shoulder and with the lightest-really-luggage in his other hand, began pushing. For the first time on this trip it was fun to shove along with everyone else—he laughed all the way down the ramp.

"I hope you have a truly great time of it here," I said, then grabbed all the change from my pocket and pressed it into his hand. "For a coffee and a *cornetto*."

"No, I cannot accept."

"Oh yes you can. I insist. Thank you again for saving me yesterday."

"Save you? The pleasure was all mine, all mine."

"*Addio*, Mimmo."

He took my hand and kissed it. "*Addio, gioia*, don't you forget me."

"As if I would." With that, I grabbed the suitcase and trekked toward the train station. I looked back once to see him. He was at some distance, glancing around at the brave new world in which he found himself, perhaps wondering which way to head first. He brought me back to myself, just as the Bronzes did. I would always love him for that.

The goddesses and gods must have been in a magnanimous mood because the train left on time and kept to its schedule. We passed through Tindari with its famous Black Madonna statue. Next time, next time. I rewrote the questions I'd been planning in capital letters on yellow legal paper, leaving plenty of room for Franca's answers. I reread them, practiced them to the sound of the train wheels, and drew stars where Maia could check my grammar, if there was time.

The sign indicated Cefalù, home of the amazing Adonis in the square. We were maybe half an hour away from Palermo still. Too much rehearsing could backfire, so I flipped over to an empty yellow page and scrawled some equations:

Pink and Black Youth in Cefalù = erotic male principle.

The abductor in Reggio = clueless, unconscious male principle.

Mimmo = the laughing healer, a good, honest, kind person, who lifted my spirits and gave me hope for men in the future.

Professor Green Eyes = marvelous fiancé fantasy. Need to complete tie for him because I'm leaving next week for Rome. Maybe we can go out for decaf?

Primo = dear friend, helper, steadfast protector, and confidant.

Guido F____, the librarian = Represents serendipity. Selfless assistant to my cause who recognized what I was trying to do, and who came through for me.

Boothe = Had my heart but not my trust. For sure, sadly, I must put him in the past tense.

Then there's Me = The irony of having freedom to choose, and making some poor choices in the past, does not preclude better choices in the future. I'm fine alone at this time, and feel complete in my own company. For now.

We pulled into Palermo with no delay. The station thrummed with urban noise. I rushed down the platform where I'd first waited for the train to Alcamo a few weeks ago. Mustache! He was leaning over two young women seated on a bench, weighed down with backpacks emblazoned with the Canadian maple leaf. They were doing their best to ignore him. I rushed out to the piazza to catch a cab.

"Natalie!"

I spun on my heel.

"Over here, *eccomi*." A familiar figure waved from beyond a slew of taxis.

"Maia!"

She had parked in a red zone, risking yet another towing. What a daredevil. We embraced.

"*The Philosopher* sends his regards."

"*Brava ragazza*," she beamed, "you made it to the other side." We kissed each cheek.

"Did I ever!"

"*Cara*, I thought I'd best be here waiting for the train, better than waiting by the phone for your call. By the way," she turned on the ignition, "notice the statue in front of the palm trees?" I twisted around. "Another Civiletti. Vittorio Emanuele the Second, of Savoia, the first king of United Italy."

"Beautiful. Regal horse. Civiletti was good at larger than life, wasn't he?"

Back home, at the appointed hour, I seated myself in the armchair next to the phone stand, placed pens in front of me, and dialed. Breathe, I scribbled across the top of the writing pad. Maia lingered a few feet away.

"*Pronto*," someone answered, maybe a woman.

"*Pronto, Signora* Franca Viola, please."

"She's cooking right now. It's lunchtime."

"When shall I telephone again?"

"*Un'oretta*." About an hour.

"Thanks so much, I will do that."

"*Prego*."

"*Ciao*."

"*Ciao*."

"It sounded like a woman, Maia. It could have been her."

"Maybe she's making sure your motives are completely sincere, that the call isn't some kind of prank."

"I see your point. She's feeling me out, listening to what I sound like, do I really have a foreign accent, am I who I claim to be."

"On the other hand, she probably *was* busy in the kitchen. Have some *caponata*. Primo made it specially for you."

"*Caponata!*" The sweet-and-sour antipasto tasted exactly the way Nonny used to make it. Diced-up eggplant with tomato sauce spiked with red wine vinegar, ribbons of mint leaf from the pot on the verandah across from Filumenu's cage, crunchy celery, salty capers and green olives, slivers of red onion and flat-leafed parsley, finished off with that secret Sicilian condiment: a teaspoonful of sugar. I tore off a ragged cushion of bread to absorb the sauce. "I'm having a memory from way back."

"*Brava*. Eat more," Maia said.

"Only if you do."

Maia had decided to rearrange the books on her shelf next to the stand when I phoned back fifty minutes later.

A young-sounding voice answered. "She's not here. She's gone into town."

"I see. What would be a convenient time for me to call again?"

"Try at maybe six o'clock this evening."

"Thank you very much, I will do that."

"What did they say?" The books in Maia's arms were on the verge of tumbling to the floor. "Tell me."

"To phone again at six, that's all. What do you think is going on? They keep putting me off."

Maia tilted her head. "I don't know, but best to do exactly as they say. *Pazienza.*"

"Yes, patience."

"To be prepared means to accept whatever outcome. If you never do actually talk with her, look what you've learned anyway."

I nodded, not resenting Maia's caution anymore. She was right, after all.

"I've filled the tank in case we are to drive to Alcamo."

"Thank you." I hugged her. "You'll make sure I understand what she says word for word."

"*Senz'altro.* Now don't forget to offer a payment for the favor she is doing you."

"Right! Of course." I wrote CONDITIONS (OFFER TO PAY) in block letters at the top of my pad under Inhale/Exhale.

For the third time, at exactly six o'clock, I sat in the big armchair. Maia, apologetic about having to leave unexpectedly to pick up her granddaughter Sabina, had rushed out the door, otherwise she would never have dreamed of missing this moment. Oh how she wished she could be here listening in. But she would be right back and ready to make the drive this evening. I was not to worry on that score, she assured me.

Light filtered through the long white translucent curtains into the living room, a gossamer veil to the great instant of now—with a sensuous, dancing flutter. The benevolent afternoon lit up the room. Hope hovered that Franca Viola and I would converse, person to person.

The phone rang many times, as it had so often here, reverberating all the way out to the province and and back again to the mother city. Sitting in this chair, waiting for someone to pick up in a land of no answering machines, I knew all at once that she would not be there, that she had made up her mind against our interview, that my chance had come and had gone. I had blown all the way around the island of the Sun, the joy of man, the world's delight, just like Odysseus except counterclockwise, only to return to this seventh-story perch and accept her decision: a sovereign right to retain privacy.

"*Pronto?*"

"*Pronto,* Franca Viola please."

"I am Franca Viola," said a sweet voice.

"Ah *signora*," I stood up and all my papers fell to the floor, "I feel so very honored and so happy to speak with you! I have been interested in your story for a long time."

"I apologize for not having been able to take the two other calls you made today. I had to go with my husband into town earlier."

"That's no problem at all. I'm calling with the hope that I might arrange an interview with you. Perhaps we could set it up for this evening? I would be accompanied by my cousin Maia Miracolo Santilli who is Palermitana, and I'm prepared to meet any conditions you may have."

"*Signorina*, I am sorry, I do not give interviews. I never have. I have asked myself why many times, and I do not really have an answer, but this is how I prefer it. I am sorry."

"I understand, I do." The immense pleasure of hearing her gentle manner and tone was enough. Just about.

"However, if you'd like to ask me some questions now on the telephone, go ahead."

"I would love to, only my Italian isn't the best and I want to make sure that I understand everything you say."

"*Signorina*, probably your Italian is better than mine, because I studied a little Italian, but here we speak dialect, and very rarely speak Italian. My Italian is worse, surely."

"Oh, that could not be, but . . . well then, yes, I do have questions. We haven't heard anything about you in America for years and years, and what we did hear in 1966 was minimal.

More than anything I would like to know how you are doing now, so long afterwards?"

"*Signorina*, everything turned out fine. Something sad finally ended well."

"I'm very happy to hear this. I'd like to know what you think of women's situation now?"

"Things have begun to improve from how they were in those times. My country people then had fixed ideas, because here they were accustomed to accepting that those who had a disgrace of that kind would accept marriage. That to say no was to remain dishonored.

"And I thought so too, *signorina*, that my soul was dishonored, because I had no education here, *signorina*. I was a poor domestic, poor like I am now. Fortunately I came to say no because I preferred to stay alone the rest of my life than be with a man who I could not feel indifferently towards, but who I would hate for my whole life. I didn't feel like staying close to a man that I not only did not love, and in fact, hated. So in that case I preferred to remain alone. Even at the risk of contradicting all my country people who did not think like I did.

"They ignored me, they did not greet me on the street. I had some very ugly moments too, because Alcamo unfortunately is not like America."

"Even now?"

"Now no. Now it's different. This was 1966. But Alcamo is still behind the times, more backward than any other part of Sicily.

"Then after, I have seen that in many parts of Sicily, I have received letters from girls who had the experience like me but who said yes; so when I said no, they said, 'I was too afraid, but I wish I had been able to say no like you did. You did what I could not do. Instead I find myself in this situation.'

"Then, after what I did, I have seen many other girls respond as I did, saying no. I was happy when I heard that other girls were saving themselves making my same choice. It pleased me to know that, even if indirectly, I was of help to them. We have the right to our liberty. We know how to evaluate ourselves." She gave a little laugh.

"Yes." I gave a little laugh too.

"Now I have seen that it has been an example that many other girls have followed, and by now many arrogant young men are no longer permitted to go take a girl like what those men did to me, because they now have the fear they will end up by going to prison because they would not be excused."

"What about those men who abducted you?"

"The men who went to prison have gotten out. They did their time."

"After the trial were your countrypeople finally on your side?"

"I'll tell you how they were. The really backward"—*arcaico* was the word she used—"the old-fashioned ones, were not with me. All the young boys and girls, the ones who were educated, who were a little more free, the ones who were moving toward a more civil country were with me. There was a part with me, and a part that was not. Also because a part of that second group of people were relatives of all the ones who participated in the kidnap. Because there were thirteen. When you think about it, the families of thirteen people in a town this size are many. But outside of all them, the majority was with me.

"And then from the whole world, because every day I received hundreds and hundreds of letters and telegrams. I have a chest full of letters because at that time when they arrived I saved them, and I haven't thrown them away yet. Many of the letters were not written in Italian and I can't read them because I do not know other languages. I would need a continual interpreter to help me to read all these letters, because I have so many."

"Do you still receive mail?"

"Some of them, people I don't know personally, always remember me with a card around the holidays. All this applause still for me. Surely, some people still remember me."

"Of course they do. I, for one, have never forgotten. For me you are a heroine."

"All the letters began with those same words: 'You are a heroine.' They gave me a big compliment, but unfortunately I didn't really realize it at the time, because of the sadness that I felt. I did not know how to take these letters. I did not see myself that way."

"How did you get through the ordeal?"

"What got me through was my faith in God, a religious faith, that I would. I prayed to God always. Sincerely with all my heart, I believed that God would take care of me. And He did. Everything did turn out well. I was strongly religious, but always with modesty. The saddest moments, I prayed to God sincerely with all my heart, and He gave grace back to me. I suffered very, very much and then I was repaid for my sufferings. He made it possible for me to meet my husband who is really such a good man. My husband has a character of gold. I am very happy about this."

"How did you meet him?"

"I had known my husband before the kidnap, because we were friends. In fact, there was an attachment between me and him before this kidnap with the other boy that I didn't prefer.

"Then I sincerely thought that my husband would not have the same ideas as the others in the country in which we live. The day after I returned he came over to visit me. He said, 'For me nothing has changed, your soul is the same as it was. What happened to your body makes no difference to me.' My husband is a very intelligent person. My husband is a marvelous man."

"I read one newspaper account which said you were engaged to 'another' after the kidnap. Would that have been your husband?"

"Yes, I became engaged to him. There was the trial, and they gave that man an eleven-year sentence. After what happened, I did not want to marry my husband because he was threatened with death by the one I didn't prefer. He [Melodia] threatened to kill him when he got out of jail. But my husband insisted that our engagement was solid."

"And how is your family?"

"My two sons are growing up well, they are sensible, they are in school. The older one is eighteen. He's studying right now for his high school final exams. The small one is twelve years old. This year he is in the third year of middle school and will have his exam. We are really very happy. Everyone is well. Just a moment, *signorina*, someone's at the door."

Her footsteps retreated. I collected my papers from the floor and tried to put them in order. Was I remembering everything? This was it. There would be no other moment but this.

"I'm back now."

"Oh yes. What do your sons think of what you did?"

"I don't want to be a symbol for them. They love me and that's enough for me."

"Did you ever want to leave Alcamo?"

"Yes, the first three years after I was married I moved to Monreale, because my husband was working in Palermo. I preferred to take a house in Monreale in order not to travel. But then my husband was transferred to Alcamo and we returned to Alcamo and have been here for eighteen years."

"And you are happy there?"

"Yes. My whole family is here, with my sisters-in-law and my brother-in-law. When you phoned earlier today, you spoke with my brother-in-law, who answered the phone when I had to go out. We live in the same palazzo together with my sisters-in-law. We get along well together. When there is peace and tranquility in the family, there is nothing more beautiful than that."

"How true, how true. I read how your father stood by you during the trial, and your mother. Your whole family backed you, is that correct?"

"Yes, exactly. My whole family was with me. My father was the first, because he was not happy to think that a daughter would marry a boy with whom she was not happy. My father, I tell you, was very modern for a father of his age, who could have been old-fashioned with old, antiquated ideas. When I said no, he didn't react even half a second. My father said, 'I will not give your hand to him and I concede to your wishes.' He supported me in my decision. He backed me. My mother too. My father and my mother, they are my good friends. I am lucky to have this family."

"I feel so fortunate that we are speaking. Many people told me that you would never give an interview. Would you care to say anything else right now?"

"When people said, mistakenly, that I sold interviews to the newspapers for money, their false statements wounded and humiliated me. I did not do that. When I hear or read about myself now, it's as if I am reading about someone else. My gesture was not courageous, I did what I felt I had to do—I followed my heart like any girl would today. Granted, that was a very different Sicily. It was the reporters later who made the event historic."

"Do you wish what happened to you had been privately resolved, without the glare of publicity and the newspapers?"

"My choice was a normal one. If I was at the beginning of that change in our society, then I am glad I was helpful to others."

"Thank you so much for speaking with me, *signora*."

"It's nothing."

"For me it's a great honor."

"*Arrivederla, e buon viaggio.*"

"*Grazie*, Franca." I bowed my head. I believed I understood everything she said. We do know how to evaluate ourselves.

Maia rushed in with Sabina. "Did you reach her?"

"Yes!"

"When are we driving to Alcamo?"

"We're not."

"Oh how disappointing."

"But look how far we got," I beamed, and held out my pages of notes.

She thumbed through the papers. "Tell me what she sounded like."

"*Dolcissima.* The sweetest. Salt of the earth."

Maia pumped and repumped me for every word *La Viola* uttered, then phoned her sister immediately. "Sofia, she was completely direct with our cousin. No pretense, just the plain truth. And very kind."

I stood by the chair, nodding. "Remind Sofia that if the *scirocco* hadn't blown through, the librarian wouldn't have needed a substitute and Franca's husband would never have been told I was here looking for her. Tell her that some of Panormus's doors opened for me, in their own way in their own time."

Sabina, jumped up and down, aware that something good, something very unusual, had happened. She squeezed my hand. She wanted to celebrate whatever it was by my taking her out for ice cream.

We were licking *gelato* on the way back when we ran into the Professor in front of the building. He was carrying a platter piled with spaghettini in olive oil. She wanted to help feed the cats so we followed him out to the lot. The pack advanced, ringing evenly around the ceramic dish.

"Delicious, *eh*?" Sabina patted their dull fur.

Had I left a carton of milk for the cats at his door last week? And had I ever found out anything about Franca Viola, the Professor wondered. Sabina beat me to the answer. "Well then, you've succeeded at something we Sicilians have not."

"That's it, Professor! I just figured out why she was willing to speak to me. I have no special qualifications except for coming from far enough away that what I asked her will not disrupt her life here."

"Give yourself some credit, *Signorina* Galli. You have persisted. You've come here with an idea that you have followed through on. But I see your point," he mused. "She always guarded her privacy. That was her choice, which she had every right to. I must say, *La Viola* put our culture to the test. She prompted us to take a position. We had to, as a society, decide our common future. We had to take our leap forward. We had to make our own human rights. It was a very critical period of time then. *Un grande fomento.*"

Sabina was dangling a strand of pasta over the runt of the litter. It was batting at the *spaghettino* with its paw, falling backward and trying again. She was in stitches. I had the feeling that the Professor and Sabina were meant for each other.

"In any event, my kudos to you." He smiled, a dazzling first. The truth was I had never heard his name. His green eyes still killed me. They were the hue of the water I could not wade into at Mondello Lido, of the swells I'd missed bobbing in at Taormina, of the tie I hadn't finished crocheting for him, of the magical inner Lake Pergusa I'd yet to visit.

"How much longer do you intend to stay in Sicily?" he asked.

"She's flying to Rome next week," Sabina answered, "but Nonna wants her to stay longer."

"The answer, Professor, is that my plans are up in the air at the moment."

"Do you suppose you might write up Franca Viola's account while it's still fresh in your mind?"

"You know," I grinned, "I just might."

Italian - English Glossary

aiutame - help me
alberghi, albergo - hotels, hotel
allattrice - wet-nurse
alta moda - high fashion
aperitivi - aperitifs
appuntamento - appointment, date
arrivederla, arrivederci - until we see each other again
auguri - congratulations
avanti - onward

basta - enough
beh, boh - well, um
brutta, brutto - ugly
buono - good
burro - butter

cameriere - waiter
capisco - I understand
capperi - capers
cara - dear
carciofi - artichokes
carina - cute, darling
carabinieri - federal pollice
carrozza - carriage, cart

centro città - city center, downtown
ciao - hello, goodbye
contadini - peasants, farmers, countrypeople
croccante - crunchy

delizioso - delicious
diavola - she-devil
duomo - cathedral

esercizio - exercise

fichi - figs
fidanzato - fiancé
forestiere - foreigner, stranger
fuitina - elopement
fumare - to smoke

gelato - ice cream
gioia - joy
guarda - look

isola - island

macchina - machine, device
magari - I wish, if it were only so
mancino - left-handed
marito - husband
mascalzone - scoundrel, rascal, no-good
melenzana - eggplant
mi fai vedere - let me see
minestra - soup
moglie - wife
moto, motorino - motor scooter

nocciola - hazelnut
nonna - grandmother
nonno - grandfather
occhi - eyes
ottimo - excellent

padrone - proprietor
palazzo - high-rise apartment building, palace (palazzi, plural)
pazienza - patience
piaga - open wound
piazza - public square, plaza
pensione - inn, hotel, bed and breakfast
pecorino - sheep's milk cheese
perché - why
permesso - excuse me, coming through
pomodoro - tomato
povero, povera - poor
prego - you're welcome; please; I beg of you
pronto - hello
purtroppo - however, unfortunately
puttana - prostitute

ricotta - twice-cooked sheep's milk curds

salumeria - delicatessen
salute - to your health
salve - hello
sarde - sardines
scusa - excuse me
scusi (formal) - excuse me
semenza - seed
senz'altro - of course
signore - mister

signora - mrs.
signorina - miss
squisito - exquisite
straniera - stranger, foreigner
strega - witch
subito - immediately
sugo - gravy, sauce
tesoro - treasure, darling, dear
terra - land, earth
tipo - type, kind
torrone - nougat
traghetto - ferry
Trinacria - ancient three-legged symbol of Sicily, also known
   as triskelion

vendetta - retribution, revenge
vergogna - shame
vietato - forbidden

zia - aunt
zio - uncle

Appendix

Sicilian's Term Increased
Palermo, Italy, July 10 (AP)
An appeal court increased by two years today the prison term of a Sicilian convicted for the kidnapping and rape of a girl he wanted to force into marriage. Filippo Melodia was sentenced to 13 years.
—New York Times, July 11, 1967

Custom Defied by Sicilian Wedding
Alcamo, Sicily. Dec 4, 1968 (AP)
Franca Viola, a 20-year-old girl who broke a thousand years of Sicilian tradition, was married at dawn today to keep her wedding trip from being mobbed.

The wedding attracted nationwide attention and the time was moved up four hours at the last moment to keep crowds from the little Catholic church in Alcamo.

Senator Ludovico Corrao was one of the witnesses, and President Giuseppe Saragat and Premier Giovanni Leone sent gifts.

Two years ago Franca refused to marry a rich[?] man's son who had kidnapped and raped her. Since the Middle Ages, this has been the sure road to the altar for a rejected Sicilian suitor. A girl who did not accept after that was dishonored and no one else would marry her.

Franca stunned the Sicilians and won approval throughout the rest of Italy when she told Filippo Melodia in court: "I do not love you. I will not marry you."

Melodia was sentenced to 11 years in prison. The charges would have been dropped if Franca had agreed to marry him.

She and her family were threatened with vengeance for her violation of the code.

Giuseppe Ruisi, a 25-year-old accountant, and Franca had known each other in school. They met again at a family reunion last year. He became a steady caller at Franca's home under the watchful eye of her parents. She accepted his proposal.

Sicilian Heroine Is Now a New Mother

Monreale, Sicily, Jan 6, 1970 (AP)

The girl who shocked Sicilians and defied the Mafia four years ago by refusing to marry a suitor who had raped her has become a mother.

The former Franca Viola, now Mrs. Giuseppe Ruisi, gave birth to a boy in her home. When Miss Viola married Ruisi, an accountant, on Dec 4, 1968, she received presents and congratulation messages from Italy's president. Pope Paul VI met the couple in a special audience.

OPINIONS ON THE STREET IN
ALCAMO AFTER THE VERDICT

A clerk: "He deserved eleven years just for the way he behaved in court."

A few begged off a reporter's questions: "What sentence are you talking about?" "I don't know anything."

A seventy-two year old man, thick-set, with few teeth: "Thirty-five years ago I found myself in the same condition as Melodia, but I behaved better. I spat in the girl's face."

"But what if you were in Bernardo Viola's place, what would you have done?"

"I wouldn't have thought twice about it. I would have shot him in the head, without awaiting the sentence."

A bricklayer: "They should treat the kidnappers just as the kidnappers treated the girl."

Signora Sacchiero, storeowner: "I think the sentence should be given for life, as an example to others. It's absurd that today a girl might not be free to choose who she wants. We are in a civil world, these kidnaps are really unacceptable."

A technical agrarian: "A condemnation would be a lesson for certain men who until now, were bossing with impunity. We have to hope then that the number of girls like Franca Viola increases. There should be boys ready to joust to win her."

Jovial father of six who wanted to have some more children 'so as not to pay taxes', walking around with the littlest, Vito, two years old: "The penalty is just, because Melodia loved the girl. If he had not loved her he would have deserved, instead, twenty-two years."

High school headmaster who agreed with the sentence but who balked at the idea of discussing the Viola case in school: "For lessons we always have the kidnap of Helen of Troy."

Professor: "They [the continental press] have generalized too
much about us. In Alcamo, out of 50,000 inhabitants there
are only ten or twenty Melodias. The others do not think
like him and condemn him . . . . the problem, however, is
the insufficiency of schools, the miserable conditions of
life. There are boys in our province who have never seen a
school nor read a newspaper. When something of this kind
happens, I do not condemn the shepherd; I condemn the
State, which has failed to create a different type of society."

Photographer: "The Trapani judges saved, as we used to say,
'goats and cabbages.' I don't consider the condemnation
excessive but, rather, mild."

Name withheld: "You must not ask me this question, because
I hate all women. And I would make a saint out of that
scoundrel!"

PEOPLE IN PALERMO WEIGHED
IN ON THE SENTENCE:

Serena Bosco, student: "Eleven years is too much. In the last
analysis, if Filippo Melodia kidnapped Franca Viola he
had had good reasons to do it."

Fernando Costantino, barber: "Melodia committed a serious
error. If the girl didn't want him, he should not have taken
her forcefully. So he deserved eleven years, logically!"

Girolamo Mangione, clerk in savings bank: "They did the best
thing to condemn him, and I have a lot of faith in the
Italian juridical system."

Signora Gulino (young, very pretty and elegant): "The sentence
is not fair because she could have refused to follow him or
could have escaped or opposed him, anyway."

Attilio Mangano, 21 years, university student: "…We should update the Penal Code. But to do that, we need to change the ruling class. And who will do that?"

The Roman newspaper, Corriere della Sera, referring to Bernardo Viola's comment during the seven-hour wait for the verdict, editorialized: "The boat came back late, but the load was not as heavy as one might have thought."

WOULD YOU MARRY FRANCA VIOLA?

In a nationally televised debate, a number of male university students responded:

"I wouldn't marry her, but only because I'm afraid of the mafia."

"I wouldn't marry Franca Viola, but another in her condition, yes."

"I would marry her, but I would not remain in Alcamo. The city is too small. For years they would continue to speak of the incident, and the slander and the gossip wouldn't be good for either her or her children. I would go to a bigger city, losing myself in the crowd . . ."

"Changes have happened, but they're not widespread. Two people who walk alone will pass for engaged, after one day for married, after two days people say they're expecting a baby. We must have the courage to admit that we still have a patriarchy. The Viola case is just one small hint. It has helped to stir you of the television and of the press. It hasn't changed things."

A woman interrupted: "None of the young men here would marry Franca Viola, and it's not for fear of the mafia, but because of the whole attitude. It's difficult to find someone in Alcamo who'd be willing to admit that his wife has had other experiences. For a man to have his woman spoken of badly is a real sin."

A judge recalled speaking with an elderly woman who had been kidnapped and raped: "She married the man, by whom she was adored, and with whom she brought into the world a half dozen children. In her old age, she said, 'I cannot stand my husband.' It is difficult after all," the judge concluded, "to build a family based on violence."

Acknowledgments

Infinite thanks to Larry Habegger for superb editorial assistance and support at so many critical points; Walton Mendelsohn for interior design; Howie Severson for typesetting; Kim Nelson for cover design and James O'Reilly, publisher at Travelers' Tales. Penelope Love of Citrine Publishing who enthused about this project as it came to final fruition; Patrick Finley, editor of the *Berkeley Monthly*, who took a chance on hiring me as a columnist; Charles Burress of the *San Francisco Chronicle* for his efforts to unearth the filler in the vault; the members of my East Bay writing group: Gwendolyn Bikis, Angie Choi, Willow, Kate Hoffman, Nikki Meredith, Loretta Sheridan, Rosalyn Jordan, Andrea Brady and Kathy Z. Georgia Hesse, Judith Wylie, Diane LeBow, Sandy Sims and Bay Area Travel Writers for seeing fit to reward my work. Linda Watanabe McFerrin of Left Coast Writers, Dr. Nicolette Collins, Kathryn McDonald, Anita Roehrick-Jones, Chana Wilson, Rebecca Foust, and Constance Hale.

Necki and Liana Springer in Cottonwood, Arizona for precise translations and warm dinners; Dr. Warren Cranmer for introducing us. Mary Burmeister, Patricia Meador, Alice Draisin, Stan and Susanne Rogers, Charlotte Lund, Mary Jean Kurlon, Anni Rachootin.

Thanks also to Roberta Brand Esberg, Elizabeth Anne Einfeld, Christopher Einfeld, Lise Maisano, Jody Stevens, Emily Odza, Marguerite Rigoglioso, Annette Pirrone, Karen

Raccanello, Teresa Dintino, Lisa Hauck-Loy, Nan Talese, Kathleen Burch, Melody Carnahan Sumner, Laurel Collins, Stephen Schwartz, Peter Richardson of UC Press, Lesley Karsten, Janell Mosgofian, Marguerite Kelly, Zoe Zuber, Theresa Tong, Joanne Miller, Oreste Torrano, Richard Giordano, William Vallivero, Karen Goldsmith, Lee Trampleasure, Dean Santomieri, Angela DeFinis, Christopher Lydon, Marie Alaimo, Barbara Truax, Constance Webb, Arielle Eckstut, David Henry Sterry, Mary Taylor Simeti, Leonello and Anna Bobo, Marilynn Zito, Stephanie Alioto Wilhelm, Paola Bagnatori and Nina at the Museo Italo-Americano, Bruno and Mary Schiro, David Cohen, Anthony Tamburri, Fabrizio Corona, Mari Ziolkowski, Michael Schiro, Jonathan Livingston, Daphne Birkmyer, Chuck Granata, Wendy Ashley, Jean Shinoda Bolen, Claire Cummings, Joan Giguiere, Elizabeth Padilla, Sylvia Anderson, Matthias Kuntzsch, Stonna and Richard Edelman, and Cyrina Anthony. Nelina, Dora, Keeno, Elise, Anna-Maria, Francesca, Leila, Cristi, Alfredo, Michele, Mario, Alberto, Anna, Silvia, Laura, Barbara, Maristella, Marilù and the hardworking employees of the National Library of Palermo. Bean, Buff, Pupick, Jasmine and The Smudge for steadfast feline support.

About the Author

San Francisco native Natalie Galli has worked as a freelance writer, editor, proofreader and columnist. She penned two illustrated children's books for Sunbath Studios: *Ciao Meow, An Italian Cat's Story* and *Spin The Hound Lost and Found, A Tale of the 1906 San Francisco Earthquake*, and edited a third: *Leelee The Lizard Wants A Pizza*. By day, she works in the field of health care. She lives in the San Francisco Bay Area.